INVENTING BILLY THE KID

INVENTING BILLY THE KID

Visions of the Outlaw in America, 1881–1981

Stephen Tatum

University of New Mexico Press • Albuquerque

Library of Congress Cataloging in Publication Data

Tatum, Stephen, 1949-
  Inventing Billy the Kid.

  Bibliography: p.
  Includes index
  1. Billy, the Kid, in fiction, drama, poetry, etc.
2. West (U.S.) in art. 3. Outlaws in art. 4. United
States—Popular culture. I. Title.
NX652.B54T38   700'.973   82-4803
ISBN0-8263-0610-1   AACR2

For
my parents,
my wife,
and
Don D. Walker—my teacher

Contents

Illustrations

Preface

This is not a book about the Billy the Kid who died, it is supposed, in July 1881. Rather, this is a book about the Billy the Kids who have lived since the historical outlaw's 1881 death. Through the years, previous studies of the Kid have characteristically demonstrated two preoccupations: separating the historical Kid from the legendary Kid; discussing the legendary Kid's resemblance to legendary heroes of other cultures. In the process we have discovered, for example, accurate facts about the number and the personality of the Kid victims, and we have learned about the Kid's kinship to Odysseus and Siegfried.

Yet the numerous efforts to understand the Kid's biography and the legend-making process have removed the extensive bibliography of Bonneyana from the course of American social and cultural history. As a result, the major purpose of this study is twofold: to examine how the Kid has been invented in the years since his death; to discuss what such visions of the Kid reveal about the cultural preoccupations of particular interpreters creating the Kid in particular years. By discussing how dominant inventions of the Kid's story emerged, were accepted, were strained to the breaking point, and were eventually replaced by more relevant concepts of the Kid, we can detect illuminating truths about the Kid and his interpreters. In particular, we can discover much about changing attitudes toward the uses and consequences of violence, the relationship of civil law and moral justice, the prospects for individual freedom in a bureaucratic society, and, indeed, even the belief in a unified society with coherent purposes.

Given this study's major purpose, it is my hope that the following pages reveal that another book on a notorious outlaw can have value beyond that of marking the centennial year of the Kid's death. For in the final analysis, this is not just a book about the changing meaning of the Kid, but about the intersection of the Kid, the West, and Modern America. This study's success, then, rests on its demonstration that discovering, inventing, and understanding the Kid is in large measure discovering crucial aspects of ourselves and our cultural history. Confronting the Kid and his West does not entail a retreat into a supposedly more attractive agrarian era when, to use novelist Frank Waters's words, men were men and the women knew it.

I should like to express my appreciation to the following persons whose ideas, suggestions, criticism, and encouragement made this study a reality. First, I am indebted to the following works by authors whose theories enabled me to approach this study's primary purpose: John Cawelti, *Adventure, Mystery, and Romance;* Hayden White, *Metahistory* and *Tropics of Discourse;* Gene Wise, *American Historical Explanations;* and Northrop Frye, *Anatomy of Criticism.* In addition, I could not have delved very far into Bonneyana without the previous publication of J. C. Dykes' *Billy the Kid: The Bibliography of a Legend;* Ramon Adams's, *Six-Guns and Saddle Leather;* and Kent Steckmesser's, *The Western Hero in History and Legend.* Any errors resulting from my use of these works are, of course, my responsibility.

For their assistance in reading all or portions of this manuscript and for offering helpful criticism, I am grateful to Hal Moore, Jan Brunvand, Ken Eble, David Frazier, and Barry Weller. My friends Robert Haynie, David Stanley, and Barry Sarchett loaned useful secondary material and made numerous insightful observations—even some that we still remember. David Mair and Stephen Ruffus supplied much of the excellent illustrative material that accompanies my prose discussion.

I have also profited from the information supplied by Richard Meyer, who graciously sent me an article on the American outlaw hero prior to its publication, and from the encouragement of Tom Pilkington, who assured the University of New Mexico Press that I could follow the Kid's trail with success.

During the research phase of this project I was greatly helped by the Interlibrary Loan Department and the Western Americana section of the Marriott Library at the University of Utah. During the writing phase of this study I benefited from a fellowship awarded by the Department of English at the University of Utah and funded by the Sherman Brown Neff family. In addition, this English department allocated research funds that enabled me to view many of the Kid movies discussed in the following pages.

My gratitude extends to Karen Donahue, who typed the entire original manuscript, and to Rhonda Reagan, who typed portions of the revised manuscript. James A. Levernier, my colleague at the University of Arkansas at Little Rock, graciously offered his services during the proofreading phase of this book.

My thanks also to Ronald Bouck of Ballet West, Robin Blazer of the Jack Spicer estate, George Wildman of Charlton Comics, and the Western History Collections of the Univesity of Oklahoma Library for permission to reproduce quoted material and/or photographs.

At the University of New Mexico Press, David Holtby expertly edited the final typescript. I want especially to thank Elizabeth C. Hadas of the University of New Mexico Press for initially approaching me about a new study of the Kid, and for her helpful encouragement during times when the split infinitive was the least of my worries.

Finally, I wish to express my special appreciation and admiration by dedicating this book to those persons most instrumental in encouraging me and this study: Robert and Bettye Tatum, my parents, who have given me tremendous support through the years; Kathy Kingdon Tatum, my wife, who assumed many extra burdens as I traced the Kid's trail, and who refused to despair when I got us lost on the dirt roads between Puerto de Luna and Fort Sumner; and Don D. Walker, who inspired me to turn this study into something far more ambitious than originally planned. And here's to the Dixie and Captain Black, boon companions on many autumnal walks never to be taken together again.

Stephen Tatum
Little Rock, Arkansas
November 1981

He who would wish to see America in its proper light, and have a true idea of its feeble beginnings and barbarous rudiments, must visit our extended line of frontiers where the last settlers dwell, . . . where men are left wholly dependent on their native tempers, and on the spur of uncertain industry, which often fails when not sanctified by the efficacy of a few moral rules.

—St. Jean de Crèvecoeur, *Letters from an American Farmer,* 1782

The essential American soul is hard, isolate, stoic, and a killer. It has never melted.

—D. H. Lawrence, *Studies in Classic American Literature,* 1923

Live and invent. I have tried. I must have tried. Invent. It is not the word. Neither is live. No matter. I have tried.

—Samuel Beckett, *Malone Dies,* 1956

INVENTING BILLY THE KID

PART ONE

Discovering the Outlaw

Not a story about me through their eyes then. Find the
beginning, the slight silver key to unlock it, to dig it out. Here
then is a maze to begin, be in.

—Michael Ondaatje,
The Collected Works of Billy the Kid,
1970

1 "The Kid Still Rides"

An Introduction to Billy the Kid's Legend and Bibliography

So the gentleman must have drawn very heavily on his
imagination.
                              —Billy the Kid to Lew Wallace,
                                            12 December 1880

Billy Bonney is dead there can be no doubt about that. But the
Kid still *lives*—the Kid still rides.
                              —Eugene Cunningham, 1935

Even a century after Billy the Kid's death at the hand of Pat Garrett on 14 July
1881, the Kid's historical record appears trivial, even meaningless, when we
consider his slight impact upon events in New Mexico territory. Although
the Lincoln county, New Mexico, range war in the late 1870s attracted the
attention of both a national and international press, Henry McCarty—alias
William H. Bonney and Billy the Kid—bequeathed no legacy in land, family, or fortune, and only appeared on the scene as a hired hand whose activities
are vague, contradictory, and confused at several key points. Unlike cattle-
king John Chisum, the Kid controlled no epic expanse of rangeland; unlike
Lew Wallace, author of *Ben-Hur* and territorial governor of New Mexico, the
Kid composed no more than a few letters, which revealed, at best, a native
shrewdness and a deficiency in spelling; and unlike the Apache warrior Victorio,
the Kid defended no ancestral homeland and possessed no unique heritage.

When we compare the Kid to such illustrious personages in New Mexican history, we find it easier to understand why academic historians and students of Western Americana have generally ignored the Kid, crusaded to demythologize the Kid, or have asserted that the facts of their research have, finally, provided a "fitting" death for the Kid and his legend. Rather than being compared to Napoleon, Faust, or Achilles—so the argument goes—the Kid is more properly linked with Baby-face Nelson, another adenoidal youth who thought bullets were brains. Yet for the Kid's defenders, even this comparison has its drawbacks, for Baby-face Nelson has never spawned the kind of mythology that has grown up around the Kid.

At present we may visit eastern and southeastern New Mexico for various reasons—to see Carlsbad Caverns and the White Sands National Monument, or to wager on quarter-horse races at Ruidoso Downs—but none of these reasons or attractions so precisely identify this geography as does the label Billy the Kid Country. On the map, the Kid's country has easily recognizable boundaries: Las Vegas and Santa Fe on the north; Silver City on the west; Old Mesilla on the south; and Fort Sumner, Roswell, and Artesia on the east. To reach this landscape of desert, forest, mountains, high plains, and rivers that empty into the Pecos or Rio Grande, we can travel south on U.S. 84 from Las Vegas to Fort Sumner and pass near such fabled Kid haunts as Anton Chico and Puerto de Luna. Or, we can travel the 120 miles or so from Santa Rosa to Carrizozo on U.S. 54 and then turn east on U.S. 380, where on the drive to Roswell we shall pass through Lincoln and Hondo, and pass near Fort Stanton and San Patricio.

The capital of Kid country is Lincoln, and its mecca is Fort Sumner, where the Kid's grave is marked by a granite gravestone and surrounded by a fence so souvenir hunters won't chip away bits of the marker as momentos of their foray into the Wild West. In Lincoln we can visit the old L. G. Murphy store–Lincoln County Courthouse building, inside of which are bulletholes from one of the Kid's six-shooters, and the adobe Tunstall store, behind which are the graves of Alexander McSween and John Tunstall. And if we are there during the first week of August, we can see the three-day pageant "The Last Escape of Billy the Kid," an outdoor drama that re-creates the Kid's jailbreak in April 1881. As one observer has commented, "You can dissolve a marriage, separate an egg, split a deck of cards and take a boy from the country—but down in Lincoln town they just can't shed themselves of Billy the Kid."[1]

Yet as the epigraphs to this chapter and our own experience remind us, not the least of ways to travel through the Kid country is the route of the imagination, a route that has known few boundaries in the century since the Kid's death in 1881. Billy the Kid's imaginative appeal continues to prosper, extend its domain, and elude those desiring to capture him once and for all and assign his undeserving carcass to the oblivion reserved for the "Catfish Kid" or the "Pockmarked Kid." The Kid has been discovered crossing paths and wits with Dracula and Mickey Mouse, and rolling in the hay with Jane Russell in Howard Hughes's *The Outlaw* (1943). The Kid's physical appearance has been preserved in a wax museum in Dallas, where he shares floor space with other famous and infamous Southwestern historical characters. The Kid's trial for the murder of Sheriff Brady has been dramatized in a float at the annual New Year's Sun Carnival parade in El Paso (it won second place), and his fantasy fling with Jean Harlow somewhere in eternity was presented in a San Francisco North Beach nightclub (this version of the Kid's story, *The Beard,* won an obscenity trial as well as an Obie award). Drugstore cowboys in 1883 and 1937 imagined themselves as desperadoes in the Kid tradition and proceeded on both occasions to shoot up a train or a town and kill people (they won prison sentences).[2] Periodically, on the other hand, old-timers have come down from the hills or emerged from the desert and imagined themselves to be the *real* Billy the Kid, a desperado who definitely was not killed on that warm, moonlit New Mexican night of 14 July 1881. Court cases have been argued over the Kid's family tree, furthermore, as well as over a 1962 motion to transport his bones from Fort Sumner to Lincoln (it failed).[3]

Even though Henry McCarty as Billy Bonney has lapsed into historical insignificance, we have, in short, discovered a significant Billy the Kid in our imaginations. It is not just old Lincoln town that can't shed Billy the Kid and his legacy of violence, loyalty, and cunning, but it is rather the countless people in countless places who have since 1881 contributed to what by now is customarily called "America's immortal legend," "the most enduring legend of the American West," or "the cattle country's most romantic legend."[4] Whether his name "causes people of the Southwest to shudder" or conjures up Robin Hood's exploits, the Kid's mysterious birth, death, and burial have made him, to quote another observer, "the most fascinating bad man in American history."[5] Even as long ago as 1952, nearly seventy-five years after the Kid's death, J. C. Dykes, in his *Billy the Kid: The Bibliography of a Legend,* compiled 437 items of Kid material, including several novels, motion pictures, biographies, and one ballet; a little over a decade later, in 1965, he conservatively estimated that the bibliography had increased to well over 800 items.[6]

At this point it seems reasonable to suppose that there will be little diminution in Kid material, and that the bibliography will continue to increase as interpreters conveniently use the Kid as a touchstone when discussing either frontier experiences or popular contemporary figures—be they country music "outlaws" or temperamental baseball managers. As with Buffalo Bill, Custer, and Jesse James, Billy the Kid's persistent presence in our imagination demonstrates an appeal that crosses and recrosses any supposedly firm boundaries between the folk, the popular, and the artistic imaginations, or any conventional boundaries between history and legend. Because every generation and every culture creates figures who embody the preoccupations of the moment, the Kid may not be as *immediately* important as any cultural hero of the moment, any Lindbergh or Luke Skywalker, but the Kid has endured like the classical figure Proteus, the "shape-shifter" who eludes the death-grips of his antagonists by changing forms as the situation demands. "As each narrative adds a bit of drama here and a picturesque detail there," wrote Walter Noble Burns in 1926, "one wonders what form the legends will assume as time goes by, and in what heroic proportions Billy the Kid will appear in fireside fairy tales a hundred years from now."[7]

One reason the Kid has endured is that even before his death his exploits were widely reported in territorial newspapers, and such reports were customarily reprinted in newspapers farther east whose editors realized that their audiences were keenly interested in sensational frontier happenings. In his own day the Kid was dubbed "The Best Known Man in New Mexico" because of the newsworthiness of his exploits, and even as he awaited trial in a Santa Fe jail, he graced the pages of the Las Vegas *Gazette* for six weeks or more as the hero of a "forty thieves romance."[8] As Dykes has documented in the Kid bibliography, the immediate growth of the legend began when a series of dime novels by different authors exploited the Kid's daring deeds and vague biography in order to transmit whatever moral lesson seemed appropriate at the moment. Some of the more interesting dime novels—*Old King Brady and Billy the Kid; Buffalo Bill and Billy the Kid*—portrayed the Kid as a murderer, counterfeiter, robber, kidnapper, ravisher, and female impersonator who was variously hanged, shot, resurrected, and converted to the side of the just.

Besides the Kid's appearance in dime novels of the nineteenth century and in later juvenile books and ballads about the Wild West, he began making periodic appearances in comic books after 1950. Some comics presented him as our familiar bandit-samaritan; others presented him as a juvenile delinquent. The most remarkable moment of the comic-book-Kid's life occurred in 1969 when *Meatball,* a countercultural comic produced in San Francisco, displayed an eighty-three-year-old Kid returning to the West to battle machine guns, mortars, air-to-ground rockets, and jet fighters (the usual symbols of the military-industrial complex) accompanied from offstage by the Hallelujah Chorus from Handel's *Messiah.*

Along with this material designed for younger audiences, the Kid's bibliography is filled with many personal narratives, histories, and articles for popular and scholarly magazines. He has been fair and attractive game for attention since his life relates to such diverse subjects as range wars, ballads and folklore, firearms, cowboys, frontier justice and violence, and the general subject of the American hero or villain. His exploits form interesting parts of the personal narratives of such cowboys as Charlie Siringo and Ike Fridge, such foreign travelers as R. B. Townshend, such territorial governors as Lew Wallace and Miguel Otero, and such women as Sister Segale of Trinidad, Colorado, and Ma'am Jones of the Pecos. His life has merited attention in the *Dictionary of American Biography,* as well as the recently released *Reader's Encyclopedia of the American West.* The Kid has also been the subject of numerous articles published in both mass-circulation and scholarly magazines since his death in 1881. Articles written by, among many others, J. Frank Dobie, Emerson Hough, Dee Brown, Eugene Manlove Rhodes, J. Evetts Haley, and Marshall Fishwick have appeared in such publications as *Life, The Saturday Evening Post, Saturday Review, Overland Monthly, Sunset, Collier's, Journal of American Folklore, Western Folkore,* and *Southwestern Historical Quarterly.*

While the amount of Kid material in histories, personal narratives, anthologies, and juvenilia can only be suggested in this introductory survey, what is perhaps most interesting about the bibliography is the attractiveness this legendary figure has maintained for writers, musicians, dancers, and film makers. He has been the subject of poetry by Omar Barker, Henry Knibbs, Jack Spicer, Michael Ondaatje, and bp Nichol. His prowess as a gunslinger, a lover, and a friend, his evil deeds and his generosity, his boyhood and his ghost have been imagined in short stories and novels by Edwin Corle, Zane Grey, Eugene Manlove Rhodes, William Macleod Raine, Dane Coolidge, Nelson Nye, Will Henry, and Charles Neider. Beginning with Walter Woods's 1903 melodrama *Billy the Kid,* the Kid has been portrayed in more than sixteen dramas in the form of radio sketches for the *Death Valley Days* series, pantomimes, fiesta plays, and teleplays. Gore Vidal's teleplay on the death of the Kid starred Paul Newman; Michael McClure's 1965 play *The Beard* dramatized a verbal and physical encounter between the Kid and Jean Harlow. Most recently a dramatist from the Playwright's Workshop at Iowa, Lee Blessing, wrote a script on the Kid entitled *The Authentic Life of Billy the Kid* that won the 1979 American College Theatre Festival Student Playwriting Award.

Just as in the literary and theatrical texts that appear in the Kid's bibliography, musical interpretations of the Kid have been written for folk, popular, and classical audiences. Such music has of course been largely in ballad and folksong form and can be discovered in John Lomax's *Cowboy Songs* and in other collections like *The Songs of the Cattle Trail and Cow Camps, Buckaroo Ballads,* and *The Bad Man Songs of the Wild and Wooly West.* Along with the numerous ballads and folksongs about the Kid's musical talents, exhumed trigger finger, racist leanings, and love life, musicians as various as Vernon Dalhart, Woody Guthrie, Ry Cooder, Billy Joel, and Bob Dylan have recorded traditional and original Kid music—Dylan most conspicuously, since his music and lyrics comprise the soundtrack for Sam Peckinpah's 1973 motion picture *Pat Garrett and Billy the Kid.* In addition, Aaron Copland composed a Billy the Kid score which, since its apearance in 1948, has appeared as a waltz, a piano solo, a suite, and of course as a well-recognized ballet score to Eugene Loring's choreography of the Kid's life and death.

As is the case with other legendary Western figures like Jesse James, Custer, and Buffalo Bill, the Kid's transformation from a folk or legendary hero into a mass-culture hero was primarily the result of Hollywood's versions of the Kid's career. In 1952 Dykes listed some twenty-five films concerned with the Kid's history and legend. Beginning with director King Vidor's 1930 MGM movie starring Johnny Mack Brown as the Kid (with Wallace Beery as Pat Garrett), we can today number at least forty movies devoted to some aspect of the Kid's biography, including three foreign films, a Disney cartoon, and a serial. Through the years since Johhny Mack Brown's 1930 performance such actors as Roy Rogers, Robert Taylor, Paul Newman, Audie Murphy, Lash Larue, Nick Adams, and Kris Kristofferson have starred as the Kid under the direction of, to choose the best known, Arthur Penn, Sam Peckinpah, Andrew McLaglen, and Howard Hughes. In addition to these motion pictures' transmission of and additions to the Kid's legend, NBC introduced "The Tall Man" during its 1960–61 television season, a series devoted to the Kid-Garrett relationship starring Clu Gulager as the Kid and Barry Sullivan as Pat Garrett. In these productions on both the large and small screen the Kid has come from Texas, Oklahoma, and thin air; has fallen in love with women and horses; has robbed, killed, drunk, and shot bullets at Dracula; has worked for and against the law; and has been killed or has been allowed to light out for a new territory with a lovely woman. To my knowledge we still await a pornographic Kid or a homosexual Kid, but then a new century of the Kid bibliography is just now beginning.

In the process of discovering the kid who still "rides" in books, magazines, films, music, dance, and oral tales, things like truth and knowledge and heroes and villains have become so intertwined that, in the metaphorical words of one author, "it would take God almighty himself to cut out his own cattle and leave the rest to the devil."[9] And if God almighty himself could work up a lather trying to muster the immense herd of Kid stories into the right pastures, then is it any wonder that generations of lesser cowboys have missed some wild mavericks out there in the pasture? Is it any wonder that the real and imagined events in the Kid's brief life simultaneously endow the Kid, according to folklorists and cultural historians, with the traits of such diverse hero-types as the Unpromising Hero, the Delivering Hero, the Avenging Hero, the Clever Hero, and—interestingly—the Handsome Coward?[10] Just how the Kid throughout the years since his death has eluded his pursuers and just how he remains "a demigod of the wild West myth" can be understood by discovering the legend that has evolved.[11]

The Kid's "golden legend," which, as one of several observers puts it, "has grown out of all proportion to the few sordid facts of his short, lightning-swift career," resembles a form associated with more respected heroes such as Theseus and Heracles precisely because of the mysterious circumstances that surround his birth, parentage, and early life.[12] As opposed to the historical Billy the Kid who *probably* was born in New York City, the legendary Kid was born not only in New York City but also in upstate New York, Philadelphia, St. Louis, rural Indiana, Cincinnati, Buffalo Gap (Texas), and County Limerick (Ireland). The mystery surrounding the Kid's place of birth extends to the Kid's date of his birth and the identity of his parents. Wherever and whenever the legendary Kid was born, and whoever was responsible for producing him, he was generally a poor wisp of a lad who in various accounts worked as a dishwasher in Arizona and a bootblack in Chicago. According to one of the earliest fictional biographies of the Kid, the outlaw was poor because his father—an Irish peasant—was ruined by the landlord's son who first seduced the Kid's sisters and then threw the father in jail.[13] Even if the Kid did have such an inauspicious debut, and even if the Kid was abused by a legendary cruel stepfather, another version of the legend tells us how the Kid went to college before he became a cattle-rustler.[14]

However he originated, the legendary Kid was seemingly destined to pursue a degree in crime, and the versions of his criminal activities are apparently as various as there are commentators on the Kid. Although some accounts stressed the Kid's violent nature by suggesting that the Kid's first violent act was braining his stepfather while the latter was abusing the Kid's mother, many more accounts developed the tale about the Kid having murdered a loafer who either insulted his mother or was about to smash a friend of the Kid with a barroom chair. Except for the earliest dime novels' portraits of his first violent crime, the legend in whatever form tends to justify the Kid's first crime as an act of self-defense, vengeance, or honor. Thus, the Kid killed a burly cook who abused him when he was a dishwasher; a miner who ran off with his sister and yet refused to marry her; a cow-camp cook who threw hot grease on him; and a group of Jayhawkers who burned his family's home to the ground. A more sensational version of the Kid's first crime has him killing a jealous husband who came home at the wrong time and found the Kid and his wife in bed; in less sympathetic versions of the legend, the Kid ruthlessly slays innocent Mexicans or Chinamen, and thus begins a bloodthirsty career of killing men "just to see them kick."

Whatever the circumstances of his legendary initiation into crime, Billy the Kid was forced into an exile's life. Like any true legendary hero, however, the Kid possessed the instinctual talents for survival in the West. According to the legend, the Kid survived as a wild man in wild times because he was an excellent marksman who could shoot off the heads of six snowbirds with only six shots or could shoot the Texas braggart Joe Grant three times and leave only one bullethole in the corpse. The legendary Kid could also aim backward over his shoulder and hit a target by merely looking in a mirror behind a saloon's bar. On another occasion, however, the Kid should have taken warning, for he lost a shooting match to Pat Garrett when the latter shot a coin positioned between the Kid's forefinger and thumb.

In addition to such tales of the Kid's physical skills, tales which also often suggested that the Kid led a charmed life and could not be killed by conventional means, the Kid survived in Southwest society because he also was an excellent musician, dancer, and lover. According to some interpreters he possessed a "beautiful tenor voice" and loved to sing "Silver Threads Among the Gold" and "Over the River"; according to others he was more of a wandering minstrel who on occasion would stop at a ranch house, and—with his chaps on and his six-shooters hanging in plain sight—pay for his supper "with marvelous renditions of 'Turkey in the Straw,' 'Swanee River,' and 'Old Folks at Home'."[15] With these attributes, it is not surprising that the legendary Kid was also "a romantic fool," to use Charlie Siringo's term for the Kid, who had a señorita in every cantina from Fort Sumner to Fort Stanton. One narrator remembered a particular October baile (dance) during which he accidentally and ignorantly danced with the Kid's girl. Because she had eyes only for the Kid, however, he quickly discovered that he himself "wuz as valuable to her as day-old chewing-gum."[16]

Such feminine devotion surfaced in certain explanations of the Kid's daring escape from jail. Several additions to the legend hold that he escaped because a faithful woman (who in some accounts was married) smuggled the Kid a pick or a key to his handcuffs by concealing the tool in a tortilla or an empanada. Another legend even offers the possibility that, if the Kid had not escaped prior to his hanging, a virgin Mexican girl was willing to substitute herself for a criminal condemned to hang. A further interesting development in the Kid's legend as romantic lover was the rumor unearthed by Walter Noble Burns which suggested that the Kid had fathered two girls and a son by different mothers.[17]

Yet the legendary Kid was an exceptional outlaw even when he wasn't gambling, womanizing, trick-shooting, or secretly placing cartridges into a campfire and gleefully watching as his mates scurried for cover when the gunpowder exploded. While some observers thought he was a harmless Boy Scout when compared to such stalwarts as John Wesley Hardin, the Kid—like Robin Hood and other noble bandits—was often fantasized as a courageous, chivalric champion of the oppressed.[18] J. Frank Dobie called the Kid "the fairy Prince not only of New Mexico but of the old West" because such sentiments as expressed in the following poem were common throughout the bibliography of Kid material:

> For the honor of his mother,
> He fought a desperate fight.
> Only a youth of tender years,
> He seemed to be in the right.
> But it made of him an outlaw,
> To range prairie broad and wide,
> And engage in many a battle,
> Before the day he died.
> He took the side of settlers,
> And natives who were poor,
> Against ruthless cattlemen,
> Who had left a trail of gore.[19]

Serving as what Kent Steckmesser has called "the American Robin Hood," the legendary Kid, after being forced into an outlaw's existence, was praised for legions of selfless acts. As a bandit samaritan, he delivered a small town held in thrall by one villainous Ruiz who was demanding tribute and preventing the marriage of two young lovers.[20] While one observer considered the Kid rather more of a Southwestern satan whose spiritual descendants were Lee Harvey Oswald and Sirhan Sirhan,[21] legend has it that the Kid gave firewood, money, food, and clothes to the poor—and once endowed an orphanage. Although the Kid might ravish a woman or two in some legendary accounts, he has been more characteristically seen killing Apaches, Mexicans, and Anglos who threatened Apache, Mexican, and Anglo women. If the Kid was correctly labeled the most notorious desperado in Western American history, a man who killed anywhere from four to forty-five men (not counting women and children), he paradoxically was extremely courteous to women and children and loyal to his friends. For example, he would not battle a group of U.S. soldiers within shouting distance of the home of a lonely widow and her sleeping children.

If the legend reveals contradictory features, the reason is because the Kid has been since his death in 1881 many things to many people—a flexible container, in other words, into which particular audiences' hopes and fears, ideals and prejudices, have been poured. As Orrin Klapp has suggested, when a historical figure by whatever means attracts popular attention, that figure is characteristically conceived according to basic heroic categories which in their general outline transcend specific cultural preoccupations. Once the hero is conceived in this manner—as a Delivering Hero, say, or as a Clever Hero—his creators select, invent, or exaggerate exploits and personality traits that support the imagined concept of the hero.[22] Thus, because the Kid's legend has in some versions emphasized his cleverness in outwitting his foes and his fighting skills on the "battlefield," the legend shares similarities with those of Ulysses or El Cid. Because his creators have stressed such episodes as the Kid's oath of vengeance sworn over his friend Tunstall's corpse—when in reality, it is now generally believed, the Kid was so insignificant a friend that Tunstall neglected to mention his name in any correspondence—the Kid, like Achilles, resembles the classic Avenging Hero. And so the process of invention continues, as various interpreters focus on the outlaw's friendship with or betrayal by Mexicans, his rugged good looks or effeminate appearance, his principled use of violence or unjustified killing of Chisum cowboys, and his supernatural ability to avoid bullets or his fatal gullibility, which thwarted his gaining large amounts of money and other valuables. As Alfred Adler has demonstrated, furthermore, the Kid's elevation into a folk and legendary hero like Moses, Siegfried, and Heracles has also occurred because of the mystery surrounding his death and burial and because of the nature of his death by treachery (the Judas theme).

The interesting fact remains that Billy the Kid is not *legally* dead because no original copy of the coroner's jury inquest has been filed in New Mexico. And even if the Kid were shot by Pat Garrett, or even if Garrett and the Kid buried another person or two bags of sand in the Kid's coffin,[23] the Kid's burial site has been located in Fort Stanton, Las Cruces, Old Mesilla, and—of course—Fort Sumner, where the official tombstone rests. As is the case with other cultural heroes, there is additional uncertainty about just whose remains, if any, are in the Fort Sumner site. In the first place, even the location of his grave in the old Fort Sumner military cemetery became problematic when army troopers at the end of the last century took target practice at the plain wooden marker, or when another person removed the marker from the site and took it home as one might the relics of a saint. In later years the Pecos River flooded and exposed the remains of several bodies in the abandoned cemetery, and in the following clean-up uncertainty arose about who was returned to what site. Finally, the government moved the bodies of the soldiers to the Santa Fe national military cemetery, and thus, given the confusion of sites resulting from the periodic Pecos River floods, the Kid might have accidentally made the journey to Santa Fe. The most recent addition to the legend concerning the Kid's gravesite is that when the road out of Santa Fe toward Española was improved a few years ago, it was built over some of the military cemetery—hence, the Kid's grave may be located under U.S. 285 near the Santa Fe Sheraton.

Whatever the fate of the Kid's grave and corpse, his death inaugurated the appearance of legends and rumors about his mortal and ghostly remains. Immediately after his death in July 1881, rumors about the fate of his remains (and any of its components) began circulating. A California woman claiming to be the Kid's sweetheart wrote the Las Vegas *Daily Optic* and requested that the Kid's trigger finger be sent to her; another legend circulated that the Kid's entire corpse was exhumed and "dressed" in Las Vegas and would hang there until the meat fell off.[24] Such rumors and requests amused the *Daily Optic* so much that within two weeks of the Kid's demise the newspaper ran a column which informed the public that the tremendous rush to see the Kid's trigger finger would cause the paper to "purchase a small tent and open a side show to which complimentary tickets will be issued to our personal friends."[25] That same trigger finger was the subject of an early ballad in which the narrator attends a Chicago side show and, after paying his dime to enter the tent, sees a finger preserved in alcohol. Of course, our narrator quickly slapped leather and blew "that *thing* clar into hell."[26] Besides the persistent desire to have possession of the Kid's trigger finger or his six-shooter, even now you can walk into a certain Grants, N.M., hardware store and be told that the skull hanging over the counter is that of the Kid's horse. Other additions to the legend extend the Kid's life after death by detailing the presence of his ghost in the mountains, plains, and villages of the West. A visitor to the old courthouse from which Billy made his daring escape a little over two weeks before he was to be hanged relates that at night he could hear ghosts playing billiards; Edwin Corle reports an old man's belief that the Kid's ghost haunted the Panamint Valley country in California; and Jack Thorp recalls that native New Mexican women would scare their children into good behavior by telling them that "Bilito's ghost" would haunt them.[27] Perhaps it was because the Kid was betrayed, according to legend, by Pat Garrett and Pete Maxwell's daughter that the Kid's ghost rides the range without rest, and that a lovely Spanish señorita haunts the Kid's grave.

Such visions of the Kid's life, exploits, death, and ghost by no means complete the portrait of the legendary Billy the Kid, but they do serve to outline the range of the legend that has emerged in the extensive Kid bibliography. Discovering the Kid throughout the years since his death in 1881 has usually meant discovering the appeals of the West and the Western, the historical landscape and the aesthetic context within which the Kid both resides and rides. Such appeals continue to preoccupy us and beckon to us, even though we no longer confront the conditions of frontier existence. We shall examine some of the reasons for this continuing attraction of Billy the Kid and his country—an attraction that ultimately resides in mental rather than topographical maps—but for the moment I wish to suggest that this attraction reveals more, on the one hand, than a mindless, subliterary, or even perverted fascination with big bad guns and bloody violence. And, on the other hand, such an enduring attraction, whether couched in positive or negative terms, reveals more than just a century's worth of infantile egos escaping into the thrilling and uncomplicated days of yesteryear to avoid the complexities of the present.

These notions are attractive on the surface, and have served some as explanations for the enduring appeal of the outlaw and the West—but these notions are simplistic. It is not just the lure of violence that draws observers to comment on the Kid. After all, his *legendary* death count of twenty-one men for twenty-one years pales by comparison to death counts of certain contemporary killers; and his *historical* death count (four killed outright; five killed with the help of others) pales by comparison to the killings recorded by Western characters in his own day. In addition, it is not just, as T. S. Eliot said in *Burnt Norton,* that "Human kind cannot bear very much reality," but that *all* of us to some degree resolve our conflicts of value and feeling in fantasy. This resolution may be grounded, at least in the Western formula, in the historical past, but in the following pages we may also learn how our discoveries of the Kid and his West have existed as strategies for encompassing cultural and personal conflicts in an audience's present.[28] Characteristically, those folklorists and historians who have commented on the tenacious growth of the Kid's legend have for our benefit traced its similarities to other cultures' heroic legends, and have suggested that heroes like the Kid arise in times of stress because they fulfill an audience's *needs*. Although there are some problems with this idea of a "need" theory, for our purposes it is necessary to recognize that in the quest for understanding how the Kid's legend conforms to archetypal hero patterns, we have often lost sight of what specific cultural needs the legend's development has fulfilled. Thus, if the strategies for inventing the Kid have been inevitably confined to what some term "the romantic," "the mythic," "the unrealistic," and "the unhistorical," then our proper task, at this point, is to understand *why* this has been the case and *what* it reveals about the culture which has been involved with the West, the Western, the Outlaw, and—the Kid.

Before we can turn to these questions, however, we need to know more about this outlaw's historical and historiographical record. If we have been successful in briefly outlining who the legendary Kid *is,* then we need also to outline who the historical Kid *was.*

2 Teaching a Burro the Beauties of Milton

An Introduction to
Billy the Kid's Biography

> "Billy the Kid" has been written up for eastern journals in all
> sorts of styles. He has been given an impregnable castle, elegant
> clothes, fine manners and great generosity. In short the accounts
> of him have been made up of whole cloth, and if eastern people
> credit them they have about as good an idea of what Billy really
> was, as a burro has of the beauties of Milton.
>   —from the Durango, Colorado, *Record* (1881)

The problem of discovering who and what Billy the Kid *really was* and of
distinguishing the historical Henry McCarty from the invented Billy the Kids
has preoccupied commentators on this outlaw since the newspaper accounts
of his career shared space with the news of President Garfield's assassination.
Yet the problem of discovering the historical Kid has never received an easy,
immediate, or even satisfactory solution. Before the Kid had exhaled his last
breath, his exploits had been reported, magnified, and distorted by both a
politically-motivated regional press and a sensationally-motivated national
press. In addition to the well-known gaps in our knowledge of his biographical facts, even the known incidents of his life have conspired to remain, in
the words of one observer, as "thick as scattered grain in the chickenyard,
and as hard to arrange in any order."[1] Because of such problems in publicity,

ignorance, and arrangement, Arthur Chapman concluded as long ago as 1911 that the Kid "must remain wholly the most unaccountable figure in frontier history."[2] In short, sometimes a burro has had a better idea of the beauties of Milton than we have had ideas of the Kid's historical record.

Some may argue with Chapman's choice of the adjective "most," but little doubt exists that this elusive figure was unaccountable for nearly eighty years after his death, due in large part to Pat Garrett's decision in 1882 to enlist Marshall Ashmun Upson's talents in writing a biography of the Kid. While staying at Garrett's ranch near Roswell, "Ash" Upson—frontier journalist, store clerk, postmaster, and justice of the peace—responded with a manuscript supposedly written to correct the factual mistakes of a host of dime novels about the Kid and to present Garrett's side in the controversy surrounding the Kid's death. Entitled *The Authentic Life of Billy, the Kid, The Noted Desperado of the Southwest, Whose Deeds of Daring and Blood Made His Name a Terror in New Mexico, Arizona, and Northern Mexico,* the Upson-Garrett effort has proved to be the foundation for many legendary treatments of the Kid, particularly the major misconceptions about the Kid's life prior to the fall of 1877.[3]

According to the Upson-Garrett account, Billy the Kid was named William H. Bonney and was born in New York City on 23 November 1859. In early 1862 the Bonney family—William H. Bonney, Sr., Katherine, and their sons William and Edward (born 1861)—left New York City for the West and eventually arrived in Coffeyville, Kansas. When the elder Bonney died shortly after their arrival in Kansas, the family emigrated to Pueblo, Colorado, where Billy's mother married William Antrim. The Antrims then moved to Santa Fe sometime in 1863 and operated a boarding house there until they moved to Silver City in 1868. After killing a man who insulted his mother, the Kid, now twelve-years-old, was exiled from the benevolent influence of family life. Before his death in 1881, the Kid rescued wagon trains from Apache raids, rescued a friend in jail after riding eighty-one miles in six hours, killed a man for every year of his life, and gambled, rustled, and loved his way across the landscape.

Since Coffeyville, Kansas, was not incorporated until 1871, and since Silver City was not in existence until the silver strike of 1870, the Upson-Garrett version has been considered unreliable by successive interpreters of the Kid's career. Often, however, the revisers of Upson's account only further confused the matter of the Kid's biography by designating different variations on his birthplace, different versions of his early life and first crimes, and different accounts of his jailbreaks and death—if, as some have questioned, he did indeed become history on 14 July 1881. Besides Upson's admittedly garbled account, for example, we have been informed that the Kid was also a bandit samaritan who nursed a sick miner back to health, an outlaw who spared the lives of Trinidad, Colorado's only doctor at the request of a Catholic sister, and a loyal friend who bought tickets from and clothing for a man who owned a traveling circus. On occasion we have learned, furthermore, that the Kid died after inhaling bat guano in a cave and that his ghost caused cattle to drift across the Staked Plains during winter blizzards.[4]

Because of the unreliability of the Garrett biography and the misconceptions fostered by later generations of interpreters of the Kid, his historical pursuers have customarily adopted an attitude of despair, resignation, and even anger toward the task of teaching the burro the beauties of Milton. However, beginning with the 1953 publication of Philip J. Rasch's and R. N. Mullin's "New Light on the Legend of Billy the Kid," investigators began uncovering evidence about the Kid's biography that enabled them to revise successfully the *Authentic Life* and to locate further Henry McCarty in the historical record.[5] During the late 1950s and the 1960s, researchers like Maurice Garland Fulton, William Keleher, and W. E. Koop discovered documents that detailed more fully the incredibly complicated web of circumstances surrounding the Kid's participation in the Lincoln County War and the probable facts of his childhood years. While the historian may never completely understand his elusive subject, at this point we can say that Chapman's insight into the unaccountable nature of the Kid's life applies more appropriately now to the persistence and endurance of his legend rather than to the Kid's historical life.

Still, several mass-market "coffeetable" books on the West or the Gunfighter have appeared even in the last few years, and while in several instances these compilations have made use of recent findings, more often these books have demonstrated the old inability to discover who and what the Kid was. Since the research accomplished by Rasch and others in the last twenty-five years has generally been published in small-circulation journals and *Brand Books,* it would be a useful service to chronicle the Kid as we now know him before turning to this study's primary concern, which is not precisely a study of who the Kid was, but is rather a study of how we have seen the Kid in the century since his death, and why a particular image of the Kid gained currency at a particular time. For the moment, then, let us briefly chronicle the Kid and, in Milton's words, "tempt with wandering feet / The dark, unbottomed, infinite abyss" of the Kid's biography, knowing full well that we also may be misled on occasion by the obscurities in his record and by the disagreement over dates and places, and knowing that this account will not fulfill the need for a full-length biography of the Kid and his times.

Many of the early settlers remember him as a street gamin in the days of longhorns.
        —Col. Marsh Murdock, *Wichita Weekly Eagle,*
                11 August 1881.

Reconstructing the beginning of the Kid's life means we also begin with a problem. Although it is generally accepted that Henry McCarty—alias William Antrim, Kid Antrim, William H. Bonney, Billy Bonney, Billy Kid, Billy the Kid—was born in New York City on 23 November 1859 to Michael and Catherine McCarty, the birthdate and birthplace may be amended if and when new evidence is uncovered. While researchers have eliminated several possible candidates for the Kid's father, it is believed that Michael McCarty was a Civil War casualty and that sometime prior to or in 1865 the widowed Catherine McCarty and her sons Henry and Joseph moved to the Indianapolis area. By 1868 the family resided at 199 North East Street in Indianapolis, and Mrs. McCarty herself told representatives of the city directory that she was the widow of a Michael McCarty.[6] During these years in Indianapolis, as W. E. Koop has discovered, Henry's mother made the acquaintance of William Antrim, a discharged Civil War veteran whose employer, Merchant's Union Express Company, was located in the area of the McCarty's 1868 residence on North East Street. This acquaintance marks the beginning of a prolonged courtship, which perhaps originated after Antrim delivered a parcel to the McCarty home.

Sometime in the summer of 1870 the McCarty family and "Uncle Billy" Antrim started a trek west and eventually arrived in Wichita, at that time "not much more than a cluster of picket shanties on the east bank of the Little Arkansas River near its junction with the Arkansas."[7] Here Catherine McCarty purchased real estate in town, and—with Antrim's help—began improvements on a vacant lot on the outskirts of Wichita. Until the family moved in March 1871 to the one-story home built by Antrim on the lot, they lived on Chisholm Street, not too distant from the town's leading hotel, where Catherine operated a laundry. Koop has suggested that perhaps an outbreak of "six-shooter promiscuity" on 28 February at the nearby hotel motivated the widow to move her family on 4 March to the improved lot and home that Antrim tended between his stints as bartender, carpenter, and farmer. Whatever the motivations for the move, Henry McCarty, nearing his twelfth birthday, performed the necessary household chores and no doubt helped Antrim complete the fencing, well, and storm cellar on the lot.

In the late spring of 1871, the hard-working yet by no means poverty-stricken existence of the McCarty-Antrim unit began to change. Even as Antrim's parents and brother James moved to Wichita from Indiana, Catherine and "Uncle Billy" began to divest themselves of their real estate and prepare for a move to a higher and drier climate. Catherine McCarty had tuberculosis. On or shortly after 25 August 1871, Henry's mother sold her lots on Chisholm Street to Henry J. Cook; with her sons and Antrim she moved to Denver and the Colorado mining camps, or perhaps to New Mexico, or perhaps even to New Orleans.[8]

Between 25 August 1871 and 1 March 1873, there exists one of the familiar gaps in the Kid's biography. Whether the McCartys and Antrim traveled among various mining camps, remained in Denver, or journeyed from New Orleans across Texas to New Mexico remains uncertain. What we now know for certain is that on 1 March 1873 Catherine McCarty, forty-four years old, married William H. Antrim in the First Presbyterian Church of Santa Fe, New Mexico. The new bride and groom, legally united after a courtship of approximately eight years, then moved the family to Silver City, lured by the prospect of silver strikes for "Uncle Billy" and better health for Catherine.[9] While Henry and Joseph attended the local school, Mrs. Antrim apparently conducted a boarding house—Upson *says* he met her while residing there—and Antrim worked in a butcher shop or prospected for minerals in the mountains around Silver City. According to Chauncey Truesdell, a classmate of Henry's in Silver City, Henry McCarty "loved to dance and sing and play end man in a minstrel show at Morrill's Theatre"; according to his teacher, Henry presented no more problems in the classroom than the next boy.[10]

However, Mrs. Antrim, remembered by one neighbor as "a jolly Irish lady, full of life and mischief," soon succumbed to tuberculosis, and died on 16 September 1874 after a four-month stay in bed. Henry was almost fifteen years old as he watched the funeral procession leave the family residence on Main Street and enter the city cemetery. For the next year he became a sort of foster son to the Truesdells and waited tables and worked in the kitchen of the Star Hotel.

Tradition has it that Henry McCarty turned into a juvenile delinquent after his mother's death, that he learned to play poker and monte, and that he associated with other juvenile toughs and fell under the sway of older men like "Sombrero Jack." Sheriff Harvey Whitehill of Silver City has stated that Henry was accused of stealing butter, among other petty thefts, and other observers have suggested that the youth began cutting his classes. It is known, though, that this "orphan," while living with a Mrs. Brown, was arrested on 23 September 1875 for the theft of clothing from Charley Sun and Sam Chung. It is well-established that "Sombrero Jack" stole the clothes and asked or demanded that Henry hide them for him; after Mrs. Brown discovered the clothes in Henry's trunk and told Whitehill, the sheriff arrested and jailed Henry to teach him a lesson. After a preliminary hearing on the charge, Henry escaped from jail on 25 September, and—with the help of Mrs. Truesdell—stayed at Ed Moulton's sawmill in the Bear Mountains. At some point the budding Kid probably saw his stepfather, who was working in a mine at Chloride Flat west of Silver City, and received some money—and advice to leave town. Henry then returned to Silver City long enough to catch a stage for Globe, Arizona, in late September 1875, approximately a year after his mother's death.[11]

> Austin Antrim shot F. P. Cahill near Camp Grant on the 17th
> instant, and the latter died on the 18th. Cahill made a statement
> before death to the effect that he had some trouble with Antrim
> during which the shooting was done. Bad names were applied to
> each other.
>
> —*Tucson Arizona Citizen,*
> 25 August 1877

If his boyhood prior to October 1875 was similar to any boy's formative years on the frontier, then the next two years were to inaugurate a life that was anything but normal, and were to begin the transformation of Henry McCarty into Billy the Kid. Disembarking the stage in Globe, alone and nearing sixteen years of age, Henry McCarty probably spent the next two years riding the grubline, working as a teamster or sheepherder or ranch hand, and learning to survive as a saddle-tramp. During this period he also learned about firearms and began adopting aliases—perhaps to protect his mother's name. At one time he was employed at J. W. "Sorghum" Smith's hay camp in Pima County; at another time he was employed at Fort Grant as a civilian teamster who hauled logs from a timber camp on a nearby mountain to the post's sawmill. According to Gus Gildea, an army scout at the time, the young Kid Antrim in the fall of 1877 "was an easy-going, likable youth still in his teens." Gildea also remembered a time when the Kid "came to town dressed like a 'country jake,' with store pants on and shoes instead of boots. He wore a six-shooter stuck in his trousers."[12]

Now known as Austin Antrim or Kid Antrim, the Kid frequented George Adkins' saloon/dance hall near the army post and took many of his meals at a nearby hotel. On 17 August 1877, as he neared his eighteenth birthday, the Kid found himself the target of Frank P. "Windy" Cahill's verbal abuse. A struggle resulted when Cahill called the Kid a "pimp," and the Kid called Cahill a "son-of-a-bitch." During that struggle the Kid worked his six-shooter free from his trousers and shot the blacksmith in the side. After Cahill died the next day, a coroner's jury—composed mainly of Cahill sympathizers—returned a guilty verdict and charged the Kid with a "criminal and unjustifiable" killing. According to Mullin, the Kid was arrested the next morning when he appeared for breakfast at the hotel dining room near the saloon; according to Rasch, the Kid entered the hotel one afternoon and was arrested by the local sheriff, who put his six-shooters on a meal tray, covered them with a napkin, and then uncovered the weapons and arrested the Kid when he reached the Kid's table.[13]

While it is uncertain how the Kid managed to escape the post's guardhouse—one version has him throwing salt in the guard's eyes—escape he did into the surrounding darkness one evening with the help of John Murphy's swift horse named "Cashaw." He made his way to Richard Knight's ranch approximately forty miles south of Silver City and stayed there for about three weeks. During this time he no doubt visited his stepfather and brother in nearby Georgetown or Silver City and saw to it that Murphy's horse was returned to Fort Grant. He may have drifted down to Sonora, Mexico, or wandered among gambling games in remote mining and cow camps; he may have begun his career as a rustler at this time, if we can believe a Mesilla *Independent* story of 13 October 1877 in which a "party of thieves, among whom was Henry Antrim," stole three horses from a coal camp.[14] However he occupied these few weeks after the killing of Cahill, the Kid eventually emerged— on foot, exhausted, alone—at the Heiskell Jones's ranch in the Seven Rivers area of Lincoln County, New Mexico, in late October 1877.

> "Advise persons never to engage in killing."
> —Billy the Kid, *Mesilla News,*
> 16 April 1881

When Henry McCarty, now known as William H. Bonney, departed the Jones ranch after recovering from an encounter with Apaches, he rode his borrowed horse northward along the Pecos River. Along his route he met George and Frank Coe and Richard Brewer, small ranchers who explained to the Kid the troubles in Lincoln County. The complications, motivations, personalities, and violent actions of the persons involved in the Lincoln County turmoil are too numerous to discuss here, where our immediate concern is to discover the Kid; however, certain facts need to be established to understand the Kid's participation in this violent time, which occupied the attention, on occasion, of territorial governors and judicial officers, a special investigator from Washington, D.C., Cabinet-level Secretaries in the Hayes administration, the President of the United States, and the foreign minister of Great Britain.[15]

The 1877–78 violence in Lincoln County has been portrayed through the years as a conflict motivated by a dispute between cattle baron John Chisum and jealous, hostile small ranchers. Without disregarding this conflict, nor the added adversary position we find in the Seven Rivers Warriors' efforts to protect their grazing and water rights, it would seem that the Lincoln County War's chief cause was the financial rivalry of, on the one hand, L. G. Murphy, James J. Dolan, and James Riley, and, on the other hand, Alexander McSween, John Tunstall, and John Chisum. The Murphy-Dolan-Riley concern was supported by Thomas B. Catron—U. S. District Attorney and President of the First National Bank of Santa Fe—and other members of the so-called Santa Fe Ring, which controlled the Territory's legal, political, and monetary matters. The complicated state of affairs in Lincoln County can be seen in a letter John Tunstall wrote to his father in Great Britain in April 1877:

> *Everything* in New Mexico that pays *at all* . . . is worked by a "ring," there is the "Indian ring," the "army ring," the "Roman Catholic ring," the "cattle ring," the "horsethieves ring," the "land ring," and half a dozen other rings. . . . I am at work at present making myself a ring and have succeeded admirably so far. [16]

In early 1877, the financial rivalry of two opposing "rings" became apparent when the Lincoln County Bank—with Chisum as president, McSween as vice-president, and Tunstall as cashier—and the John H. Tunstall Company opened for business in Lincoln in direct opposition to J. J. Dolan and Company.

By the time the Kid entered the Pecos country and began working for Tunstall in the late fall or early winter of 1877, the Dolan people, heavily mortgaged to Catron's bank, had initiated a series of legal maneuvers to combat the financial inroads made by the new "ring." These legal maneuvers were founded on complications arising from the disposition of the will of Emil Fritz, a former partner of Murphy's who had died of dropsy while visiting his native Germany in 1874. Upon Fritz's death, his brother and sister living in New Mexico, Charles Fritz and Mrs. Emelie Scholand, retained McSween's legal services to collect the $10,000 life insurance policy held by Emil Fritz. When the settlement was delayed by a dispute over the cause of death, McSween traveled to St. Louis and engaged a New York law firm to obtain the policy's full amount. The New York firm was successful in its efforts, and McSween deducted their fee of $2,800, as well as his own fees and expenses from the settlement's full amount—yet he failed to return any remaining monies to the Fritz heirs. Finally in December 1877 the Fritz heirs, persuaded by Dolan and guided by Catron's law firm, obtained an indictment in Judge Warren Bristol's court against McSween for embezzlement. Soon afterward, the Fritz heirs learned that McSween had been arrested in Las Vegas as he, his wife, and John Chisum prepared to board a stage for a St. Louis business trip. [17]

As the new year's first weeks passed by and McSween remained in the Las Vegas jail until his hearing in the Mesilla district court, several important events occurred that ultimately led to the single act—the murder of Tunstall—precipitating the 1878 violence in Lincoln County. As the Kid travelled between Tunstall's Rio Feliz ranch and the Tunstall store in Lincoln to protect his employer's interests, Tunstall composed what some have called his "death warrant": a letter to the Mesilla *Independent,* published on 26 January 1878, which charged Dolan, Riley, and Sheriff Brady with using county tax money to finance their fraudulent operations. Also in January Dolan mortgaged his entire holdings in land, stock, and buildings to obtain further financing from Catron. Shortly after these events, McSween traveled to Bristol's court in Mesilla and learned that his bail was $8,000 and that his case was to be continued in the April term of the district court in Lincoln. As the McSween-Tunstall party returned to Lincoln from Mesilla, Judge Bristol approved a writ of attachment against McSween's property since District Attorney Rynerson refused to accept McSween's bond. On 8 February 1878 before McSween and Tunstall reached Lincoln, Sheriff Brady began attaching both men's property, even though their partnership was not yet legally in effect.[18] Because the refusal of his bond meant he would be placed in Brady's custody until April, and because San Miguel County Deputy Barrier decided not to become involved in Brady's affairs, McSween was "allowed" to escape custody before the party reached Lincoln. McSween soon wrote a letter to Secretary of the Interior Carl Schurz and charged that the Dolan company, in league with local Indian agents, had stolen cattle to meet government contracts and had sold supplies in the Dolan store that were intended for the Mescalero Apache reservation.

The questionable legal right for Brady to seize Tunstall's property in Lincoln did not prevent him from deputizing Billy Mathews and others and dispatching them on 12 February to Tunstall's Rio Feliz ranch with orders to attach the livestock and property there. However, when this posse, among whose members were a group of escaped rustlers led by Jesse Evans, reached the ranch they discovered—as the Kid later told Special Investigator Frank Angel—that the defenders had "cut portholes into the walls of the house and filled sacks with earth . . . this course being thought necessary as the posse was composed of murderers, thieves, outlaws, and desperate characters. . . ."[19] The posse relinquished the field on this day to Tunstall's defenders and turned back to Lincoln to consult with Brady; on the next day the Kid, Robert Widenmann, and Fred Waite also returned to Lincoln. It was not until 23 February that the Kid and other surviving friends of Tunstall managed to recover Tunstall's store from Brady's men.

As Dolan was drumming up support from area ranchers who owed him in one way or another, the Kid and other Tunstall hands returned to the ranch and prepared for the expected return of a more formidable Dolan-led posse. However, Tunstall reached the ranch on the evening of 17 February and informed his supporters that he intended to pull out with only a few of his horses, which were not included in the writ of attachment, and to allow the courts to decide the matter. Around 8:00 A.M. on 18 February 1878 Tunstall, the Kid, Dick Brewer, Fred Waite, Bob Widenmann, and John Middleton started driving nine horses to Lincoln. After they had departed, the expected large posse arrived and discovered Tunstall's absence. Mathews then authorized Billy Morton and several others to pursue the Englishman and return with the horses. Later that day, around 5:00 P.M., Tunstall and his crew were about thirty miles from the ranch when a flock of wild turkeys rose into view. As some of the group began to hunt them, thus leaving Tunstall momentarily alone, the Kid and Middleton noticed, from their vantage point a few hundred yards in the rear, the large Morton posse top a ridge and begin shooting in their direction. The two spurred forward to warn the others, and while Billy, Brewer, and Widenmann headed for a defensive position on a nearby hill, Middleton yelled to Tunstall to follow the rest towards safety. Middleton himself then spurred off to join the others. Tunstall was left alone, evidently having been unable to comprehend what Middleton said.

However, Tunstall was soon surrounded by the lead contingent of the posse. As Tunstall approached Morton, Jesse Evans, and Tom Hill, Morton shot him in the breast and, as Tunstall lay dying on the ground, Hill or Evans shot him in the head. Another bullet was necessary to kill Tunstall's horse. The trio then fired two shots from Tunstall's gun and claimed to the rest of the late-arriving posse that Tunstall had fired first.[20] Meanwhile, the Kid and the others managed to reach Lincoln around 10:00 P.M. that night and told McSween of the day's gruesome events.

Within the next few days an autopsy was performed on Tunstall's body, and Justice J. B. Wilson of Lincoln issued warrants for the arrest of the murderers. When Brady refused to serve them on posse members that were frequenting Dolan's store in Lincoln, the Kid, Fred Waite, and Atanacio Martínez attempted to serve them. Brady in turn arrested the trio and put them in jail. Because of this arrest on 20 February, the Kid and the others were forced to miss Tunstall's funeral—contrary to the traditional notion that the kid swore an oath of vengeance over Tunstall's coffin. After the funeral, however, he and the other two were released at the demand of local citizens. The Kid then joined a special posse called "The Regulators," a group formed by the local populace and authorized by Justice Wilson to seek out Tunstall's murderers. Most significantly, as all this activity was happening in Lincoln, Pat Garrett and two other buffalo hunters arrived in Fort Sumner, about ninety miles northeast of Lincoln, after a journey from the Texas panhandle.

Armed with their own legal status, "The Regulators" began the process of avenging Tunstall's murder while McSween—fearing rearrest and confinement by Sheriff Brady—left Lincoln for the safety of the surrounding hills and sheep camps. On 4 March Brewer and his posse left Lincoln for the Pecos country and soon caught up with Billy Morton and Frank Baker near the lower Penasco; on 6 March, after a six-mile chase, Morton and Baker were captured. On 9 March after hearing that Dolan was organizing a large group of men to free Morton and Baker, the special posse, under circumstances that are still cloudy today, killed Morton and Baker.[21] Presumably the pair were killed during an escape attempt in which the two prisoners also killed William McCloskey, but the pair were probably executed by the entire posse—not just the Kid—since at least nine wounds were found in each corpse and since the prisoners would have been allowed to "escape" if placed in Sheriff Brady's jail.

After this bloody episode, Territorial Governor Axtell soon cancelled both Justice Wilson's authority as justice of the peace and Dick Brewer's status as special constable. As a result of this action, "The Regulators" forfeited their legal status and were thereafter pursued by both Brady and U.S. Army troopers from Fort Stanton. Around 10:00 A.M. on April Fool's Day, the Kid and several others ambushed Sheriff Brady and Deputy George Hindman as the latter two walked from the Wortley Hotel to the Lincoln courthouse. The sheriff and his deputy were followed at a distance by three others—one of whom was Billy Mathews—and when this trailing trio saw Brady and Hindman fall they quickly reached cover and returned fire, supposedly giving the Kid a flesh wound in the thigh when he rushed out from behind a plank gate next to Tunstall's store to retrieve the victims' weapons. Accounts of their fight vary: some narratives have it that the Kid hid in Lincoln in a barrel or under a bed until his wound received treatment, but he and his companions ultimately reached their mounts and escaped safely into the hills surrounding Lincoln.[22]

After the slaying of Brady and Hindman, the Lincoln County Commissioners authorized a $200 reward for their killers. On 4 April, Andrew L. "Buckshot" Roberts (Bill Williams), after verifying the truth of this reward offer, left Lincoln on a mule and headed for Blazer's Mill, situated on the edge of the Apache reservation on the banks of the Rio Tularosa. Unfortunatey for Roberts, he reached the mill, or more likely returned to the mill after an earlier departure that same day, while "The Regulators" were inside eating dinner. When he refused to surrender peaceably to Frank Coe, the shooting commenced: Roberts immediately received a mortal wound in the lower stomach from Charlie Bowdre's six-shooter, but his initial blast hit Bowdre's belt buckle, ricocheted, and tore off George Coe's trigger finger. Before he died, however, Roberts, who was also a member of the posse that killed Tunstall, managed to kill Dick Brewer and to wound Frank Middleton, as well as to stand off any attempt by the Kid to storm his position.

Between the remainder of April and the infamous July siege in Lincoln, the combatants for each side harassed each other in court, exchanged gunfire across Lincoln streets and the open stretches of landscape, and rustled stock from each other's herds. Armed cowboys frequently sat in McSween's parlor on Sundays to sing hymns and listen to Dr. Ealy preach on Paul and Silas at Philippi.[23] The grand jury at the district court in Lincoln County was empanelled in mid-April, and—despite Judge Bristol's prejudicial directions to the jury—dismissed charges against McSween, charged Governor Axtell with negligence of duty, and formally indicted several persons, including William H. Bonney, for the murders of Tunstall, Brady, and Roberts. By the end of April, Dolan relinquished his business affairs to Catron; by the end of May, Governor Axtell had installed the pro-Catron George Peppin as Sheriff of Lincoln. Furthermore, as an indication of how serious an issue was the corruption and violence in Lincoln County, Judge Frank W. Angel, special investigator from the Department of the Interior, arrived in Lincoln and began taking affidavits on the county's recent history. He heard the Kid's testimony on 8 June 1878.

There were several skirmishes between "The Regulators" and Peppin's men, who for the major portion of this period had the support of army troopers and John Kinney's gunslingers. On 5 July the Kid, McSween, and a few others left Chisum's South Springs ranch and saw their numbers grow as they neared Lincoln. McSween and his group of about forty men reached Lincoln on Sunday evening, 14 July and positioned themselves in strategic houses along the town's main road. When Peppin and his men later reached Lincoln they realized that the strategic positions held by McSween's group made the process of serving warrants tenuous at best. Peppin set up his headquarters at Wortley's Hotel west of McSween's house and sent some men into the hills above town for long-range target practice.

From the Sunday evening deployment of the opposing forces to Col. N. A. M. Dudley's arrival on 19 July with troopers, a howitzer, and a Gatling gun, the opposing forces exchanged desultory fire, and the McSween group was confident of victory. In retrospect the most important bullet fired during this stage of the siege was one that narrowly missed one of Dudley's troopers on 16 July. Peppin claimed that McSween's men fired on the lone soldier and requested Dudley's assistance in dislodging the McSween people. Although the law prevented the use of federal troops to aid local law officers, Dudley left Fort Stanton and entered Lincoln around mid-morning on 19 July. He subsequently forced McSween men stationed in the Montano and Ellis houses to leave town, and he forced Justice Wilson to swear out a warrant against McSween for firing on a United States Army trooper. He also threatened military action against McSween if any shots were directed at his troopers.

Around mid-day on 19 July, Peppin-men John Long and "Dummy" attempted to torch the rear kitchen in the east wing of McSween's house but were driven to cover by shots from George Coe and Henry Brown, stationed in a bunkhouse behind the nearby Tunstall store. Long and another man named Buck Powell discovered that their only available cover was the open trench exiting from McSween's two-holer backhouse, and they were thus forced to wait until dark before they could leave the scene. Meanwhile, as the burning shavings were being extinguished by the Kid and others in the house, Andy Boyle torched the west wing's rear kitchen. As the day progressed the steadily-burning fire forced the McSween people to move back toward the last available room, the aforementioned rear kitchen in the east wing.

Although the Kid would later testify at the Dudley Court of Inquiry that "we all tried to escape at once," and although legend has it that the Kid, after lighting a cigarette on one of the burning embers in the kitchen, was the last to leave the house, it is well established that two separate groups attempted to escape in two different directions at two different times. The first group of men, including the Kid and Tom O'Folliard, ran out of the kitchen's east door and toward an opening in the east picket fence surrounding the McSween house. Except for Harvey Morris, this group managed to reach the safety of Tunstall's store and ultimately the Rio Bonito. The other group of men, including McSween, met such a devastating round of fire on their exit from the kitchen that they retreated toward the nearby woodpile, backhouse, and chickenhouse. After a few minutes McSween offered to surrender, but when Bob Beckwith stepped forward to claim his prisoner one of McSween's men in the chickenhouse killed Beckwith.[24] McSween was quickly killed by the other Peppin men stationed around the house, and the ex-partner of Tunstall joined in death his allies Vincenté and Francisco Romero.

The Kid and his few remaining friends traveled among the hills, deserts, and outlying villages and camps in Lincoln County during the weeks between the escape from the burning house and a visit to old Tascosa in the fall. He established a base of operations at Fort Sumner and at times visited Sallie Chisum at the Bosque Grande and gave her small presents. He also furthered his acquaintance with Pat Garrett in Beaver Smith's Fort Sumner saloon. Meanwhile, Frank Angel concluded his investigation and presented it to Secretary of the Interior Carl Schurz; in September 1878, the nineteen-year-old Kid heard that Schurz had succeeded in persuading President Hayes to remove Axtell from office. Axtell's replacement was General Lew Wallace, Civil War veteran and author.

> I am not afraid to die like a man fighting but I would not like to be killed like a dog unarmed.
> —Billy the Kid to Lew Wallace,
> 20 March 1879

During the fall of 1878 Billy the Kid and his companions were seen in Old Tascosa delivering stolen horses to prospective buyers. While there they reassured the locals that their interests were not in rustling Texas livestock for New Mexico markets by instead engaging in horseraces, shooting matches, and gambling games, and attending the area bailes (dances). At one baile the

Kid and Henry Hoyt left during intermission and walked a short distance away; on their return to the dance they decided to have a foot race for the remainder of the journey. The pair started running, but as they neared the door of the dance hall, the Kid tripped over the threshold and went sprawling across the dance floor as several men—uneasy at the sudden interruption—drew their six-shooters and covered the Kid.

By late November 1878 the Kid was back in the Fort Sumner area, and there he heard about the governor's amnesty proclamation as he gambled and rustled his way across the New Mexican landscape. While Wallace, Dolan, Mrs. McSween, and her lawyer Huston Chapman wrangled over the conflicting interpretations of recent Lincoln County events, Billy and Tom O'Folliard decided to make peace with the Dolan outfit so as, according to Billy, "to be able to lay aside our arms and go to Work."[25] On 18 February 1879, exactly one year after Tunstall's death, the Kid and O'Folliard rode into Lincoln and met Dolan, Jesse Evans, and Bill Campbell. Around 10:00 P.M., after an apparently agreeable meeting, the group started for a saloon to celebrate their peace. During their walk to the saloon, however, the group crossed paths with Huston Chapman. As the Kid and O'Folliard looked on, Dolan and Campbell shot Chapman and then set fire to his body after probably soaking the lawyer's clothes with whiskey.[26] To their dismay, the Kid and O'Folliard found themselves Dolan's hostages since they had witnessed the murder. Although forced to continue to the saloon with the Dolan crowd, the Kid and O'Folliard later managed to slip away—Billy by volunteering to return to Chapman's charred corpse and place a pistol in his right hand so as to make the murder look like self-defense. Instead, of course, he headed for the hills.

The nineteen-year-old youth who had hoped to conclude a peace treaty with his enemies now found himself dodging the posses and troopers dispatched by Wallace to capture him to obtain his testimony concerning the Chapman murder. Furthermore, his indictment for the murder of Sheriff Brady made him ineligible to receive Wallace's offer of amnesty. Nevertheless, when Wallace arrived in Lincoln in March 1879 the Kid began his correspondence with the governor on the subject of his safety and a pardon in exchange for his testimony. As he told Wallace in one letter,

> I have no wish to fight any more. Indeed I have not raised an arm since your proclamation. As to my character, I refer to any of the citizens, for the majority of them are my friends and have been helping me all they could.[27]

On 17 March, the Kid—armed with a rifle and a six-shooter—left San Patricio and met Wallace around 9:00 P.M. in Squire Wilson's house in Lincoln. Billy agreed to submit to a mock arrest and to testify before a grand jury if Wallace would ensure his safety while he was in jail and would guarantee his freedom after his court appearance. Even though Evans and Campbell escaped from Fort Stanton within a day of the Kid-Wallace meeting, thus endangering the Kid's safety in the event of his testimony against Chapman's murderers, the Kid on 21 March surrendered to Sheriff Kimbrell and was eventually confined to Juan Patrón's vacant storeroom until the April term of court. While there the Kid was interviewed by Wallace, who desired information on cattle rustling by John Selman and other desperadoes. Wallace also heard local minstrels serenade Billy, who, all in all, had to be the least of Wallace's worries during this time of depredations by both Apaches and John Selman.

During April and May the Lincoln County Grand Jury and the U.S. Army Court of Inquiry began their deliberations into Dudley's actions during the McSween siege. Although Evans and the Seven Rivers Boys saw their indictments thrown out of court due to Wallace's amnesty proclamation of the previous November, Billy discovered that Wallace could not obtain District Attorney Rynerson's approval of a pardon in exchange for Billy's testimony regarding Chapman's murder. Instead, Rynerson asked for a change of venue to Dona Ana County, and Judge Bristol agreed to the request. Billy remained under house arrest in Lincoln, and in late May he testified at the Army's inquiry into Dudley's behavior the previous July at McSween's house. Upon learning later on that Dudley was exonerated after a three-minute deliberation by his fellow officers, and hearing that Evans and Campbell were still eluding Wallace troopers, the Kid realized that Wallace, however well-intentioned, was unable to completely enforce any of his desires on Rynerson, Bristol, the U.S. Army, and—in the background—Catron and the Santa Fe Ring. In late June the Kid, perhaps with the consent of his "jailers," rode to freedom on a horse supplied by Doc Scurlock.

Between this escape and Pat Garrett's election as sheriff in November 1880, the Kid and his few remaining allies worked and played in the Fort Sumner, Anton Chico, White Oaks, and Puerto de Luna area. Their work was rustling; their targets were Chisum, Mexicans, and other Anglo ranchers. At one point the Kid returned to Arizona with some cattle he sold to one Patrick Shanley. "When Shanley asked for a bill of sale and title for the cattle, the Kid said 'You'll have to go down the road 200 miles and get it'."[28] During this eighteen-month period the Kid was also indicted for keeping a gaming table in Las Vegas, was said to have met Jesse James in a Hot Springs, N.M., eating place, and was also said to have given Pat Garrett a case of beer to help the latter celebrate the opening of his restaurant in Fort Sumner.[29] In August 1879 Wallace's soldier-posse apparently surrounded the Kid in a cabin six miles south of Lincoln, but the Kid, as he did when he was twelve years old, waited until dark and escaped through the cabin's chimney to avoid capture.

A few months later, in January 1880, the Kid killed Joe Grant in Bob Hargrove's Fort Sumner saloon after the gunman drew his six-shooter and fired at the Kid. Contrary to the legend, the Kid, as Maurice G. Fulton concludes, did not borrow the drunken Grant's six-shooter and turn its cylinder so the next round would be an empty chamber; rather, if the incident happened at all, Grant's revolver—as was frequently the case with frontier firearms—failed to fire at the critical moment when he had the drop on the Kid. Whatever the case, by the early summer the Kid's "gang" was solidified into the group composed of Tom O'Folliard, Charles Bowdre, Dave Rudabaugh, Billie Wilson, and Tom Pickett. By the early fall the Kid learned of Garrett's candidacy for sheriff, and he probably conducted an informal campaign against Garrett's election. The night before the election, for example, the Kid dropped in at George Curry's ranch and told his audience that he had campaigned against Garrett at a dance held earlier that evening—the next day the precinct voted for Sheriff Kimbrell.[30] However, Garrett was supported by Chisum, J. C. Lea, and other Pecos area ranchers who wanted to dispose of this symbol of defiance to the law, and Garrett—ex-bartender, gambler, buffalo-hunter, and restaurant owner—defeated the incumbent Kimbrell on 11 November 1880.

Although Garrett was not officially installed in office until January 1881, he had already been appointed by Thomas Catron to the post of deputy U.S. marshal. Thus, Garrett was not prohibited from crossing county lines in his search for the Kid, who was still under federal indictment for the killing of "Buckshot" Roberts. In late November 1880 the Kid, Rudabaugh, and Wilson rustled eight horses from a Puerto de Luna storekeeper-rancher named Grzelachowski and drove them to Jim Greathouse's stage station on the road to White Oaks. After entering White Oaks, supposedly to see Judge Ira Leonard, the gang was spotted at the West and Dedrick stables by Barney Mason, Garrett's brother-in-law who at that time was investigating counterfeiting in the area. The next few days saw sporadic pursuits and shooting by the local posses—in one encounter the Kid and Wilson had their horses shot out from under them at Coyote Springs. On 27 November, however, the Kid and his friends were surrounded at Greathouse's Station. According to a letter the Kid wrote Wallace on 12 December, Billy decided his pursuers were "nothing more than a mob" and told them that they could "only take me a corpse." Instead of the Kid, however, it was James Carlyle—posse member held hostage by the Kid's group—who became a corpse, apparently killed by one or all of his captors as he jumped through one of the station's windows.[31] After the Carlyle killing the Kid's group left the station on foot and eventually reached the Wilcox-Brazil ranch about twelve miles from Fort Sumner.

Approximately two weeks after Carlyle's death Garrett initiated the series of moves that resulted in the Kid's capture at Stinking Springs on 21 December 1880. Garrett and Mason united on 14 December at Anton Chico with a group of Texas cowboys sent over to recover stock stolen from the Texas panhandle. Because of heavy snowstorms and gusty winds, Garrett's posse endured a tedious trip to Fort Sumner. They quietly arrived there on 17 December and occupied the old Indian Hospital at the eastern edge of the fort. After sending a native youth to the Kid's hideout at the Wilcox-Brazil ranch with a note stating that the posse had left for Roswell, Garrett and his men began their wait for the Kid's appearance. The next night, as the Kid's small group approached Fort Sumner to resupply their needs before leaving the country, Garrett's men ambushed them and killed O'Folliard, who was riding point at the time because the Kid supposedly turned back to the rear to get some chewing tobacco from another rider. The rest of the Kid's party escaped the trap, but they were soon captured at the deserted Perea house at Stinking Springs, after a day-long siege during which Charlie Bowdre was killed.

Garrett and his posse transported the Kid, Pickett, Wilson, and Rudabaugh to Las Vegas without incident, although in Fort Sumner Charlie Bowdre's wife clobbered one Texas cowboy with a branding iron when she heard the news of her husband's death. As the group entered Las Vegas on the afternoon of 26 December, "groups of people flocked to the jail and hung around the corners straining their necks to catch a glimpse of Sheriff Garrett, Frank Stewart and the brave fellows who had brought in the outlaws."[32] In the Las Vegas jail, which the Kid thought was "a terrible place to put a fellow in," the Kid granted a short interview to a local reporter who described the Kid thusly:

> He did look human, indeed, but there was nothing very mannish about him in appearance, for he looked and acted a mere boy. He is about five feet eight or nine inches tall, slightly built and lithe, weighing about 140; a frank open countenance, looking like a school boy, with the traditional silky fuzz on his upper lip; clear blue eyes, with a roguish snap about them; light hair and complexion. He is, in all, quite a handsome looking fellow, the only imperfection being two prominent front teeth slightly protruding like squirrel's teeth, and he has agreeable and winning ways.[33]

The next day, after a short verbal skirmish with local Mexicans who wanted to detain Rudabaugh for his murder of Antonio Valdez, Garrett and his party boarded a train for Santa Fe, where the Kid and the others remained in jail until their various court appearances.

Between 1 January and 27 March the Kid again resumed his correspondence with Wallace in an attempt to gain a pardon, but Wallace was completing *Ben Hur* and—because of Garfield's recent election—was preparing to leave New Mexico for a more prestigious position (he was appointed minister to Turkey). On 4 March Billy complained to Wallace that he was "getting left in the cold," and that he guessed "they mean to send me up without giving me any show but they will have a nice time doing it. I am not entirely without friends."[34] On 28 March Billy Bonney and Billie Wilson were quietly boarded on a Santa Fe railway train and moved to Mesilla for their trials. When Billy and his legal counsel Ira Leonard disembarked the train at Las Cruces, "an inquisitive mob gathered around the coach and someone asked which is 'Billy the Kid'. The Kid himself answered by placing his hand on Judge Leonard's shoulder, and saying, 'this is the man'."[35]

The Kid began his court appearances on 6 April in Judge Bristol's courtroom. Leonard managed to quash the federal indictment against the Kid for the killing of "Buckshot" Roberts on the grounds that the incident did not take place on federal land. However, the Kid was immediately rearrested and placed on trial for the murder of Sheriff Brady. This case was heard by a prejudiced judge and an unsympathetic jury; the Kid was unable to summon any witnesses for his defense since such witnesses were either dead, in hiding, or in jail. The jury returned a guilty verdict on 9 April, and four days later Judge Bristol sentenced the Kid to hang by the neck in Lincoln on 13 May 1881, between the hours of 9:00 A.M. and 3:00 P.M. Although the Santa Fe *New Mexican* thought the Kid should be flattered by the fact that the execution "will probably attract more people than any similar event that ever occurred in the Territory," the Kid told a Mesilla *News* reporter that "I think it hard that I should be the only one to suffer the extreme penalty of the law."[36] Not only were Evans and Campbell still free after the killing of Chapman, but Dolan was eventually acquitted of the Chapman murder in a Socorro courtroom.

Lacking the funds to finance an appeal, the Kid was turned over to Garrett's custody and transported to Lincoln in a wagon guarded by seven deputies. On 21 April the caravan reached Lincoln and the Kid was installed in a second-floor corner room of the old Murphy-Dolan-Riley store, which had been purchased from Catron by the Lincoln County Commissioners and converted into a courthouse. A week later the Kid escaped his confinement and rode to freedom after killing his two guards, Robert Olinger and J.W. Bell. Versions of this escape are as numerous as there are people to comment on the event—versions which focus on slipped handcuffs, dropped cards, and knives smuggled in a tortilla. Nevertheless, it appears likely that Sam Corbet, an ex-clerk in Tunstall's store, slipped Billy a note informing him that a six-shooter, wrapped in old newspapers, would be hidden in the jail's outdoor privy.[37]

Around 5:30 P.M. on 28 April, when Pat Garrett was away collecting taxes or (as some believe) buying lumber for the Kid's scaffold, Olinger escorted prisoners from the Tularosa Ditch War over to the Whortley Hotel for dinner. The Kid then visited the privy, obtained the six-shooter, got the drop on Bell, and—when back inside the courthouse—killed Bell when the latter tried to escape. Olinger heard the shots and was killed by blasts from his own shotgun as he walked across the street to investigate the cause of the shooting. After killing the two deputies, the Kid managed to loosen one shackle and to tie the chain to his belt. He then mounted a spirited horse owned by Billy Burt and was bucked off, but he then remounted the horse and rode out of town. After loosening the remaining shackle with the help of José Córdova and Sepio Salazar, and borrowing a horse for the long ride to Fort Sumner, Billy began his last days of hide-and-seek with Garrett, his fugitive days and nights among sheep camps, friendly homes, and old Fort Sumner.[38]

In early July 1881 John Poe, a Garrett deputy stationed in White Oaks, learned from a man that the Kid was still in the Fort Sumner area and not in old Mexico. At first Poe was inclined to doubt the story, since the man claimed to be sleeping off a drunk in West and Dedrick's stable when he overheard a conversation. However, he decided to tell Garrett. Poe reached Garrett on the latter's ranch near Roswell and eventually convinced Garrett to leave for Fort Sumner. On 13 July, Garrett, Poe, and Tip McKinney camped near Taiban Spring below Fort Sumner; on 14 July Poe rode into Fort Sumner to reconnoiter. Although Poe was selected because he was not familiar to Fort Sumner residents, he learned nothing. He left around mid-day for Rudulph Milner's ranch north of Fort Sumner.

At moonrise Poe reunited with Garrett and McKinney at La Punta de la Glorietta, and the trio traveled to the outskirts of Fort Sumner. After waiting for two hours in a peach orchard on the edge of the fort, Garrett decided to call on Pete Maxwell and ask him if he had seen the Kid in the area. As Garrett entered Maxwell's bedroom and as Poe and McKinney stationed themselves near the picket fence surrounding Maxwell's house, the Kid—in stocking feet and armed with a butcher knife and a Colt .41 in his waistband—left Bob Campbell's room (next to Celsa Gutiérrez's dwelling) to go to Maxwell's meat locker to cut a steak from a newly-butchered carcass. Earlier that night he had attended a baile in Fort Sumner and, when the dance was ended, he had returned to the nearby sheep camp of Ramón Trujillo. For some reason—perhaps love, or a business meeting with a cowboy—the Kid had returned to Sumner. Upon passing the old dance hall and coming across the two deputies standing outside Maxwell's house, the Kid became disconcerted, perhaps frightened, at the presence of these strangers. He entered the house and then the bedroom where, for once in his life, he asked a question instead of firing at an unknown presence, there with Maxwell and himself. Garrett instantly shot the Kid in the chest. Within seconds Billy the Kid was history, was the past; Pat Garrett, according to Deluvina Maxwell at the funeral, was "a piss-pot," a spoiler.

A candle-lit vigil over the Kid's body lasted the rest of the night, and in the morning the Kid, dressed in an oversized, borrowed white shirt, was buried in the Fort's cemetery next to Bowdre and O'Folliard. During his short life of an estimated twenty-one years, seven months, and twenty-two days, Henry McCarty killed four men and participated in the killings of five others during his travels in New Mexico and Arizona after a boyhood spent in New York City, Indianapolis, Wichita, Colorado, and Silver City. Of such stuff legends are created, and in such legends interpreters have been interested since the Kid's anticlimactic death in Pete Maxwell's bedroom.

PART TWO

Inventing the Outlaw

. . . one of the things the Western is always about is America rewriting and reinterpreting her own past, however honestly or dishonestly it may be done.

—Philip French, *Westerns,* 1973

3 "We Ain't None the Sadder"

Visions of the Kid and the American Search for Order, 1881–1925

Billy was a bad man
And carried a big gun,
He was always after Greasers
And kept 'em on the run.
. . . .

But one day he met a man
Who was a whole lot badder.
And now he's dead,
And we ain't none the sadder.

—John Lomax (ed.), *Cowboy Songs*, 1916

After Billy the Kid died on 14 July 1881 territorial newspapers voiced relief at the news of the Kid's demise and loud hosannas for Pat Garrett, New Mexico's deliverer from the Kid's bloody reign of terror. Within a week of the Kid's death, the Las Vegas *Daily Optic,* a newspaper that relentlessly boosted the territory's opportunities for development, called for donations to reward Garrett for his accomplishment and concluded that with the death of such a "bold thief and cold-blooded murderer . . . all mankind rejoices and the newspapers will now have something else to talk about."[1] On 23 July, *The New Southwest and Grant County Herald,* published in Silver City, proclaimed that "despite the glamour of romance thrown around his dare-devil life by sensation writers, the fact is he was a low down vulgar cut-throat with probably not one redeeming quality."[2] Perhaps the most noteworthy of all the territorial obituaries about this "vulgar cut-throat" was that published by the Santa Fe *Weekly Democrat,* which explicitly linked the Kid with our most familiar avatar of death, sin, and destruction:

> No sooner had the floor caught his descending form which had a pistol in one hand and a knife in the other, than there was a strong odor of brimstone in the air, and a dark figure with wings of a dragon, claws like a tiger, eyes like balls of fire, and horns like a bison, hovered over the corpse for a moment and with a fiendish laugh, said "Ha, Ha! this is my meat!" and then sailed off through the window. He did not leave his card, but he is a gentleman well known to us by reputation, and thereby hangs a "tail."[3]

What distinguished Billy the Kid from other local desperadoes like Dave Rudabaugh or Jesse Evans, of course, was that newspapers for a while talked of nothing else but this devil's "meat," and that these reports of his death were reprinted and circulated across the United States and also even in Great Britain. In New York City eight newspapers published notices of the Kid's death, ranging from one sentence to extended paragraphs.[4] While the *New York Times* and the *Post* briefly mentioned the fact of Garrett's killing of the Kid in the line of duty, other papers like the *Sun,* the *Mail,* the *Globe,* and the *Daily Graphic* exaggerated, fabricated, and derided the Kid's career at the same time they began circulating the famous twenty-one men for twenty-one years notion about the Kid's murder count. The *Sun* believed the Kid to be a Brooklyn native who became in his short life "the scourge of the Southwest," a notorious "blood thirsty young outlaw with murder in his heart." The *Globe,* indulging in an ethnic slur, believed the Kid to be a native of Ireland who after crossing the plains at the age of twelve "became a cattle rustler and . . . killed twenty-one men and a large number of Mexicans and Indians." The *Daily Graphic,* on the other hand, more than lived up to its name when it summarized the Kid's career as concluding when, "with fangs snarling and firing a revolver like a maniac, W. H. Bonney (alias Billy the Kid) fought his way out of his ambushed robber castle at Stinking Springs where he lived in luxury on his ill gotten gains with his Mexican beauties. . . . " According to the *Daily Graphic,* in the final analysis the Kid

> had built up a criminal organization worthy of the underworld of any of the European capitals. He defied the law to stop him and he stole, robbed, raped, and pillaged the countryside until his name became synonymous with that of the grim reaper himself. A Robin Hood with no mercy, a Richard the Lion Hearted who feasted on blood, he became, in the short span of his twenty-one years, the master criminal of the American southwest. His passing marks the end of wild west lawlessness.

Those New York City newspapers that commented at some length on the event did, like the territorial New Mexican papers, imply their agreement with the *Daily Graphic's* verdict that Garrett's action was admirable. And in case anyone questioned Garrett's summary justice in shooting the Kid, the *New York Tribune* was ready with a defense by noting, how such an action displayed "more of justice, rude as it is, than in many of the decisions of the courts, aided as they are by all the machinery of civilization."

These newspaper accounts not only introduced tales about the Kid's career that would fuel the development of his legend, but in statements such as those by the *Tribune* and the *Daily Graphic* about the slow movement of law enforcement a leitmotif of frontier justice was projected into the Kid-Garrett story. Along with responses of newspapers in New Mexico and New York City to the Kid's death, other papers in other places repeated and lightly publicized similar themes about the end of lawlessness, the desire for an immediate justice, and the barbarous nature of the Kid's exploits. News of the outlaw's death and rumors about the disposal of the Kid's remains prompted requests from distant readers to have parts of his body forwarded to them. On a more serious level, the Kansas City *Journal* suggested on 30 July that "in Missouri is needed just some such man as Pat Garrett," a manhunter "who will follow the James boys and their companions in crime to their den, and shoot them down without mercy. . . . " By performing such a deed, the *Journal* concluded, such a man would "be crowned with honors by the good people of this commonwealth, and be richly rewarded in money, besides."[6] On 18 August *The Times* of London reprinted the Santa Fe *New Mexican* obituary of the Kid on the same page that it informed its audience of the deteriorating state of President Garfield's health after he was wounded by an assassin. Significantly, this reprint noted Garrett's role as "the mainstay of law and order in Lincoln County, the chief reliance of the people in the dark days when danger lurked on every hand. . . ." In fulfilling this role, "the faithful and brave" Pat Garrett, readers of *The Times* learned, "accomplished the crowning feat of his life by bringing down his fierce and implacable foe single-handed. . . ."[7]

Within a few weeks of the Kid's death, there emerges in the printed obituaries from Las Vegas to London the outlines of a distinctive manner in perceiving the significance of the Kid's short, but bloody career. Images of the Kid clustered around the popular mythology of Satan and thus personified the outlaw as the devil's lieutenant, a prince of darkness, or the chief agent of "the dark days when danger lurked on every hand." Although we shall see how in later years the Kid's image would evolve from a "Robin Hood with no mercy" to a Robin Hood with mercy, in 1881 it was customary for observers to portray him as an unredeemable ally of those forces opposing the advance of law and order into the territory.

For those familiar with Kent Steckmesser's study of the growth of the Kid's legend, the immediate emergence of this "satanic" Billy is not surprising; however, we should also notice other elements at work in these brief obituaries which suggest something more revealing than just the predominance of a certain Kid image.[8] The fact is that for too long the visions of the Kid have been divorced from specific cultural contexts, and it is only by examining more than the image of the Kid that we can begin to make a connection between the Kid's creators and their cultural values. By examining also the form of the visions of the Kid and the characterization of others in the Kid's story, we should begin to notice that at the same time the Kid is being conceived as the latest incarnation of the grim reaper, Garrett is perceived as "the mainstay of law and order," the redeemer whose actions delivered the commonwealth from evil and brought an end to "wild west lawlessness"—thus making the country safe for women and children. This achievement, however, is accomplished only after a perilous struggle with what one obituary called "a fierce and implacable foe," and—significantly—the extralegal violent action necessary to rid society of this foe is in several places considered to be a legitimate response which ensures the preservation of society's ordered existence—and ensures the Kid's place in hell. In short, what we should notice even in these brief portrayals of the Kid is how the struggle between the Kid and Garrett is envisioned as an adventure story, which is resolved when the hero overcomes his deadly antagonist and restores civilization.

That the Kid's obituary writers interpreted his death in this manner reveals how easily both the Kid's real and imagined exploits were offered in the structural pattern of the romance, one of the four fundamental story forms in our culture (besides comedy, tragedy, and irony).[9] In its complete form, the romance story we are concerned with here does not, as its name implies, center on the hero's love interests, nor is it limited to the specific form of prose fiction practiced by such authors as Nathaniel Hawthorne. Rather, as Northrop Frye has demonstrated in his *Anatomy of Criticism,* the central plot of the romance is the adventure of a hero who undertakes a quest to achieve an important goal. The hero's quest characteristically is composed of three main stages: a perilous journey, a climactic struggle, and, finally, a recognition or exaltation of the hero by an admiring society. Because this quest assumes two main characters in conflict, a heroic protagonist and a villainous antagonist, Frye suggests that the central form of this story is dialectical:

> Everything is focussed on a conflict between the hero and his enemy, and all the reader's values are bound up with the hero. Hence the hero of the romance is analogous to the mythical Messiah or deliverer who comes from an upper world, and his enemy is analogous to the demonic powers of a lower world. The conflict however takes

place in, or at any rate primarily concerns *our* world, which is in
the middle, and which is characterized by the cyclical movement
of nature. Hence the opposite poles of the cycle of nature are as-
similated to the opposition of the hero and his enemy. The enemy
is associated with winter, darkness, confusion, sterility, moribund
life, and old age, and the hero with spring, dawn, order, fertility,
vigor, and youth.[10]

Except for the fact that the Kid is of course a youth, we can see how his
deadly conflict with Garrett, at least in the obituaries' accounts which extended the details of the Kid's death, reveals the emerging outlines of this
romance story. Not only do the Kid and Garrett become analogous respectively
to the demonic powers of the lower world and to the mythical deliverer, but
each is also associated on occasion with opposing cycles of nature: the Kid as
an agent of darkness and decay; Garrett as a representative of a renewed, vigorous society. In addition, Garrett's pursuit of, struggle with, and final defeat of the Kid results, as we have seen, in his exaltation by a grateful society,
and thus we notice how his heroic success illustrates the central moral fantasy
of this story by affirming the emergence of order and control over the competing human and natural forces of chaos, anarchy, and disorder.

In our cultural tradition the romance story appears in such various narratives as Christ's resurrection, the saintly knight's quest for the Holy Grail,
and St. George's slaying of the dragon. Since several cultural historians have
identified this narrative form as characteristic of interpretations of the American historical experience, it is not difficult to perceive the outlines of the
romance at work here in the short obituaries of the Kid. Even more to the
point, of course, is the fact that commentators from Owen Wister to Mody
Boatwright have noted the Western story's affinity to the quest romance of
medieval knights. Still, even if we can accept the structural parallels between
the stories of St. George and his dragon and Pat Garrett and his Kid, we need
also to consider how the Kid's interpreters embedded specific cultural conflicts of value and feeling within this narrative structure. By examining how
specific cultural conflicts were presented within this larger story form, we
can approach an understanding of how the Kid's meaning at this time functionally related to the American cultural context, and also an understanding
of what purposes the Kid's story served for his creators.[11]

When we place the Kid's obituaries' vision of his career into the context of
the historical evolution of the Western, we can isolate what particular conflicts and preoccupations were displaced into the Kid's story. It is important
to recognize, as John Cawelti has stated, that the significant point about the
Western formula is its dramatization of that epic historical moment in our
national past when the opposing forces of civilization and wilderness confronted

each other and shaped the course of American history.[12] Whether this struggle symbolized the conflict between social control and individual freedom, industrialism and agrarianism, or East and West, the Western hero, unlike the progressive pioneer or the savage outlaw and Indian, resided in both the savage and civilized worlds. Because the hero observes social proprieties and possesses a personal code of honor, he is "civilized"; yet because he is also well-versed in the ways of frontier survival and the uses of violence, the hero is also identified with the wilderness. Since the hero's interests are ultimately aligned with the advancing civilization, however, his acts of violence are legitimated and ensure the founding of an ordered, progressive world.

By the time the Kid died in 1881 this dialectic between civilization and wilderness, which authors like Fenimore Cooper had formulated, had been simplified into a moral fantasy that basically opposed the clearly-defined forces of good and evil in order to dramatize the triumph of good over evil. As we have seen in the newspaper responses to the Kid's death, any complex attitudes toward the conflict of outlaw and sheriff are nonexistent, and the Kid's death reaffirmed all the enduring values Garrett represented literally and symbolically. At the same time, any potential conflict between Garrett as hero and the settled community never surfaced because his potentially anarchic extralegal use of violence ensured—rather than subverted—both his and his community's welfare. As one version of the Western formula, the visions of the Kid as they develop in his obituaries reveal not only the structural outlines of the romance story but also project a specific preoccupation with the meaning of justice, the establishment of a progressive social order, and the moral worth of violence in an America rapidly evolving into an urban-industrial society.

When the Kid died, then, the formula used to explain his career emerged as an examination of the conflict of civilization (Garrett) and savagery (Kid) within a romance story form. With this formula in mind, it is little wonder that a New York reporter who read the bare fact of the Kid's death in Pete Maxwell's bedroom would invent a running gun battle throughout the house leading up to the Kid's death: the romance tradition demands that the triumph over evil be the result of a perilous struggle. If that were not the case in history, then it should have been to match what the imagination nurtured or what cultural expectations demanded. Although interest in the Kid declined after the immediate excitement caused by news of his death, as we shall see in the rest of this chapter, explanations of the Kid between 1881 and 1925, however complex and in whatever genre, tended like the obituaries not to beatify but rather to barbecue the Kid within an imaginative, sometimes desperate, reaffirmation of traditional values in a time of immense changes and varied searches for order. Before addressing why this formula was successful at this time, and before understanding what relationship it bore to the larger historical context, our first task it to consider how this emergent vision of the Kid became accepted and extended in the hands of the dime novelists, and in the books by Pat Garrett, Emerson Hough, Charlie Siringo, and others.

At the time of the Kid's death, large numbers of the American reading public who were bothered by the late nineteenth-century rift between Darwinian science and traditional theology were turning to historical romances. One of the most popular historical romances of this era was Lew Wallace's *Ben-Hur,* a work completed in New Mexico amid rumors that the Kid was planning to assassinate the territorial governor in his study. Along with the escapist fare offered by the historical romances of the era, another of the most important expressions of American popular taste at this time was the "dime novel," an inexpensive papercovered work of entertainment and, sometimes, education that was designed for juvenile and working-class audiences—but which was read by masses of Americans regardless of age or occupation.[13] Beginning with the June 1860 publication by the house of Beadle and Adams of Anne Stephens's *Malaeska: The Indian Wife of the White Hunter,* several publishers throughout the latter half of the nineteenth-century released cheap pulp thrillers in various series and formats ranging from newspaper size to the larger twelve-by-eight-inch papercovered edition of sixteen to thirty-two pages. Whether selling for five or twenty-five cents, most dime novels were printed in 60 to 70,000 copies, and some titles were reprinted several times under different titles. Even though series devoted to pirates, noble rogues, desert chieftains, and juvenile detectives were frequently popular, an estimated three-quarters of the dime novels produced by Beadle and Adams were set in frontier landscapes populated by such wilderness types as the backwoodsman, the plainsman, and the outlaw.

At the time of the Kid's death, furthermore, the dime novel's heroic outlaw was replacing in popularity such earlier favorites as the buckskin-clad backwoodsman modeled after Cooper's Leatherstocking figure, Natty Bumppo. Between the October 1877 appearance of Edward Wheeler's *Deadwood Dick, the Prince of the Road* and 1903, by which time over 270 stories about Jesse and Frank James had appeared, whole series of dime novels were published devoted to the outlaws, the most prominent among them being *Morrison's Sensational Series,* Street and Smith's *Log Cabin Library,* and Frank Tousey's *Wide Awake Library* and *New York Detective Library.* Such was the extent and notoriety of these outlaw dime novel series that as early as 1883 Frank Tousey was forced by the U.S. postmaster general to withdraw certain titles from his outlaw series to retain his second-class mailing privileges. One of the withdrawn titles from his *Wide Awake Library* was an 1881 effort by John W. Lewis entitled *The True Life of Billy the Kid.*[14]

Between August 1881 and June 1906, dime novels specifically devoted to the Kid's real and imagined exploits were published and sometimes reprinted in New York City, Chicago, St. Louis, and Denver by such houses as Beadle and Adams, Street and Smith, Richard Fox (publisher of the *National Police Gazette*), Frank Tousey, and John W. Morrison. Seven dime novels appeared within a year of the Kid's death and thus continued the publication of the Kid's name for weeks after the news of his death and the queries over the disposal of his corpse ceased creating headlines. Notwithstanding the Morrison series' self-congratulatory blurb which states on one of its numbers that "100,000 copies of Billy the Kid have already been sold," what stands out when we consider the production of Kid dime novels is just how few there were. As opposed to the James gang series, for instance, which numbers more than 270 titles, Kid dime novels number about 15. Between 1883, only two years after the Kid's death, and 1906, furthermore, only four original titles appear in the Dykes bibliography, two of which are reprinted once. What also strikes us when we consider the dime-novel Kid is how these cheap mass products—whether the 1881 *The Life and Deeds of Billy LeRoy, alias the Kid, King of American Highwaymen* or the 1906 *Buffalo Bill and Billy the Kid; or, the Desperado of Apache Land*—envisioned the Kid in a formula similar to that we have noticed emerging in the Kid obituaries. Like the obituaries, the dime-novel Kid narratives appear as romance stories of heroic adventurers overcoming a dastardly Kid who conspires with other plunderers of the common man to prevent a fledgling civilization from taking hold in the Western wilderness.

For the few dime-novel authors who discuss the Kid, the outlaw's story was significant in the annals of American history because opposing forces of wilderness and civilization were locked in struggle and the outcome hung in precarious balance. As John W. Lewis stated in his *The True Life of Billy the Kid,* the isolated New Mexican landscape was "a land that is stranger to civilization, and where the strong arm of the law seldom reaches its victim, where might is right. . . . "[15] In Edmund Fable's *Billy the Kid, the New Mexican Outlaw,* the fact that New Mexico was awaiting the completion of its first railroad made towns like Lincoln symbolically important in the struggle to transform the desert West into the golden West, for such towns were "standing between the civilization of the new west and the barbarism of the frontier." For Fable, this frontier barbarism was of course evident in the fact that the frontier's highest "civilization" was that "of the knife and rifle, with the number of their victims cut on the stock; of savage Indian raids and massacres; of ruthless vendettas and assassinations; of wars among stock kings and cattle thieves, and of lawlessness in every form."[16] Given this troublesome state of affairs at such a dramatic moment, the struggle for control of the territory was likened in *The Cowboy's Career; or the Daredevil Deeds of Billy the Kid* to a "war of the Roses" fought between rival houses. More prosaically, one character in Francis Doughty's *Old King Brady and Billy the Kid; or, the Great Detective's Chase* simply stated on the opening page that "these is tight times."[17]

The times were "tight" indeed, and dime novelist after dime novelist projected into this symbolic setting and into their portraits of frontier characters contemporary anxieties about antidemocratic monopolies, excesses of individual freedom when "might is right," and corruption of political offices. Thus, the Kid's deadly skills and inhuman personality—when allied with John Chisum's schemes to monopolize the public domain or when supported by corrupt politicians, judges, and law officers—existed as convenient metaphors for the dime novelist's vision of this "border civilization": depraved men, who have yet to establish a social contract, fight for control of barren landscape that is yet to experience cultivation. It is in this alien world that the Kid, in Lewis's *The True Life,* is at one point even made constable, and at another point is offered a pardon by a weak-chinned Lew Wallace—this happening within paragraphs of the one describing the Kid dipping his finger into the blood of his victims. It is an upside-down world: in *Old King Brady,* the nominal sheriff of the area appears at the Kid's secret hideout to get his share of the loot; in at least three other dime novels the Kid serves as Chisum's ally during the cattle king's battle with small ranchers; and elsewhere the Kid even thinks of standing for governor.

The outlaw's villainy is apparent not only in his support for Chisum, but also in his defiance of any restraints and in his "absolute delight in murder." That the Kid represented the demonic forces of the lower world was evident in Thomas Daggett's description of the Kid's recognition "by his cloven-footed, long-tailed majesty as a very promising lieutenant who . . . would certainly be an effective aid in working to his scheme to gather mankind into Hades."[18] As a devil's lieutenant, the Kid in various scenes through the years of the dime novels murders unsuspecting miners, drovers, and handcuffed prisoners; kidnaps heroines and kills to prevent marriages; rustles cattle and robs stagecoaches; and even disguises himself as a saloon's soprano entertainer who could trill "notes that would baffle the majority of female throats."[19] Although in J. C. Cowdrick's *Silver-Mask, The Man of Mystery* the Kid's efforts to confiscate a hidden treasure result in his unimaginative title of "common cut-throat," in other dime novels his scheme to gather recruits for Hades results in particularly abhorrent deeds. In Lewis's *True Life,* the Kid kidnaps and presumably rapes a young woman who is later found wandering insanely in the desert. In Doughty's *Old King Brady,* the Kid kills a clergyman and kicks the corpse over a cliff while the man's daughter is watching. Comparisons of the Kid in other novels to Napoleon or the worst New York City wretch further supported the early depiction of this "fiend incarnate" whose career was unmatched "in the annals of crime":

> How many murders he committed, how many cattle he stole, how many daring deeds of deviltry he performed, will never be known until the dark deeds of cow-boys, congressmen, governors, thieves, lawmakers, are laid bare to the world.[20]

Given the romance story's dialect of antagonists, it is not surprising that in these dime novels there are arrayed against the Kid, Chisum, and other corrupt figures such admirable people as good-hearted small ranchers, army troopers like Harry Ringwood, frontier heroes like Buffalo Bill, elderly detectives like Old King Brady, and—of course—sheriffs like Pat Garrett, who met, in manly fashion "the tacit defiance of law, the reign of terror and bloodshed inaugurated by the Kid. . . . "[21] Such authorites as Harry Ringwood respected traditional legal and moral codes, and—in opposition to the Kid's anarchic violence and to Chisum's rangeland autocracy—their actions aimed toward an ideal utopian society of comfort and equality in a Southwestern Eden that synthesized civilized values and a close contact with Nature's beneficent influence. This dream would be worthless without a titanic struggle confirming the morally superior values of civilization, and just such a conflict is always enacted. After typically opening with an instance of the Kid's devilry, the dime novels' narrative of adventure begins with figures of authority pursuing the Kid. In Daggett's *Billy LeRoy* the Kid, after a four-day drunk, robs a stagecoach and kidnaps a woman who turns out to be a willing accomplice. The Kid is naturally chased and escapes capture twice by posing as a woman, until a group of concerned citizens and ranchers finally organize to stop this menace. In *Old King Brady*, the Kid's stagecoach robbery of the Army payroll and his kidnap of Harry Ringwood's fiancée begin a series of escapes and pursuits through ranchhouses and secret caves as the twin heroes—Ringwood and Brady—attempt to stop the "youthful fiend." In *The Life of Billy the Kid*, the third number of *Morrison's Sensational Series*, the Kid also robs, ravishes, kills, and dresses in drag, but here he also escapes hanging because the noose was too large for his delicate throat—and the chase begins anew.

After a final battle, which at some point typically reveals the Kid's cowardice when cornered, the dime-novel Kid is typically shot or hanged by resourceful figures like Pat Garrett who, when things looked bleakest for civilization, "bid farewell to his family, and armed with a short repeating rifle and a pair of revolvers, set out to find the Kid."[22] Even if the Kid were allowed to escape so the series might continue, authors customarily alluded to the Kid's ultimate death, as in the conclusions to *Old King Brady* and *Silver-Mask*. In this manner, if the usual flight-pursuit plot was "fearful in its beginning the reader must judge the righteousness of the end," which established honest figures of authority, held out hope for a rural democratic community of small ranchers and productive merchants, and blessed the commonwealth with new marriages. Whether the Kid was killed by Buffalo Bill (*Buffalo Bill and Billy the Kid*), hanged in Del Norte, Colorado (*Billy LeRoy*), or shot by Pat Garrett (in several dime novels), it is clear that by eradicating the Kid and exalting a Garrett-like figure the Kid dime novelists were, in the words of Doughty, pointing out how

> All is fair . . . in a warfare against so vile a specimen of mankind as this bloodthirsty boy, whose chief delight was murder.
> His fate was well deserved, and was the only one which could have come to him.
> The rifle ball in the heart or the gallows rope about the neck was the only choice for Billy the Kid, and his fate should be a solemn warning to all who fancy that there is either pleasure or profit, in the long run, to be had in an outlaw's life.[23]

When we closely consider the images of the Kid and the plot dynamics of the Kid dime novels, it becomes very difficult to accept the general notion that the Kid was canonized along with Jesse James and other outlaws of the time, or that portraits of him were filled with "a disrespect for the law and the proprieties. . . . "[24] To be sure, a typical effort like Lewis's *The True Life* at times glamorized the Kid's daring deeds. By romanticizing the life of reckless adolescents banding together to defy several parental figures of authority—as in *Old King Brady* where the Kid's inaccessible hideout (The Devil's Bowl) in New Mexico is reached only by a treacherous underground river or by a secret trap door to a cave—a certain attraction was held out to those juveniles wishing to establish a place free of adult supervision. It may be true also, as John Cawelti has suggested, that such standard plot devices involving characters disguised as the opposite sex appealed to adolescents uncertain about their own identities as they approach maturity. Yet this same outlaw was presented as a thick-skulled ignoramus who could not read or write, as a murderer who killed friends, and as—importantly—a defeated, not triumphant, outlaw. Such blatantly anti-social activities as the Kid's making a secret sign with his victim's blood no doubt was attractive to those readers imaginatively rebelling against their assigned duties and social roles, yet all Kid dime novels of the period patronizingly suggested that his seemingly wonderful energy and remarkable bravery in the face of danger were entirely misdirected. Although, in one author's words, "with proper culture, Billy the Kid might have made his mark in the world,"[25] the dime-novel Kid was ruthlessly self-centered, dishonest, a loser, and anything but a successful romantic interest. That the Kid appears as a worthy opponent whose pose astride a rearing stallion would attract the admiration of certain audiences perhaps can be seen as one of the dramatic demands of the romance story form: for dramatic purposes the villain who confronts the hero must be a worthy antagonist whose skills serve to attract audience interest, create additional suspense, and deepen the hero's commitment to his values.

More to the point than a numbering of daring or demonic images, however, is the fact that the dime-novel Kid did not achieve heroic status because his creators did not give him qualities possessed by other outlaw heroes like Deadwood Dick and Jesse James. As Daryl Jones has demonstrated in his study of the dime novel Western, the outlaw hero evolved only when authors solved the artistic problems associated with the outlaw's status and his use of violence. The eventual solution worked out by the dime novelists was to endow the outlaw with a veneer of gentlemanly respectability, thus making him an eligible romantic interest, and to give him a revenge motive that justified his violence and his outlaw status (a conventional one being that society's legal system was unable to bring the real villains to justice). Except for one Kid dime novel published in Denver, Edmund Fable's *Billy the Kid, the New Mexican Outlaw* (1881), the Kid—however daring and reckless—was not given a revenge motive for his violent career, and, instead of observing the social proprieties and looking like a handsome gentleman, the Kid flouted the proprieties at every turn to the point of being unable to decide whether to wear male or female attire in some dime novels. And even Fable's novel, while certainly finding the Kid's life of crime justified in the sense that the Kid was persecuted and forced into crime, details the dangers of the Western landscape, which offers total freedom, and characterizes the Kid as a vain, cruel, and flashy Southwestern Scarlet Pimpernel.[26] The Kid, in short, is a badman, whereas in the dime novel Jesse James is an outlaw, and the Kid's resulting failure "to attain heroic status in the dime novel illustrates the public's refusal to condone unjustified violence."[27]

Because he was just a badman the dime-novel Kid, who appears as a villain in a romance story, lacked the artistic devices necessary to sustain his popularity throughout the 1880s and 1890s when other dime novels with scores of misunderstood, defiant rebels were attracting large audiences. With no motive for his violence except a ruthless blood lust, and without a handsome appearance, the Kid was reduced to being a foil, an obstacle to civilization's westward progress. With the Kid as an unsympathetic figure and with the heroes of the Kid dime novels firmly committed to the traditional values of civilization, these novels lacked the characterization and the dramatic framework by which to criticize the slow-moving bureaucracy of civilization. The Kid dime novels failed to sustain interest because his creators failed to combine successfully both criticism of society and an affirmation of society.

At the same time, however, we should also notice something else. If we enlarge our perspective and compare the Kid dime novels to the popular books of the era, we can see that while the Kid's dime novel creators lacked the necessary creativity to sustain his appeal, their formula for explaining the Kid's story did thematically parallel another level of American literary taste. That is, the public taste which demanded historical and utopian romances and which consumed numerous titles of business success stories could have been satisfied by the same rags-to-riches success ethic as it appeared in the Kid dime novels. Only a year after Andrew Carnegie's *Gospel of Wealth* was a self-help best seller, young Harry Ringwood galloped across the sagebush in pursuit of the Kid, and—with Old King Brady's mature guidance—gained his wife and achieved his version of the American Dream. Ultimately, as we have seen, the Kid dime novels dramatized a Horatio Alger-like success story— but success in both history and fiction was not the Kid's fortune. In these dime novels the young outlaw's irrational, cowardly, and deadly behavior guaranteed his moral failure. The appeal this morality tale would present to audiences worried about the American transition to an urban-industrial nation is perhaps obvious, but it remained for Pat Garrett and Ash Upson, Charlie Siringo, Emerson Hough, and William Macleod Raine to relate the Kid as villain to such audiences between 1881 and 1925.

What is curious about the Kid bibliography during this period is how the Kid ever became a popular outlaw figure. The years we shall cover in the next chapter (1925–55), for instance, produced over three times as many entries in the bibliography as the years covered in this chapter. That the Kid's story did not become extinct is mainly because Charlie Siringo's *A Texas Cowboy,* which included a chapter on the Kid's capture at Stinking Springs and also a chapter on the Kid's life according to Ash Upson and Pat Garrett, was in print for over forty years after its initial publication in 1885. Between 1897 and 1909 the Kid was kept in the public's mind by popular authors like Emerson Hough, who reintroduced the outlaw's story to a national audience. It is no exaggeration to suggest in fact that except for the excitement caused by the Kid's death, interest in this boy outlaw was extremely low—especially when we compare his published appearances with those of Custer and Jesse James— until Hough's articles, stories, novels, and informal histories discovered a meaning in the Kid's story relevant to the cultural preoccupations and anxieties during the Progressive era.

Because Garrett's *Authentic Life* was a marketing failure and only sold a few copies in the New Mexico region, it was not until 1885 that a sketch of the Kid's life appeared that would compete with the dime novel's formula for inventing the Kid. By the time Siringo's sketch appeared, however, over ten dime novels had been published, and their interpretations of Billy's real and imagined exploits were well-entrenched in the popular culture. As a result, whether writing personal narratives or impersonal histories of Western happenings, image-makers characteristically opened their accounts with declarations of an intent "to correct the thousand false statements that have appeared in the public newspapers and in yellow-covered cheap novels."[28] Other authors attempted to curry audience trust by suggesting that the Kid's exploits they were presenting only gave "the *impression* of having torn pages at random from the superheated literature that now and then quickens the pulse of the American District Telegraph service"; still others declared that the Kid "was not the typical character depicted by yellow-covered magazine and newspaper writers. He was about the last person one would select for a 'gun man'."[29] Because of such strident criticism of the popular press creation of the Kid, what happens during these years is that observers successfully developed more completely humanized portraits of the Kid. Yet because such portraits still offered the Kid as a villain in a romance story dramatizing civilization's triumph over savagery, these observers who kept the Kid's name alive during these years reproduced the basic idea of the Kid's meaning for American history as it had emerged in the popular press.

Of course some writers were still content to echo the popular press conception of the Kid as a satanic cutthroat fiend who inaugurated a reign of terror, irresponsibly defied the law, and cruelly slew men "just to see them kick." In such accounts the authors followed the dime novelist's formula by emphasizing the Kid's prominent buck teeth and feminine behavior, his cowardly personality, and his limited intelligence.[30] Although little agreement existed on the color of the Kid's eyes and hair, the typical description of Billy offered him as a soulless and beardless youth who was

> about five feet high, small hands and feet, dark, swarthy complexion, with hair as black as the ravens which infest those plains in great numbers. The distinguishing mark about the Kid were his eyes. They were black and very bright. They seemed to glow with something like the fierceness of the cougar or mountain lions when he became excited. At such times his expression seemed to be that of unconquerable determination, and that was his peculiar characteristic.[31]

What is important here is not the description's accuracy or inaccuracy, but its efforts to classify the Kid as an evil force by diminishing his height to a dwarfish five feet and by using the color black to describe his eyes and hair.

In later years, more favorable descriptions of the Kid's appearance emphasized his blonde hair and his blue eyes, and added up to eight inches to his height—thus making the Kid eligible for heroic status. In addition, the note struck here about the Kid's beastly eyes glowing when excited reveals another short-hand manner of confirming Billy's unheroic status: good guys are always in control of their emotions. Such allusions to wild beasts like cougars and mountain lions, furthermore, actually become in several accounts as convenient a method for portraying the Kid's villainous qualities as were the earlier satanic allusions. For others, the Kid was "an animal born with a cat soul," a "tigerish" and "foxy" stripling who possessed such a "pure wanton love of carnage" that he "was the youthful monster of wickedness."[32]

In support of these accounts, which echoed the dime novelist's vision of the Kid, also emphasized was his commission of "outrage after outrage with the blind recklessness of a maniac."[33] Tales of the Kid's murders of defenseless Eastern salesmen, handcuffed prisoners like Morton and Baker, and harmless Chisum cowboys or Mexicans were highlighted, as were tales of his treachery in fixing Joe Grant's revolver so the hammer would fall on an empty chamber. Although the Lincoln County War was historically a conflict between two rival financial groups, several dime-novel accounts conceived it as a conflict between a greedy robber baron named Chisum and a group of small ranchers supported by Murphy and Dolan. Not only was the Kid portrayed as fighting on Chisum's side, but one account even labelled the Kid *the* perpetrator of the war. And although the Kid was viewed in most accounts as a skillful horseman and an excellent marksman, his skills were so coldly and cruelly demonstrated in support of unjust causes that many agreed with one writer "that it affords one a great deal of pleasure to print the account of his being killed and one can at least realize that he is dead enough to stay dead."[34]

However dominant and appealing was this image of the Kid as the stark embodiment of lawless devilry, most interpreters during this period objected to the stereotype. They were at least willing to consider the possibility that Billy was as much a human being as he was a serpent or Satan's lieutenant. This theme was first voiced in Garrett's *Authentic Life* when the sheriff declared his intention "to do justice to his character, give him credit for all the virtues he possessed—and he was by no means devoid of virtue—but . . . not spare deserved opprobrium for his heinous offenses against humanity and the laws."[35] To give the Kid credit for what virtues he possessed, writers considered three possible means of qualifying the Kid's crimes. In the first place, some considered briefly that "many of the men killed by Billy the Kid were gangsters, too," and that little, if any, "moral gulf" separated the Kid from his enemies. Besides suggesting that the Kid was no worse than his contemporaries, others characterized him as "an avenging demon" whose violent actions were performed "to make the guilty suffer for the murders of his parents and friends."[36] Along with justifying the Kid's violence or doubting his moral difference from his enemies, other themes were introduced to render him more believable. Some writers occasionally introduced questions about Garrett's failure to give the Kid a chance in Pete Maxwell's bedroom; others briefly softened the Kid's devilish demeanor by noting his considerable cow-punching or letter-writing talents.

But it was in recounting the Kid's noble deeds that writers were most ef-fective in muting his lawlessness. The Kid's first appearance in a short story saw him hold up a wedding celebration and unknowingly kill his father, but he apologized to his victims by saying that his booty would be used to main-tain an orphanage.[37] Even in predominantly negative portraits, the Upson-inspired account of the Kid saving his friend from jail or saving wagon trains of women from violation by Apache warriors would be recited. Such deeds led more than one author to acknowledge that the Kid was not in fact as cruelly vindictive as an imitation badman like Bob Olinger or the Kentucky "Night Riders" who lynched black women.[38] In addition, in what later would become a major element in the Kid's portrait, it was noted on more than one occasion that the Kid "never took anything from a poor man, but, on the contrary, with true bandit nobility, took from the rich in order that he might give to the poor."[39] As a result of such bandit nobility, one author commented that "many grateful blessings followed the little fiend as he rode from the doors of squalor, poverty, and distress."[40] The conjunction of "little fiend" and Robin Hood-like acts precisely indicates this period's often paradoxical response to the Kid's career.

Realizing that such beneficial actions, however few in number, could not be accomplished by a little fiend who was known only by his oily tresses and baleful black orbs, observers also revised the dime novel's typically negative portraits of the Kid's appearance. Garrett's biography, for instance, described the Kid as an outlaw who forgot to don Claude Duval-like flowing capes, who remembered to swear only in picturesque phraseology, and who retained more gentlemanly manners than "some of the 'society' men of today":

> He was about five feet and eight inches in stature, stood straight, and weighed about 135 pounds. His form was well-knit, and he was very muscular, tough and light and active. His hair was of a dark brown, glossy and luxuriant, and not worn long as depicted by 'fake' magazinists. His eyes were a deep blue, dotted with spots of hazel, and were bright and expressive. His face was oval, the most noticeable feature being two projecting upper front teeth, which was not a disfigurement, but sufficiently prominent to at-tract attention. Newspaper fakers have described these as 'fangs' and depicted him as an ogre. He was handsomer than the major-ity of men.[41]

Whether for stylistic reasons or merely as an accurate description, Garrett's portrait lightens the color of the Kid's eyes and hair and drops allusions to beasts and devils, and in so doing reveals a more sympathetic approach to the matter of the Kid's prominent front teeth and directly attacks the popular press invention of the Kid's appearance. While this process of humanizing the Kid's appearance occurred throughout the period after Garrett's lead, we can witness it happening within the mind of a single author. In 1901, writing for *Everybody's Magazine,* Emerson Hough described the Kid as "a miscarriage in the aeons of evolution," a "short, undersized little man, with legs none too good, and the habit of a riding man. His eyes were bluish gray. His chin so far from being broad and strong, was narrow and pointed"; later, in his 1907 *The Story of the Outlaw,* Hough's conversations with Pat Garrett led him to a more charitable description of the Kid as "a pleasant mannered youth" who was "always slight and lean, a hard rider all his life, and never old enough to take on flesh."[42]

The relative truthfulness of these descriptions of the Kid's appearance and actions is not our concern here; rather, the point to be emphasized is that authors in the dime novel's wake attempted to invent a believable Kid who could thus be understood and explained. Still, however much such descriptions granted the Kid handsome teeth, a humorous wit, some honorable qualities, and a partial motive for his crimes, they yet ultimately transmitted the same idea of the Kid as that held by the dime novelists: the blue-eyed laughing Billy Bonney who never betrayed a friend was only significant as a supreme antagonist whose deadly skills and art of daring tested civilization's determination, manliness, and moral vigor. The Kid's significance was not as a coolheaded, clear-eyed, resourceful and courageous hero who upheld truth and justice and was thus respectable; rather, he was "the most dangerous lawbreaker of the century," a man all bad who had to be tamed.[43] Even the fact that he was *the* most notorious Western desperado, and that the wild West had never "produced his equal in sheer inborn savagery" was not sufficient for those who additionally termed him "the worst outlaw in the history of crime," and the "only white man who slew out of pure wantonness."[44] His chivalrous impulse to reward the poor was noted, to be sure, but it was noted as his only "redeeming quality, unless his attachment to a Western girl could be so considered." "His pastime, his greatest amusement and delight," according to one old-timer, "was the taking of human life."[45] He might be called by Siringo "the good-natured 'Billy the Kid'," but Siringo also detailed the Kid's casual murders of salesmen and cowboys; Garrett may not have given the Kid a fair chance the night of the Kid's death, but, after all, the sheriff was facing a man who was "a murderer of the worst type," a man who may have been "a half-breed Indian."[46] Finally, if the Kid was "one of the most picturesque criminals in the bloody annals of the Southwest," it was not because he was gallant and good-looking but rather because he "summed up in his debonair person the vices of the white race in a land where the arm of the law did not reach."[47]

Given this superlative antagonist "who had about him none of the attributes that usually gain the Western desperado a certain sort of admiration,"[48] the Kid's image-makers conveniently dramatized his confrontation with the law as a momentous event occurring in a significant time and symbolic landscape. "Here on this great battle ground of lonely desert wastes, of virgin forests, and rolling tracts of bunch grass," wrote one author, "respectable cattlemen battled horse thieves and cattle rustlers for the control of the future and the defense of private property."[49] Emerson Hough argued that the barren New Mexican setting revealed a situation where "nowhere in the world was human life held cheaper, and never was any population more lawless. There were no courts and no officers, and most of the scattered inhabitants of that time had come hither to escape courts and officers."[50] Because of such anarchic conditions, another writer declared that the times could be identified as "the Dark Ages" of southeastern New Mexico.[51] Another manner favored by authors to describe this setting was to open the account with a symbolic description of a single line of railroad track traversing a desert landscape of shifting sands, hidden wild animals, and dangerous, wild men like Billy the Kid.[52]

I think many interpreters of the Kid and his times were attracted to him because they found in the historical resolution of the confrontation of an advancing civilization and a resisting savage wilderness a parallel to the dramatic resolution that the romance story form demanded. That is, unlike Custer's last stand, Garrett's last stand with the Kid required no heroic manipulation of evidence to portray effectively the moral righteousness of his triumph: the Kid's failure to kill Garrett was a moral failure, while Garrett's success revealed manifest destiny's sign of election and approval by Providence. When describing the resolution of the conflict between the outlaw and the sheriff, few were able to resist an allegorizing tendency and, like Siringo, merely voice the notion that the Kid, a killer of a man for every year of his life, was no more. In a manner reminiscent of the Kid's obituaries, later interpreters typically termed the Kid's demise a symbolic conclusion to an anachronistic way of life. Thus, as one person argued, "he died as he had lived, a wild, untamable, remorseless human fiend. With him passed the old order of things. The reign of the revolver in New Mexico was over forever."[53] "With the death of Billy the Kid," concluded the second novel to feature Billy, "outlawry in New Mexico fast gave way to times of peace and security."[54]

That this historical confrontation of the Kid and Garrett was understood as an adventure story, one which dramatized the evolution of a reign of lawless terror into a period of peace and prosperity, can best be summarized by comparing the conclusions of an early and a late contribution to this era's understanding of the outlaw. The last page of Garrett's *Authentic Life,* for instance, draws on conventional romance images of a restored world to illustrate, however flamboyantly, the regeneration of the human and natural worlds after a perilous conflict with the Kid's demonic vision of experience:

> Whatever may be the cause of the effect, Lincoln County now enjoys a season of peace and prosperity to which she has ever, heretofore, been a stranger. No Indians, no desperadoes, to scare our citizens from their labors, or disturb their slumbers. Stock wanders over the ranges in security, and vast fields of waving grain greet the eye, where, not a stock of artificially-produced vegetation could be seen.
>
> > 'When late was barrenness and waste,
> > The perfumed blossom, bud and blade,
> > Sweet, bashful pledges of approaching harvest,
> > Giving cheerful promise to the hope of industry,'
>
> Gladden the eye, stamp contentment on happy faces, and illustrate the pleasures of industry.[55]

Having accomplished the crowning feat of his life, this Southwestern Cincinnatus can return to his ranch and await the call to join the Rough Riders in quelling another threat to peace and security by a Spanish civilization. In 1922, as this explanation of the Kid was becoming less and less acceptable, similar images were invoked to describe the aftermath of this conflict of the law and the lawless: "To-day [1922] fat prairie corn-fields stand tasseled in the sunlight, the smoke of lusty young cities rises black against the sky," wrote an old Lincoln County resident, "while automobiles speed upon concrete highways over the forgotten graveyards where their bones lie."[56] Although nostalgia for the past would soon prompt serious questions about the worth of automobiles, smoke, and cities, for the moment Garrett's triumph demonstrated that the American people would successfully tame their continent and that the guardians of civilization—including Garrett—were ready and able to defend their country against lawlessness.

Whether as the dime novelist's fiend incarnate or as the magazine journalist's unaccountable stripling with feminine features, the Kid was generally perceived as the romance story's villainous foil to the hero's progress through a depraved landscape. In the beginning it was enough for the dime novelist to create action scenes that depicted the Kid as a conventional threat to authority; in later publications, however, more thoughtful observers writing for more sophisticated audiences also speculated about the forces that spawned a Billy the Kid. Besides just inventing the Kid's image, in other words, it became important to understand him—even if he was "entirely unaccountable" to one person, or for another person accountable only by the Providence who knew how "the soul of some fierce and far-off carnivore got into the body of this little man."[57]

Human behavior is usually explained in terms of hereditary or environmental influences. There were those who suggested that the Kid was "naturally depraved," an anomaly who possessed "an inherent criminal nature," who seemed "to have been born without the usual sense of values."[58] Although some, like Garrett, hedged their bets and decided the Kid was a product of both unfortunate circumstances and an ungovernable inherited spirit, most traced the reasons for his career to his environment. Thus, observers charitably blamed the Kid's behavior on early association with the cowboys who taught him how to drink, womanize, and kill; others noted the harmful effect of the Kid having a cruel stepfather, or his reading of inflammable dime novels about heroic outlaws.

Still, most discussions of the Kid's evolution from bad boy like Huck Finn to an even worse badman like Injun Joe indicted the western landscape, which exercised few formal controls over its inhabitants. Particularly during the first decade of the twentieth century, Hough and others who preserved the Kid's reputation in large-circulation magazines explained him as a bastard product of the frontier culture, which repressed the good and developed the evil instincts of his character. Thus, as Hough wrote,

> turn the white man loose in a land freed of restraint—such as was always the Golden Fleece land, vague, shifting, and transitory, known as the American West—and he simply reverts to the ways of Teutonic and Gothic forests. The civilized empire of the West has grown in spite of this, because of that other strange germ, the love of law, anciently implanted in the soul of the Anglo-Saxon.[59]

For our purposes, this statement is highly interesting for at least two reasons. In the first place, it reveals how easily an interpreter of the Kid during this period framed the subject matter—in this case in only two sentences—in terms of a romance story's conflict and ultimate resolution, which verified civilization's progress over the savage ways of the forests. It is also interesting because it shows the tendency of the Kid's interpreters to endow his story with epic significance. As in the popular Western in general, antagonists must be created to match a setting seen in epic terms; here, the Kid can never just be the Kid nor can Garrett be just Garrett. Instead the conflict of the two ex-friends marks "the legal challenge from law to lawlessness."[60]

More often, however, the conflict was extended to more significant proportions, at times resulting in comparison of the Lincoln County War to the

War of the Roses or even the Trojan War. Most writers agreed with Hough that the conflict was a significant event in the evolutionary progress of the Anglo-Saxon race. "It was not a challenge from Billy the Kid," as Hough wrote in 1901:

> There was nothing personal about it. Simply Civilization, new come upon the land, had sent its challenge to Savagery; the law had issued its ultimatum to lawlessness. . . . He [Garrett] stood for the new order of things. Billy the Kid clung steadfastly to the old order.

"Naturally," Hough concluded a few pages later, "the Anglo-Saxon civilization was destined to overrun this half-Spanish civilization."[61] Through statements like these, we can understand that the Kid became Clio's bastard not only because the dime novelists distorted the Kid's career, but also because commentators like Hough denied either the Kid's or Garrett's qualities as human beings in order to discuss the symbolic qualities of each as opponents to or defenders of manifest destiny.

In 1901 Hough might just as well have been describing the Rough Riders' 1898 conquests in Cuba, though in fact he was discussing Garrett's 1881 conquest in New Mexico. Both triumphs revealed the emergence of a new order of Anglo-Saxon civilization, which loved justice more than the lure of primitive plains or jungle; both conquests were destined to succeed—as late nineteenth-century thinking would have it—because desperadoes, Indians, and Mexicans or Cubans were unable or unwilling to transform the wilderness into a pastoral garden. While we might wish to consider with Hough that "it is enough to say that the outlaws who were at the bottom of it were gradually defeated,"[62] the point is that Hough and others were not content with saying *just* that. The historical resolution of the Kid's career became ritualistically dramatized as a conventional triumph of civilization over savagery, and it is evident that the past existed as a usable imaginary landscape into which present concerns about the direction of the historical process were projected, dramatized, and resolved. After all, Hough himself voiced the opinion in *The Story of the Outlaw* that "the lessons of our dealing with our bad men of the past can teach us . . . the best method of dealing with the bad men of today."[63]

Just who the bad men were and just how the idea and image of the Kid functioned to encompass a historical period can best be understood by first briefly considering the dominant cultural preoccupations during this period of the Kid's bibliography. Whether this time is understood as Mark Twain's "the Gilded Age" or as Vernon Parrington's "the Great Barbecue," the first visions of the Kid were circulated in an era that witnessed, in the words of one prominent historian, a culture's search for an order that could explain and control the bewildering and swift changes in American society wrought by industrialization, urbanization, immigration, and mechanization.[64] Certainly the turbulance that characterized attempts to subjugate Native Americans and Western desperadoes was a common factor for all Americans during this period: two presidents (Garfield and McKinley) were assassinated; two foreign wars were fought; numerous legislative acts to control "dangerous" ethnic minorities and economic combinations were passed; and several labor disputes were turned into violent episodes such as at Haymarket Square and the Pullman factory. Supported by *laissez faire* economic thought and Social Darwinism as an ethic, capitalists like Jay Gould and J. P. Morgan amassed tremendous fortunes by exploiting laws and labor in the process of creating various trusts, monopolies, and holding companies. In addition to the challenges to the traditional fabric of American society by plutocrats and labor organizers, increasing numbers of immigrants and rural Americans flooded the cities and, while supplying cheap labor for industry's needs, transformed the urban environment into what some called a threatening jungle of conflicting cultures. As a result of depressed wages, labor troubles, and insufficient capital to cover extensive investments, America experienced a series of financial panics between the Civil War and the turn of the century. With such general economic uncertainty amid the financial leaders' conspicuous consumption, with the continental frontier expansion completed, and with traditional moral assumptions based on village values becoming increasingly outmoded, America was, in James Hart's words, a "paradox," since it was

> confused by internal class struggle, secure as it turned a bold front upon the world. Sure of its industrial might, elated by its mechanical contrivances, boastful of its national wealth, proud of its form of government . . . and lordly in welcoming hundreds of thousands of immigrants, America was yet torn by economic and political dissension.[65]

The vibrancy and complexity of the forty-odd years between 1881 and the 1920s are glimpsed in such events as the introduction of the light bulb, telephone, model T, and Prohibition; the march of Coxey's unemployed army in 1894 and the creation of the U. S. Chamber of Commerce in 1912; the rise of the Populist and women's suffrage movements, and the publication of Stephen Crane's *Maggie* and Eleanor Porter's *Pollyanna*—each introducing different extremes of feminine decorum. While problems and triumphs, hopes and fears, are present in any era, the point here is that the transition of America from a predominantly rural agrarian society to a predominantly urban industrial society was such a wrenching experience that it created a kind of crisis mentality as many Americans witnessed the emergence of a sociocultural environment they could neither understand nor identify with. The human response to the new, the different, or the unknown, is often to counter it with a rigid defense of old ways and values, so it is not surprising that many Americans responded by organizing clubs like the DAR and by joining the Temperance Union; by urging the passage of legislative acts to regulate trusts, interstate commerce, and labor unions; by denouncing such alien forces as Catholics, Mormons, blacks, railroad companies, immigrants, and absentee owners; by attempting to exorcise the evils of machine politics, which had corrupted the political system; and by searching for and embracing simple solutions like Henry George's single tax theory, Laurence Gronlund's brand of Christian socialism, and the Populist's crusade for the silver monetary standard.

Such efforts to impose the known upon the unknown, to replace the impersonal with the personal, and to purify the present by preserving the past—such efforts are further evident in the era's popular books which emphasized both escape and romance. During the late 1880s, at a time when *Huckleberry Finn* was banned from the Concord, Massachusetts, library shelves because of its unrelenting exposure of American hypocrisy and greed, Andrew Carnegie's *Gospel of Wealth,* Orison Marden's *Pushing to the Front,* and Russell Conwell's *Acres of Diamonds* offered dazzling stories of personal success that reaffirmed the self-reliant individual's ability to conquer his environment and satisfy his dreams. In addition to stories of personal success, throughout the century and the first decade of the new century millions of readers were granted release from religious doubts by books like *Ben-Hur, Quo Vadis?,* and Charles Sheldon's *In His Steps.* Besides an escape into the past via historical romances, there was the equally popular escape into the future via the utopian romance in the manner of Edward Bellamy's *Looking Backward.* Also popular during this period were the books of Kipling, Stevenson, H. G. Wells, and Anthony Hope, which dramatized heroic adventures in exotic landscapes far removed from labor unrest and what many perceived to be the Populist threat to national unity.

The American reading public also preferred historical romances about the national past because they affirmed traditional values in a troublesome time, and thus books by Harold Bell Wright, Gene Stratton-Porter, and Helen Hunt Jackson became best sellers. In this concern with the national past the frontier experience was especially significant because it presented an intriguing, symbolic landscape which, as a result of heroic individual actions, underwent a transition to a newer civilized order and simultaneously regenerated the individual jaded by life in the crowded East. As the industrial East became more crowded, ethnically mixed, and polarized, the popularly accepted idea of the West in books and articles did not focus on the IWW, the Populists, striking miners, or Mormon polygamists. Rather, in the vision of Owen Wister, Theodore Roosevelt, Frederick Remington, Emerson Hough, Stewart Edward White, and, later, Zane Grey, the West became an ideal golden world of heroic Anglo-Saxons whose courage, common sense, stoicism, and willingness to fight for what is right affirmed and preserved true American ideals of democratic freedom. Roosevelt's Rough Riders, Wister's Virginian, and Remington's dashing horsemen promoted an image of the adventurous male that was consonant with the popular concept of the self-reliant American hero, and which was suited to the era's popular thirst for a subject matter which in troubled times dramatized individuals controlling their own destinies. Where earlier in the century the West had been imagined as a "desert" wilderness resisting the advance of American civilization, the Western landscape during this period was conceived as a crucible which formed such unique national traits as self-reliance, love of democracy, practical thinking, and extravagant wastefulness. Notwithstanding the naturalistic West of Stephen Crane and Hamlin Garland, the popular West of numerous authors, rather than being seen in strictly negative terms as a land of barbarism, was now believed to represent a positive natural moral force that was opposed to the ugliness of industrial life.

The triumphant affirmation of traditional American values, such as in the resolutions of Roosevelt's *The Winning of the West* or Wister's various fictional works, became the dominant meaning of the West; however, as one scholar has argued, this vision of the West could not be separated from the concerns of the present—indeed, for Roosevelt and Wister, the leading image-makers of the West at the turn of the century, knowledge of past achievements provided a clue to the qualities needed for America to succeed in the present and future.[66] And what the recently completed achievement of winning the West demonstrated to Roosevelt, furthermore, was that

> The crisis demanded that they [backwoodsmen] should be both strong and good; but, above all things, it demanded that they should be strong. Weakness would have ruined them. It was needful that justice should stand before mercy; and they could no longer have held their homes, had they not put down their foes, of every kind, with an iron hand. They did not have many theories; but they were too genuinely liberty-loving not to keenly feel that their freedom was jeopardized as much by domestic disorder as by foreign aggression.[67]

The backwoodsmen faced and overcame disturbances caused by Indians and desperados during their taming of the frontier, and similarly the contemporary tumult caused by labor anarchists and Populist sympathizers had to be resisted with the same forthright strength frontiersmen had. Wister, Roosevelt, and Remington characteristically projected their concern over the invasion of the West by Wobblies and bearded anarchists and the attendant threats to democratic freedom and national unity into stories and articles of the past frontier experience in which backwoodsmen, cowboys, and army troopers were "subjected to battles and darkness, to nature in the raw, to the fierceness and generosity of the desert"[68] before emerging triumphant over these obstacles to American progress. This emergent civilization, it should be stressed, resembled neither the lawless landscape of Indians and the Kid nor the circumscribed landscape of the urban present; instead, civilization resembled a landscape that synthesized both the cultured elegance and primitive vigor of, respectively, Eastern and Western life.

If we were specifically studying the West of Wister, Remington, and Roosevelt as G. Edward White has done, we should of course detail the changes in this interpretation of the West, just as we should notice the distinctions among the Wests of these leading image-makers.[69] Since we are more specifically interested in the Kid, it is sufficient for our purposes to outline the network of assumptions that dominated the popular concept of the West and the larger historical context. What happens in the popular culture at this time, then, is that historical romances involving overseas adventures, utopian societies, and primitive frontier landscapes offered escapes into environments that contained problems which were ultimately resolved as heroic individuals overcame threats to freedom and the community. As part of the national past, the Western formula in the hands of the dime novelists, Wister, Remington, Roosevelt, and Hough dramatized successful individuals triumphing—often through violence—over opponents. The West, then, became not only an avenue of escape but also a moral lesson that established the need for heroic individual achievements by strong, self-reliant, stoic, male adventurers. In popular magazines and novels, the West became not just the repository of wilderness freedom but the true location of American ideals, which were in danger of extinction from an elitist, ethnic, and industrial society that was transforming America into a replica of Europe. If there were those concerned about the direction of American history, they could read in *Century* magazine an extended series of articles on "The Great West," articles that demonstrated in the editor's words that "no climax of national achievement seems difficult of belief."[70] Articles in this series, often illustrated by Remington or J. N. Marchand, presented particular climaxes of achievement supporting this assertion, whether it be taming the landscape by irrigation, railroads, and dams—or taming the Kid by Pat Garrett.

The Kid's interpreters never forget that Billy was just one among many badmen, and with that association in mind we can begin to connect the visions of the Kid to the sociocultural context of the era. The Kid was first invented during the years before World War I, when familiarity with the West was highly shaped by the works of Wister and Roosevelt. But the vision of the Kid figured prominently as well, and we can construct a tight relationship between the Kid, his creators, and this context by noting a few key points. In the first place, the characteristic manner of emplotting the Kid's story in the romance mode parallels the reading public's preference for the romance, which offered an imaginative escape from current anxieties. Envisioning the Kid's story as one of taming the border outlaw or the end of the reign of the revolver thematically served the same purpose as the Virginian's marriage to Molly Stark Wood or the Rough Riders' detachment which synthesized New Englanders and Southwesterners: division and turmoil evolve to unity and stability. Moreover, the discovery of the Kid during the years of Roosevelt's ascendancy was accomplished in the pages of such popular magazines as *Outing, Century, Everybody's, Harper's,* and *The Overland Monthly*—magazines that were also publishing Wister's stories, Remington's stories and illustrations, and Roosevelt's essays. In theme, structure, and place of publication, visions of the Kid reveal the era's cultural assumptions about the meaning of the West for American history.

That the formula for explaining the Kid had specific connections with the larger cultural context can best be understood by examining the work of Emerson Hough. He is important for our purposes because he was a best-selling author who seemingly was able to articulate in his work cultural preferences and preoccupations. In addition, Hough knew Garrett, travelled through the Kid country, campaigned for Roosevelt, and embraced the then emerging cause of conservation at the turn of the century. His specific contributions to the Kid bibliography, particularly his 1901 *Everybody's Magazine* article, recapitulated the earlier ideas of the Kid and also influenced several other magazine accounts of the Kid that appeared before World War I.

Hough is further important for he, like Wister and Roosevelt, consciously connected past achievements and present concerns. In his chapter "Beef and Freedom" in *The Story of the Cowboy,* Hough identified the cowboy, as did Wister, with authentic American ideals, purposes, and goals. Like many other observers of the time, Hough feared that uneducated immigrants and marauding capitalists constituted serious danger for the country because both endangered figures of American strength like the grim, self-reliant cowboy. In *The Story of the Outlaw,* furthermore, Hough believed not only that the lessons of dealing with the badmen of the past would instructively reveal how to deal with the badmen of the present, he also thought that "the old vigilante principle" of the lynch law and a "dozen town marshals of the old stripe would restore peace and fill a graveyard in a day of any strike."[71] Whether explicitly calling for the return of a virile male code, which would save America from the threats of strikers and other evils, or whether symbolically portraying the overthrow of outlaws who carried guns or manipulated votes and finances, Hough fearlessly noticed the macrocosmic workings of history within the briefest microcosmic event. Stories of cowboys and outlaws, as a result, were clearly allegorical examples drawn from

> that frontier whose van, if ever marked by human lawlessness, has, none the less, ever been led by the banner of human liberty. May that banner still wave to-day, and though blood may again be the price, may it never permanently be replaced by that of license and injustice in America.[72]

Readers of Hough's words and other interpreters of the Kid during this era would have no trouble identifying whose blood may spill in defense of human liberty, just as they would have no trouble recognizing what elements were fomenting injustice in American life. The search for order during America's transition into a predominantly urban industrial society caused many to return to the past for reassuring evidence of national achievement. And with the paucity of creators who knew how to formulate a justification for his violent career, Billy the Kid could hardly occupy a place in the hearts of those who celebrated Cody and Custer, and who elevated Wister, Remington, and Roosevelt to the peaks of popular success. As we have seen, the imagery used to depict the story of the Kid's life conventionally endowed the chief protagonists in the encounter with opposing values and experiences. When presented in the romance mode, which demanded a conflict of hero and villain, a dialectical relationship like the following was created at the time of the Kid's death:

Billy the Kid	*Pat Garrett*
devil	redeemer
outlaw	law
reckless	control
immature	mature
effeminate	virile
disguise	honest
selfish	socially responsible
cruel	sensitive
savage	civilized

Savagery	*Civilization*
wilderness	community
hunting	pastoral cultivation
wild beasts	domestic animals
anarchy	order
reversion	progress
Dark Ages	rebirth
death	life
Spanish	Anglo-Saxon

The Kid was in all but one major account highly irredeemable.[73] He was a cowboy and rustler, but he was no Western Andrew Carnegie as was the Virginian; he was a colorful sort, to be sure, but he was not the principal sort Remington painted, and J. N. Marchand only illustrated the Kid being brought into Las Vegas as Garrett's handcuffed captive. When the respective values personified by the Kid and Garrett were projected into a violent confrontation in the recent national past, the Kid's interpreters dramatically affirmed a benevolent historical process as the values in the right-hand column succeeded those in the left-hand columm.

Furthermore, when it is understood that the values the Kid and Garrett stood for also symbolized—either explicitly or implicitly—conflicting ideologies in the interpreters' present experience, then we can see why this formula for inventing the Kid was accepted at this time and realize what cultural functions it served. The Kid's domestic disorder no doubt reminded audiences of the anarchic forces threatening the values of the mainstream American culture; the record of New Mexico's corrupt judicial system no doubt reminded audiences of an equally inefficient system that allowed labor strikers and J. P. Morgans to disrupt the economy. The rustlers in the 1878 New Mexico legislature and the corrupt Lincoln peace officers no doubt prompted audiences to remember that bribery and graft were prevalent in the present. As all these current anxieties were being displaced in the legendary past, the visions of the Kid as a romance villain enabled authors and audiences—precisely at the moment of the Kid's death—to reassert the triumph of traditional values and to reestablish the necessity for America to continue producing men like Garrett, the Rough Riders, the Virginian, and Roosevelt in order to maintain control over the forces of chaos. Instead of the Kid's personal quest to realize total individual freedom, and instead of Chisum's quest to monopolize private property, Garrett's triumphant restoration of civilization symbolically affirmed the moral worth of a culture that asserted faith in order, reason, stability, individual freedom, a natural aristocracy of talent, and the irresistible progress of society.

The point is that when such values were increasingly regarded as anachronistic or were threatened by the emerging forces of an industrial society, the story of the confrontation of the Kid and Garrett projected the necessity for preserving such values and thus offered another kind of stability to audiences searching for a way to address the forces of change and disorder at home and abroad. Besides creating an imaginary landscape that affirmed the survival of such values, this vision of the Kid also resolved the often ambiguous, if not contradictory, responses to the meaning of the law and the relationship of the individual to society. The defeat of the Kid meant that a villainous obstacle to manifest destiny had fallen, and in Garrett's achievement we see a successful resolution of the disruptive antagonism of the individual and society. That is, Garrett's conquest resolved the conflict between the individual's desire to escape the restrictions of an increasingly standardized society and the same individual's awareness that he must submit to societal restraints in order for the community to exist.[74] By dramatizing an individual's decisive violence on behalf of the community's interests, Garrett's achievement, instead of destroying the social contract, served rather to establish the social contract. Furthermore, Garrett's victory resolved any disparity between the law and true justice, for his killing of the Kid, however potentially anarchic it was in bypassing the courtroom, served to inaugurate true justice and moral law. Thus, such fantasies as Garrett's unrestrained expression of individual freedom operating on behalf of the community reconciled what were in reality patently irreconcilable conflicts of values.

By envisioning the Kid as the deadliest, cruellest outlaw in the history of the West, authors created both a worthy antagonist and a supreme example of what experiences the culture thought forbidden. By further using this antagonist in a romance story form, authors were also free to create daring actions that might attract audience identification toward the villain, because in the end this villain and his vision of experience were defeated. Thus, the Kid's appeal was not only in the manner in which his story reaffirmed traditional values and resolved cultural conflicts; his story also appealed to audiences because through it they could cross over into the forbidden world of the barbarous Kid for a brief moment before returning to the ordered daylight world of restraint and responsibility Garrett validated by shooting the Kid.

By understanding the functions the Kid served for his creators and audiences, we also notice how this vision of the Kid enabled changes in values to continue in the traditional framework of the romance pattern. In 1881, when the Kid died and many people like Chester Arthur could not distinguish between cowboys and outlaws, it became customary to envision the Kid as a conventional symbol of irrational, savage behavior in order to indict the barbaric nature of the Western frontier, which had not yet experienced the grace of the genteel world. When the Kid was revived during the Roosevelt years and only the woefully ignorant could not distinguish between, say, the Virginian and Trampas, it was necessary to explain the Kid as a badman and to distinguish his world from Garrett's settled West.

The meaning of wilderness changed from that of a savage, hostile nature to that of a positive aesthetic and ethical force in the decades between the Civil War and the turn of the century. While we might expect the Kid to be revised in positive terms since he was associated with wilderness values, what happens is that Garrett instead becomes the representative of an ideal agrarian West, which exists as a middle ground between the Kid's barbaric West and the industrial East of a refined elite class and an undereducated lower class. In Emerson Hough's novel *Heart's Desire,* for example, an ideal state of affairs comes about when the conflicting claims of aggressive Eastern coal investors and sleepy Western villagers can be synthesized by a hero who understands how railroads and remudas can coexist. Just as Coalville (the Easterners' intended name for the village) by itself lacks beauty, and Heart's Desire (the Westerners' name for the village) by itself is a false paradise out of touch with reality, so the novel's reconciliation demonstrates how creators of the West and the Kid during this period could still reconcile industrialism and agrarianism.[75]

Whether the West was imagined as a wilderness to be ruthlessly tamed or as the repository of true American values, the Kid was only useful as a symbol of values to be discarded. For a nation facing disorder at home and abroad, the Kid's anarchic defiance of the law was not heroic, but was rather a doomed effort to prevent civilization's advance. At the same time Custer's biographers were portraying him as a poor boy who rose to be manifest destiny's standard-bearer, the Kid's biographers were offering him as a poor boy who died because he stood in the way of manifest destiny. Even more significantly, at the same time a ballad was calling Jesse James a friend of the poor and a victim of the rich, another ballad was proclaiming the Kid's penchant for murdering a poor "greaser" for his daily breakfast. And if he was seen as an anachronism in a society devoted to confirming that railroads and the wilderness could coexist, then the Kid was easily forgotten during the coming war years when the Germans became more immediate and useful symbols of chaos to be controlled.

This explanation of the Kid as a strategy for encompassing a particular cultural situation could be strained to the breaking point as both the Kid's interpreters and the cultural context changed. When the conservative morality affirmed by Hough and others in the Roosevelt era was considered to be restrictive, then the Kid's death could be seen as a tragic event rather than as a triumphant affirmation of traditional American village values. Furthermore, when the white Anglo-Saxon genteel world's faith in reason, order, and evolutionary progress was viewed as an irrelevant and an incredibly simplistic outlook, then the Kid's anarchic defiance of that ordered world could be perceived as heroic rather than as atavistic. In addition, when the conflicts in values are no longer evident in the audience's daily experience, then the Kid-Garrett confrontation could be seen as an evasion of the deep-seated ethical conflicts about the definition of justice and the meaning of individual freedom. When the creators of the Kid emerge with a new vision, which aligns the outlaw with these kinds of recognitions, then the Kid could be accepted, along with Jesse James, as someone other than an "atrocious and uncompromising, cowardly murderer."[76] Instead of existing, in short, as a man all bad, the Kid might attract the interest of those who believed nobody was all bad.

William H. Bonney or Billy the Kid. (Western History Collections, University of Oklahoma Library)

The mother of Billy the Kid. (Western History Collections, University of Oklahoma Library)

Old county jail and courthouse at Lincoln, New Mexico, where Billy the Kid made his famous escape. (Western History Collections, University of Oklahoma Library)

Invitation to a "necktie party," a poster warning Billy the Kid and others to stay out of Las Vegas, New Mexico. (Western History Collections, University of Oklahoma Library)

Johnny Mack Brown as the Kid in director King Vidor's *Billy the Kid* (1930). (MGM)

Roy Rogers as a singing Kid in Republic's *Billy the Kid Returns* (1938).

Jack Beutel as the Kid and Jane Russell as Rio in Howard Hughes's *The Outlaw* (1943).
(Universal City Studios, Inc.)

Robert Taylor as the Kid gets the drop on Brian Donlevy in MGM's *Billy the Kid* (1941).

A publicity shot of Lash Larue, well-known "B" Western actor who played the Kid in *The Son of Billy the Kid* (1949).

Audie Murphy (far left) as the Kid examines a wanted poster in *The Kid From Texas* (1950). (Universal-International)

Paul Newman as the Kid in Arthur Penn's *The Left-Handed Gun* (1958). (Warner Bros.)

Chuck Courtney drawing on an approaching Dracula in Embassy's *Billy the Kid versus Dracula* (1966).

Michael J. Pollard commits his first crime as the youthful Kid in Stan Dragoti's
Dirty Little Billy (1973). (Columbia Pictures)

Kris Kristofferson as the Kid beckons to Matt Clark as Deputy Bell in Sam Peckinpah's
Pat Garrett and Billy the Kid (1973). (MGM)

Joseph Clark as the Kid in Ballet West's 1980 production of Eugene Loring and Aaron Copland's *Billy the Kid*. (Photo by Peter C. van Dyck, courtesy of Ballet West.)

Joseph Clark and Karen Kuhn during the *pas de deux* of *Billy the Kid*. (Photo by Kenn Duncan, courtesy of Ballet West.)

Cover of John Woodruff Lewis's (Don Jenardo) 1881 dime novel *The True Life of Billy the Kid*.

The comic-book Kid, circa 1980. Lewis's glowering, dark-haired evil Kid is in this production a blonde, blue-eyed bandit samaritan who delivers a native village from the evils of pet vultures. (© 1981 Charlton Publications, Inc.)

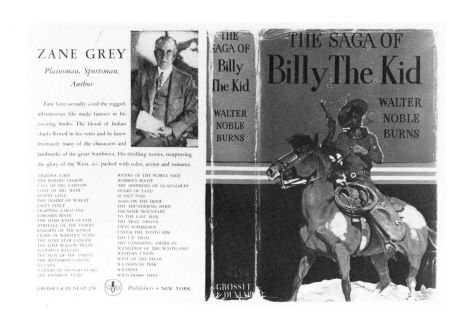

Dustjacket to an early edition of Walter Noble Burns's *The Saga of Billy the Kid* (1926). Zane Grey's shadow cuts across what is arguably the most important book in the Kid bibliography.

Charles M. Russell's pen-and-ink drawing of the Kid's legendary murder of Morton and Baker.

4 "Nobody's All Bad"

Visions of the Kid from Prohibition to the Cold War, 1925–1955

Billy: "Not even the devil, Miss Haskel, can be as black as people make him out to be!"
—E. B. Mann, *Gamblin' Man*, 1934

Billy: "I don't know Mr. [Robin] Hood or where he rides, but if he just rustled a few cows to help out a widowed mother, I hope the Sheriff's posse will never cut his trail."
—William Lee Hamlin, *The True Story of Billy the Kid*, 1959

The initial vision of the Kid as a deadly obstacle to civilization's displacement of savagery faded during World War I. Although Zane Grey's fictional West and William S. Hart's cinematic West were extremely popular with the American public between 1915 and 1925, Billy the Kid's West had declined to such a low level of interest that Harvey Fergusson, writing in 1925 for H. L. Mencken's *American Mercury*, opened his article on the Kid with this question: "Who remembers Billy the Kid?"[1] Certainly Fergusson's question was well-taken, for those who did remember the Kid immediately after the war usually encountered him in privately-printed publications, which naturally reached smaller audiences than the numerous commercial magazine articles on the Kid that appeared in the century's first decade. John Poe's eyewitness account of the Kid's death, for example, first appeared in a London magazine in 1919 and was then later privately reprinted in Los Angeles in 1922 and 1923. Besides the fact of its limited circulation, Poe's account also marked the dormant state of interest in the Kid by seemingly clearing up any remaining controversy about whether the Kid did die in 1881. And if, in the words of one commentator, "one can at least realize that he [the Kid] is dead enough to stay dead,"[2] then there was apparently no need to resurrect him in a century that experienced the evils of chemical warfare and gangsters.

Yet the Kid's legend was resurrected and saved from an early death, as we know, and Fergusson's question is important, for it not only indicated the dearth of interest in the Kid by 1925, it also marked a revitalization of the initial formula for explaining the outlaw's significance. For those observers who continued to believe with William Macleod Raine that "lil'l' red school-houses and diapers is in; six-shooters is out," it was easy to accept even as late as 1945 the familiar verdict that the Kid "was just a little, small-sized cow- and horse-thief who lived grubbily and missed legal hanging by only a few days."[3] Yet when other observers after World War I daily saw things that were at odds with what they heretofore believed to be the American way, and when observers like Fergusson who experienced this discrepancy did not re-treat from or sublimate this disquieting truth, then at such moments a new form of historical explanation might emerge which would more successfully relate to the current cultural scene.[4] If we recall that the initial explanation of the Kid affirmed a benevolent historical process and resolved a potential conflict between self and society, we then find that the most vulnerable points in this explanation of the Kid would be recognitions that the process of histori-cal change did not guarantee progress, or that the conflict between self and society could not be resolved by an Horatio Alger ethic of success.

We discover the weakness of the initial explanation of the Kid precisely in those instances where uncertainty appears about the definition of the words "outlaw" and "hero." As Emerson Hough, for example, became disgusted in 1907 with the news of brutal rapes and murders committed by contemporary urban criminals, he decided that even as evil as were outlaws like the Kid, "if we were forced to make choices among criminals, then by all means that choice should be, must be, not the brutal murderer of the cities, but the desperado of the old West."[5] In addition to dismay at urban criminals, as Charlie Siringo grew older and began to regret his earlier activities as a Pinkerton's agent working for mine owners against striking miners, he suggested that "behind the doors of polite society today, just about as many things are done on im-pulse, which are fully as bad, considered morally, as anything the cowboys pulled in their wild, free, open style."[6] While the Kid was perhaps more than a mere free cowboy who let off steam at a Kansas railhead, Siringo concluded his 1920 biography of the Kid by blessing the outlaw's ashes. Despite the Kid's many faults as a murderer, Siringo believed him to be "a young hero outlaw," a romantic "fool" who died for love rather than leave the country.

Siringo's and Hough's statements are entwined with a nostalgic recall of what was believed to have been a simpler, yet more vigorous era when men were men and women knew it. Yet at moments of recognition so pivotal that the definition of hero could include the Kid, or that the actions of urban criminals and polite society were just as bad—if not worse—than the Kid's exploits, such authors as Siringo and Hough did not pass over the critical threshold and advance a new vision of the Kid that would transform the initial explanation. All too often Hough's heroes were in the mold of the Virginian; Siringo's heroes, on the other hand, resembled Siringo. However much Siringo's 1920 biography opened new ground in treating the Kid's legend, and however sympathetic Siringo was to the Kid's fate, the Kid was for Siringo different from the leathered cowboys who paved the way for civilization. In addition, while by 1920 Siringo was attuned to the cultural changes that would accept a new vision of the Kid, his biography was only privately-printed in New Mexico, thus ensuring its relative insignificance when compared to the *Saga of Billy the Kid,* which appeared in 1926 as a Book-of-the-Month Club selection.

But if occasionally Siringo and Hough failed to popularize a new explanation of the Kid, one author before Fergusson did envision a Kid as something other than a romance villain. In 1903, one year after *The Virginian* appeared, Walter Woods published a melodrama entitled *Billy the Kid.* In it a dashing, resourceful, handsome young man named Will Wright was transformed into an avenging outlaw named Billy the Kid in order to punish the crooked shyster (who turns out to be his father) who had defrauded and murdered his mother and stepfather. Although Woods's melodrama only capitalized on the notoriety of the phrase "Billy the Kid," it demonstrated during its successful twelve-year tour beginning in 1906 that the Kid—like the dime-novel Jesse James—could be a conventional hero *if* he were given a justification for his actions and *if* he were endowed with a gentlemanly sense of social proprieties.[7]

Yet because it had completed its tour by 1918, and because Fergusson's question reminds us how much the postwar recovery diminished interest in the Kid, we can discover a more sustained reappraisal of the Kid in 1925 when Fergusson's essay appeared and when Walter Noble Burns's *Saga* was being completed. Furthermore, Fergusson provides an appropriate transition from the earlier visions of the Kid for, as he mentions in his essay, he had seen the melodrama prior to the war, had read Garrett's *Authentic Life,* and also had interviewed Frank Coe, one of the Kid's colleagues.

The differences between the new vision of the Kid advanced by Fergusson and the previous vision formulated by Hough and others can best be seen by contrasting Fergusson's essay with Hough's 1901 article about the Kid for *Everybody's Magazine*. Although both men mention the Kid's "true bandit nobility" and his tricks of genius with firearms, they offer different notions about the Kid's appearance, personality, and cultural significance. Where Hough's outlaw appeared most frequently as an undersized, weak-chinned miscarriage in the evolutionary process, Fergusson's later version of the Kid's appearance dropped allusions to wild animals, gave the Kid a chin and decent height, and generally concluded the Kid was rather good-looking except for his two prominent front teeth. Where Hough's outlaw was a purely savage personality motivated by an instinctual blood lust, Fergusson's Kid possessed a recognizable personality: "Billy was a quixotic romantic, who cared nothing for money. He lived and died an idealist. . . . He had in immense measure that uncompromising vanity which makes human destiny spectacular, and . . . is the chief difference between heroes and ordinary men."[8] Unlike Hough's outlaw, Fergusson's hero did not lust for blood but was violent to avenge the deaths of his mother and his friend Tunstall. And where Hough judged the Kid by the standards of the genteel world, Fergusson placed the Kid in the context of frontier conditions and decided that he was actually "a distinguished member of society, the most feared and admired man of his time and place."[9]

Besides representing in appearance and personality "the perfect specimen of the bandit hero," Fergusson's Kid differs from Hough's in terms of historical significance. Where Hough saw the Kid's death as emblematic of an advancing civilization's triumph over an obsolete order of savagery, Fergusson envisioned the Kid as the key figure of the pastoral epoch that spanned the years between the Civil War and the completion of the transcontinental railroad. On the surface these versions of the Kid's significance appear similarly to present him as a symbol of an irretrievable past; however, the difference in tone is crucial, for unlike Hough's optimistic celebration of the Anglo-Saxon's triumph over a lawless half-Spanish civilization, Fergusson's tone is more somber, even elegiac, as he ponders the loss of the Kid's fame in the era of Coolidge's business ethic. What bothers Fergusson is that his perception of Billy's gallant and engaging qualities appears irrelevant to the concerns of an age that could portray Jesus as a go-getter super-salesman like George Babbitt. Thus, Billy's "idealism" for Fergusson is more highly valued than the materialistic spirit of the James gang, those "hard-headed businessmen who made crime pay."[10] Essentially, the muted, perhaps elegiac, tone of the essay is due not so much to any regret that the Kid has been forgotten, as to a regret that the values the Kid is now seen as personifying—romance, chivalry, unmoneyed idealism—are, after the Great War, gone.

This essay restated themes that were internal strains in the initial explanation of the Kid: as in Woods's melodrama, the Kid is a hero justified in his actions; as in Siringo's biography, the Kid is an eligible romantic interest "foredoomed to be a fool for women"; and as in Hough's later publications, the Kid—however ruthless and deadly—personified the spirit of the frontier whose primitive individualism was unfortunately becoming extinct in contemporary America. Fergusson in 1925 was critical of some of the historical choices made in the last century, and he thus introduced the possibility of envisioning the Kid as a bandit hero of the romance or as a figure in a tragic story—a figure who for a moment spectacularly defied destiny and a materialistic society before succumbing to defeat.

Although Fergusson's interpretation of the Kid could be granted only provisional acceptance at the time it appeared, within five years Burns's *Saga* (1926) and the 1930 MGM movie so successfully popularized these two possible visions of the Kid that few people aware of popular cultural trends could say they didn't remember the Kid—or that their memories of him would not be dominated by a noble bandit image. In the years between Fergusson's essay and 1950, over three times as many entries appear in the Kid's bibliography than in the period from 1881 to 1925. During this era the Kid appeared in ballets, movies, ballads, books, and—for the first time—*The Dictionary of American Biography*.[11] Whereas in 1925 Fergusson had asked who remembered the Kid, in 1941 *Life* magazine called the Kid one of America's "best-loved badmen," and by 1950 William Keleher remarked that nine out of ten Santa Fe tourists requested Billy the Kid picture postcards.[12]

The era of Fergusson and Audie Murphy (war hero and movie star who played the Kid) should be remembered as the classic era, one which transformed the Kid into a figure of cultural significance. The reasons involve the diversity of persons interested in the Kid, the Kid's presence in several movies that sustained his appeal, and—in the aftermath of Wister, Grey, and Hart—the general popularity of the Western in fiction and film. Along with these developments, we need also to consider how the emergence and acceptance of a new idea of the Kid functionally related to the cultural context of the 1920s and 1930s. As we shall see in the next few pages, while Fergusson's essay marks a convenient transition from Garrett's *Authentic Life* to the era of Burns's *Saga*, it appeared in an environment markedly different from that of Hough's *Heart's Desire*. After the war, in short, the possibility of envisioning the Kid as a sympathetic, misguided youth who defied a corrupt establishment meshed during the years of the flappers and Shirley Temple with audience uneasiness about the results of the late-nineteenth century decision to model America along the lines of an urban-industrial society.

Before World War I, the meaning of the Kid and the West was conditioned by attempts to reaffirm what were considered to be basic American values under siege from developments in a rapidly-evolving urban-industrial society. This moralistic effort to shore up traditional values was successful during the Progressive years before the war, but after 1920 it was increasingly difficult to sustain such an effort. What social historian Frederick Lewis Allen has called "the Revolution in Manners and Morals" occurred in the 1920s as the combined pressures of feminism, science, Freudianism, political corruption, credit buying, and postwar hedonism corroded earlier ideals of religious piety, sexual chastity, sobriety, and frugality.[13] With Freud's adherents (and his distorters) discussing society's repression of the individual self, with war veterans returning home after experiencing different moral climates, and with basic ethical standards coming to seem irrelevant, even comical, and certainly immature, the reform ideals of Theodore Roosevelt and Woodrow Wilson were being displaced. A new generation searched for the pleasure of the moment. By the time Fergusson's essay appeared in 1925, bootlegging in the streets and scandals in the Harding administration had eroded faith in the legal and political systems. The jazz age had begun a sweeping transformation of social and cultural life, and the cultural spokesmen of this era—including Sinclair Lewis, Mencken, and Hemingway—complained of American mediocrity, conformity, and loss of identity. Several biographies also appeared which debunked traditional heroes and saints by portraying their failures, vices, and personality complexes. Instead of George Washington or Abraham Lincoln, Al Capone and John Dillinger mesmerized America, and in this change of taste we can understand how Americans would be receptive to a sympathetic vision of the Kid.

If the 1920s represented an assault upon the dominance of traditional rural Protestant American values, the Depression of the 1930s amounted to a scattering of the faith many Americans had in their economic system. By the time the first Kid movie previewed in 1930, few Americans could blithely assume that ambition, hard work, thrift, and company loyalty would guarantee success. Few Americans could assume that poverty was the result of ignorance or lassitude. Cynical about the past and yet searching for a usable past that would help address current moral and economic problems, shocked by the economic chaos of the present, and disillusioned about future prospects, large numbers of Americans were undergoing a fundamental change in how they saw themselves and their world. In the political, economic, social, and cultural upheaval of the 1920s and early 1930s, two events in the na-

tional scene contributed directly to the changing vision of the Kid's significance—Prohibition and the related rise to prominence of the gangster film
melodrama.

Millions of Americans between 1920 and 1933 technically became *outlaws*
every time they bought, drank, or distilled alcoholic beverages. Ratified in
1920, Amendment 18 was supposed to regenerate American life. Before its
repeal in 1933, however, Prohibition had effectively demonstrated that legis-
lating morality was one task; enforcing it was an altogether different, and
difficult, enterprise. Though federal agents did make 500,000 arrests during
a ten-year period (and secure 300,000 convictions), illegal bootlegging and
drinking were, to understate the case, widespread. However "wet" or "dry"
proponents explained the rise and fall of the temperance movement, the significant point about Prohibition, in the exemplary words of one observer,
was that "a virtue is passing out of the American people. We make laws and
can no longer enforce them."[14]

Many Americans focused their fears upon the most obvious example of the
decline in respect for law—the inefficiency and corruption of the judicial system exposed by the urban gangster's spectacular rise to public prominence.
At the same time Fergusson was asking his *American Mercury* audience if anyone remembered the Kid, Al Capone assumed control of the Chicago underworld by paying off police, bribing politicians, and killing his rivals. Whether
or not Prohibition created the gangster, such incidents as the St. Valentine's
Day massacre and the O'Bannion Flowershop murder captivated a national
audience and created the Capone legend.

It was Capone's legend that also inspired the gangster film boom between
1930 and 1933.[15] While Johnny Mack Brown was portraying the Kid in 1930,
millions of Americans were paying to see Edward G. Robinson in *Little
Caesar*. One year later the public could choose to see around 50 gangster
films, the most predominant one being *Public Enemy* with James Cagney. Although the Western movie *Cimarron* won the Oscar for Best Picture in 1931,
gangster melodramas consistently outdrew Westerns at the box office. With
the popularity and subsequent success of the gangster film, some critics and
reviewers confidently predicted the Western's ultimate demise.

Such developments as the rise of the gangster in the streets and in the
movies, the debunking of traditional heroes, the flouting of traditional moral
standards, the changing roles of women, and the popularity of authors like
Erskine Caldwell reveal an American public anxious to discard outmoded codes
of conduct and belief. Incidents of political corruption, economic disruption,
and moral breakdown certainly lend credence to the traditional view of America
in the 1920s and 1930s as a tired, disillusioned nation searching for ways to
address a strange new world. Yet the questioning of traditional values was

but one response to change; as one scholar has recently suggested, we should remember that many Americans during this period were supporting and resurrecting preindustrial American ideals as alternatives to the present.[16] Church attendance and family life were still important elements in the lives of many Americans. During the same decade when Americans endured Harding's corrupt Republican administration, Americans yet elected Republicans Coolidge and Hoover to the presidency. Amidst greater frankness in treatments of sex and violence, the Legion of Decency and Production Code Administration established moral standards for the movies to follow. The revolt against Roosevelt and Wilson's Progressive politics was not unanimous, for La Follette and Norris were still actively pushing Progressive legislation in Congress.

During the Kid's revitalization in the 1920s and 1930s, then, many Americans displayed an ambiguous response to the postwar environment. While many Americans were dissatisfied with the cultural norms they inherited and thus explored newer codes, these same people were also reluctant to make a complete break with conventional values. This ambiguous response to inherited traditions can be seen in the fate of the Cagney and Robinson gangster characters of 1930 and 1931. In these films a gangster's rags-to-riches success story naturally reaffirmed the possibility of the self-made man realizing the American Dream; yet the gangster's ultimate destiny of defeat and death re-established what we might call the Legion of Decency moral judgment about those who break the law. That the film gangster both succeeded and died allowed audiences simultaneously to criticize a society which would condone such antisocial behavior and to affirm that success was still possible if one utilized his talents.

The Kid's renewed popularity also demonstrated how the creators and consumers of popular culture revealed a mixed response to the general loss of faith in traditional explanations of life. As we have already seen in our brief discussion of Fergusson's essay, this youthful outlaw—once considered the worst man alive—was portrayed after 1925 as a quixotic, romantic idealist who symbolized a lost pastoral world. The resurgence of interest in the Kid after this essay is of course due in part to old-timers offering their recollections of the Kid, as well as to Siringo's and Hough's highlighting the Kid's noble deeds and questioning whether the Kid's taming by Garrett achieved a more civilized world. But the most important factor behind renewed attention to him was that many of his creators considered the idea of the outlaw as a response not just to the general decline in faith in the law, but also to the American experience with Prohibition and gangsters.

It is tempting to assume that the Kid's revaluation occurred because his legend could assimilate the appealing qualities of the popular Capone legend. Like Capone, for example, the Kid might be regarded as a romantic rebel both challenging a corrupt system and befriending the dispossessed. It is also conceivable that some people could identify the Kid and Capone as isolated loners, embodying disillusionment with a hypocritical mainstream society, or as tragic figures defying destiny with daring exploits. Though on one occasion the Kid's rustling activities were considered as innocuous a crime as bootlegging, the few observers who did associate the Kid with gangsters usually did so in a negative manner. After reading Burns's *Saga* in 1926 and viewing the 1930 MGM movie, one writer complained that "since observing the gradual deification of Billy the Kid I have come to the conclusion that King Arthur was probably the leading racketeer of his day, and Galahad the local Don Juan."[17] On at least two other occasions the Kid was perceived as neither a martyr nor a quixotic romantic, but as "the Dillinger of 1879."[18] Even as late as 1945 Jack Thorp believed the controversy over the deteriorating state of the Kid's gravesite meant that "maybe somebody will be erecting a monument one of these days to every paid killer hired by Al Capone."[19]

Regardless of the similarities drawn between the Kid and the gangster, however, by far the greatest number of observers revised their estimate of the Kid because they saw crucial *differences* between the Western desperado and the urban gangster. Whatever their personal views of the Kid, most observers preferred the outlaw's appearance, personality, mode of violence, and milieu to those of the gangsters. Owen White, a writer not overly fond of the Kid, was one of the first to contrast favorably the Kid and gangsters by asking if anyone ever called outlaws "nuts":

> You never did, and it wouldn't have been healthy for anybody to have done it. Those men would have resented such an insinuation with a six-shooter. They were sane and wicked, damnably, gloriously wicked after a courageous and manly fashion. They were bad, proud of it, and willing to pay the price, whereas the modern Clarences of the profession, the overdressed, slick-haired, girl-chasing bandits of Broadway and Michigan Avenue are vicious, low down and cowardly.[20]

Between 1926 and 1953 little disagreement arose over White's assessment of each outlaw's values. "The leaders of those cowboy-outlaws of the plains," wrote one cowboy in 1927, "must not be catalogued with the type of modern pay-roll and bank bandits of big cities of America."[21] In 1934 Eugene Cunningham favored Billy over "the litter of sneaking out-of-doorway thugs spawned by any metropolis"; in 1941, at the same time actor Robert Taylor's version of Billy reminded audiences of George Raft's characterizations of gangsters, another writer asserted that "to compare the modern gangster with the typical bad man of the West is absurd."[22] And even in a 1951 book dedicated "to the man who brought law and order to the frontier," the author suggested that "the gunfighter of the old days was not the same type as the bandits and hijackers of more modern times."[23]

Western outlaws were favored over the gangster because of observers' prejudices against the gangster's racial heritage and urban environment. Whereas the Western outlaw was a "gloriously wicked," shrewd, hearty, rough, and *manly* Anglo-Saxon, the urban gangster was typically seen as a slick-haired, shifty-eyed, treacherous "child of racial degeneration"—a "saffron hued Yegg" who was raised "without discipline, religion, education, or common decency of thought or action."[24] Whereas the Western outlaw's evil occurred in the wild, free, and primitive canyons and plains of the sparsely-settled and unrestrictive Western setting, the gangster was viewed as "the degenerate product of the city slums, brother to the sewer rats of the same districts," cowardly thugs who were "weaned on crook plays in the cinema and contempt for women in the tenements."[25] Even the fact that the Kid was a New York City product was seen to be a favorable fact, for the Kid and his family had the good sense to migrate to New Mexico.[26] Another person suggested that Western outlaws such as the Kid were to be preferred over their modern descendents because the outlaws drank tequila, not "east side dago red."[27] The point to make here is that while before the war the Kid was given an Irish, Mexican, or an Indian heritage to validate racist allegations, after the war such racist remarks were directed not toward the Kid, but toward the gangster.

In the eyes of the Kid's observers, the major problem associated with the gangster's racial heritage was that these criminals were thought to possess no code of honor, and were known to employ vicious, impersonal, and unchivalrous methods. Throughout this era observers typically juxtaposed the gangster's bullet-proof automobile and the outlaw's horse, the gangster's machine-gun and the outlaw's revolver, the gangster's heroin and the outlaw's fresh air. While the gangster ambushed women and children and other helpless victims, the outlaw fought only duels and never shot defenseless persons; while the gangster perfected cement overshoes and time bombs and gang slayings, the outlaw more gallantly fought his opponent face-to-face and relied only on his native skills, intelligence, and exposed—not concealed—weapons.[28] "Modern gang butchery would nauseate any old-time outlaw I ever run across," wrote Emmett Dalton in 1931, himself one of the last surviving old-time outlaws.[29] And one of the Kid's last surviving friends, Yijinio Salazar, admired the fact that unlike the gangster 'rats', the Kid at least "had a horse. A pair of six-guns. . . . He fought face to face with his enemies. He gave them a chance to draw."[30]

Besides this response to the distressing rise to prominence of the gangster, the Kid's observers were similarly distressed by the record of political and judicial corruption in the late 1920s and early 1930s. "Driven from their spectacular roles," one essayist wrote, "the bad men do not vanish from the sight of God. They bob up in a new place, namely politics."[31] One old-timer concluded his account of New Mexico's turbulent 1870s by stating that "instead of cattle thieves, bank robbers, and outlaws, we now have statesmen who practice nepotism, pad the public payrolls and graft as much as they think they can get away with . . . just like the folks back east."[32] This statement is important, for it typifies the reaction of many people who were disillusioned not only by what they saw or read about Eastern happenings, but also by the fact that such declining standards occurred in the supposedly pristine Western landscape. Others were also disillusioned by the government's inability to enforce its laws, a condition which naturally bred a disrespect for law and order. In an article "The Strong Men of the West," one observer suggested, in a manner reminiscent of Emerson Hough in 1907, that the FBI needed an Earp or a Hickock to control those who ruthlessly exploited personal lives and property.[33] In this view, the only way to impress any criminal with "the beauty of morality" would be "to set up a new Police Department, elect new judges, import a new brand of mayor, and build a completely new political organization."[34]

The Kid's legend was revived during the boom and bust years of the late 1920s and 1930s. Moreover, in this revival the Kid and other outlaws were basically defined in opposition to the technological society that spawned Capone, the shyster, and the corrupt politicians. If we can accept the American public's attraction to or abhorrence of certain modes of criminal behavior as an extended metaphor of social tension, then the above responses to the results of Prohibition reveal a deep-seated conflict between the past and the present, between the values of agrarian and industrial America. If the choices made during the last century to invent an urban-industrial America produced such unfortunate results, if this state of affairs was *civilization,* as one Kid observer wrote as late as 1953, "perhaps a throwback on survival is in order."[35] Other authors were convinced that "we are living on wheels now and have not time to kneel," and, after the stock market crash in 1929, that "Big Money = Hell for Everybody."[36] The commonly voiced frustration with post-World War I society is nicely captured in a 1935 poem, which featured the Kid:

> The wooly West has got effete,
> It makes me sore to think
> That nowadays a guy must sneak
> Outside to take a drink
> All I can do is set an' think
> Of good old days of yore.[37]

The national mood was such that in combination with either nostalgia for a past when people controlled their destinies or anger at the present context of lost ideals and limited freedom, it led the Kid's creators to identify their contemporary society with savagery, and to imply that in the old West reposed civilization's real values. That outlaws could become heroes is understandable when the nation was believed to be dominated by organized crime, restrictive legislation, corrupt politicans and judges, and rapacious big business.

The sympathetic response given to the Kid after 1925 reflected in part the widespread dissatisfaction with the evolution of horses into getaway cars, revolvers into tommy-guns, and the Virginian's West into a place where a man couldn't even drink like a man. When, as was the case during Prohibition's existence, every American who surreptitiously took a drink internalized a conflict between individual morality and social prescription, it became easier for an audience to understand the Kid's legal dilemma during the Lincoln County War. And when the legal and economic system was known to betray individuals and reward corruption, it became more credible for an audience to voice and accept the idea that the Kid was framed and betrayed by this system. In the face of such skepticism about the results of our historical decisions, in the face of a changed attitude toward the criminal, and in the face of the public's awareness of the ambiguous nature of justice, it was evident that one who defied the status quo could be envisioned as a hero of democracy, as "our fighting vicar against aristocracy, against power, against law, against the upstart, the pretender, the smugly virtuous, and the pompously successful person or corporation whom we envy."[38] A defiant Kid who symbolized the positive values of a vanished pastoral epoch could be and was accepted in this cultural context as a tragic figure of another lost generation, or later, during the Depression, as a romance hero whose moral sense and skillful use of deadly force protected democratic ideals from the alien threats of big business, organized crime, and other dispossessors of the populace. However, just as large numbers of Americans were paradoxically attracted to both Capone and Coolidge, so too those who created the Kid as a benevolent outlaw were rejecting and yet affirming the direction of American society. Just how this response to sociocultural developments was specifically embodied in the changed vision of the Kid is the subject of the rest of this chapter.

For those willing to see the Kid in sympathetic terms—a semiheroic figure vastly preferred to modern gangsters—it was yet necessary to justify his violent exploits and to spruce up his scruffy, if not demonic, appearance. That the Kid was eventually accepted as something other than a misfit and murderer was made possible in part by the writings of Zane Grey and the films of William S. Hart. In characters like Jim Lassiter and Blaze Tracy, Grey and Hart popularized the benevolent outlaw figure who existed outside society to avoid misguided social persecution during a quest to avenge injustice. In works by Grey and Hart, justice was often viewed as helpless before the truly pernicious elements in society, and the good-badman's violent actions, rather than being seen as a threat to an established order, actually purged a helpless society of its evil elements and thus regenerated familiar ideals. Because of such beneficent results to a potentially subversive display of power, the Grey and Hart good-badman was typically domesticated by marriage, or was last seen in the heroine's company as the duo entered a secret, idyllic landscape in which violence had no place.[39]

By the mid-1920s, when such examples of the good-badman were before the public, and strident criticism of the modern criminal was beginning to surface, the Kid was also emerging as a good-badman along the lines of, say, Hart's Draw Egan. Interestingly, Grey provides an effective transition from the 1912 Lassiter to the 1920s Kid in his novel *Nevada* (1928). At one point he presents a respected judge lecturing the novel's heroine about a crucial distinction that must be made when anyone considered lawless activities:

> There are bad men and bad men. It is a distinction with a vast difference. I have met or seen many of the noted killers. Wild Bill, Wess Hardin, Kingfisher, *Billy the Kid, Pat Garrett* an' a host of others. These men are not bloody murderers. They are a product of the times. The West could never have been populated without them. They strike a balance between the hordes of ruffians, outlaws, strong evil characters like Dillon, and the wild life of a wild era. . . . And such as we could not be pioneers, we could not progress without this violence. . . . The rub is that only hard iron-nerved youths like Billy the Kid, or Jim Lacy can meet such men on their own ground.[40] [emphasis added].

Besides the explicit contrast drawn between badmen and good-badmen, we notice that by 1928 Garrett and the Kid are not distinguished from each other, but are rather yoked together as examples of men whose violence enabled pioneers to found a new world. Furthermore, instead of condemning the Kid as a ruthless murderer, Grey's character indicates a willingness to see the Kid as a wild product of a wild era, and—in the last sentence—to place even the Kid for a brief moment on the same level as the novel's hero.

As is indicated in Grey's passage, one essential feature in legitimizing the Kid's violent legacy was to view his career as a natural product of a frontier environment. Earlier Kid observers also identified the outlaw with the frontier, but both were judged to be "savage." By the 1920s and 1930s, though, when the definition of civilization and *hero* were ambiguous and when the Kid's observers were increasingly critical of a settled, urban industrial America, the Kid and his frontier were viewed favorably. That the Kid could be seen as an understandable, even ordinary, frontier product in the 1930s is consistent with that era's belief that gangsterism and juvenile delinquency were the manifestations of their decadent, slum-ridden environment. Since this simple environmental determinism argued that setting causes conduct, the Kid as a frontier youth was preferable, on the one hand, to the city-bred delinquent, and, on the other hand, was just one among many frontiersmen who slapped leather holsters instead of written subpoenas on their enemies. "In justice to Billy the Kid," one typical commentator argued, "it is necessary that the persons judging him put themselves in his position. He had not been trained in the finer arts of civilization, he had been reared in the prairies, and the only law that he knew was that dealt by his ready gun. . . . "[41] The Kid, though, had tried to adjust to change around him by foregoing direct action in favor of testifying in court. Moreover, unlike others of his era, he never robbed banks and trains. All this suggested that he was not a true desperado but perhaps a misguided youth.

Another essential feature of the frontier was the arbitrary nature of justice and the inconsistent application of the law. Whereas before the 1920s a contrast between outlaw and sheriff was clear-cut, such unambiguous definitions of good and evil or guilt and innocence were difficult to stipulate, much less believe, after the American public had witnessed Harding, Capone, and corrupt law enforcement officials. The good-badman and the bad-goodman were realities in life and in art. In the Kid's case, people began to realize that what law did exist in territorial New Mexico was fickle, ill-defined, and basically corrupt. Harvey Fergusson voiced this notion in 1933 when he declared that any cowboy in the 1870s was "at times a cattle thief and at times a hired gunman on one side or another in a struggle where ethics and issues were alike confused."[42] Because it was accepted that such confusing ethics and issues could mean a man might be an outlaw on one day and a deputy on the next, the Kid in a 1940 play told a nun that "in this part o' the country the line that divides the law an the outlaw is as near as fine as a frog's hair."[43] Without any clearly-defined concept of the law (and thus the outlaw), and with a willingness to see the Kid betrayed by Wallace's amnesty offer and promise of a pardon, many accounts echoed Miguel Otero's judgment that the Kid was a scapegoat, "a man more sinned against than sinning."[44] "How was it," wrote one contributor to *Ranch Romances,* "that he was the only one ever brought to trial for any of the numerous killings from 1878 to 1880?"[45] Thus, while the Kid was viewed as no more amoral than others of his time, he was—given this skepticism about the even-handed application of justice—increasingly considered to be an exceptional instance of misapplied justice.

The discovery of strong motives behind the Kid's killings served to legitimate his violence. The Kid was no longer perceived solely as a blood-thirsty wild beast who slew men, in Emerson Hough's words, "just to see them kick." Instead, authors traced the Kid's penchant for violence to a cruel stepfather who abused both him and his mother. A more common and successful manner of justifying the Kid's violence was to highlight the Kid's vengeance motive. While certain authors deplored the application of an Old Testament "eye for an eye" concept of justice, the fact remained that such an ethic explained the important motive for the Kid's first killing. Whereas earlier the Kid was seen as a murderer of friends, authors during this era characteristically echoed the Garrett version that the Kid's first murder occurred when the twelve-year old youth stabbed a degenerate loafer who insulted his mother. The Kid's later killings were also typically explained as actions avenging the murder of his friend Tunstall. Thus, after Tunstall's death the Kid "became a man—grown, grim, and experienced—whose sole aim in life was to get revenge for the death of his friend."[46] In this changed attitude toward the Kid's violence, observers conveniently recalled the Kid's enemies' despicable acts of shooting Tunstall's horse or dancing around McSween's corpse while forcing McSween's servants to play music for the celebration. Even if accounts failed to mention the Kid's heinous killing of Joe Grant, the fact that historical researchers were questioning his sole responsibility for the murders of Bernstein, Roberts, and Brady only added to the Kid's growing appeal as a good-badman. And though vengeance alone could hardly justify the nature of the Kid's killings after the Lincoln County War was terminated, the Kid's deadly deeds between 1879 and 1881 were often compressed in time so that, for example, Carlyle's death in 1880 seemingly occurred shortly after Tunstall's killing in 1878.[47]

Along with attention to the hypocritical nature of frontier justice and the Kid's justifiable vengeance motive, the Kid's career was portrayed as a violent, perhaps misguided, dedicated attempt to further a just cause. On several occasions in the late 1920s the Kid was described as a desperate youth battling organized gangs controlled by a Capone-like J. J. Dolan or L. G. Murphy. In the 1930s the Kid's personal quest for vengeance was given an added social dimension when he was perceived as a martyr for oppressed peoples persecuted by wealthy landowners who wished, by controlling the public domain, to sever the tie between the people and the land. By the 1940s, as Kent Steckmesser has argued, the association of the Kid as a Robin Hood who befriended the poor was the inevitable result of presenting his violence as defense of a just cause.[48] Where the initial vision of the Kid portrayed him as Chisum's henchman, during this era the Kid was viewed as the enemy of a haughty, aristocratic Chisum who conspired with Santa Fe bankers to defraud small farmers of their dreams of an independent existence in nature's bosom.

Yet because Tunstall was killed and McSween was a pacifist (before he too was killed), the Kid was also viewed as a persecuted figure who singlehandedly combatted the more powerful forces destroying society from within. Like Tom Joad in *The Grapes of Wrath,* the Kid did not want to hurt anyone, but was driven to his actions to defend a personal code of honor, one usually aligned with Jeffersonian agrarian ideals: as the Kid explained to a friend in one piece, "They made me this way! . . . Drove me to what I am. Cattlemen wanted to steal the home right of the people, the homesteads of the settlers, the grants of the natives. They have done this and hounded me to death. I'm mad from fever or persecution."[49]

Although brief instances of the Kid's noble bandit characteristics cropped up in accounts before the 1930s, a veritable eruption of stories occurred in the next twenty years presenting the Kid's affinity with Robin Hood or Claude Duval.[51] Whether hounded by an oppressive society or in pursuit of vengeance, the Kid was portrayed performing a range of both monetary and nonmonetary samaritan exploits. On various occasions the Kid was seen shooting a crooked Mexican faro dealer and outfitting cowboy gamblers in new clothes; nursing a sick prospector to health and leaving him a new mule packed with mining equipment; giving money and/or sides of beef to poor Mexican families; and, incredibly, paying Pat Garrett's hospital bills. Besides these grants of financial aid, the Kid also was revealed to have prevented the rape of a Mexican girl by Apaches, to have killed Joe Grant for insulting an Indian, to have helped some boys capture lost horses and then cross a stretch of treacherous quicksand in the Red River, and to have allowed a Colorado town's only doctors to live even after they had refused to treat an injured outlaw. In a 1930 story entitled "Nobody's All Bad," the Kid is seen helping the narrator battle a band of Mescalero Apaches, and, because of this act, the narrator is unable to shoot the fugitive Kid.[51] The thematic difference between this Kid's exploits and the former Kid's exploits can of course be seen in the contrast of this story's title with that of the earlier title "A Man All Bad." But a more dramatic contrast between the old and the new formula can be seen when we contrast the Kid's role in two stories set at wedding feasts: in Forbes Heerman's 1887 "Wedding at Puerto de Luna," the Kid robs the guests and kills an old man who turns out to be his father; in Frank Applegate's 1932 "New Mexico Legends," the Kid delivers the little Mexican village from the thrall of an oily outlaw and creates the conditions for a proper wedding to take place.[52]

By highlighting the Kid's noble deeds as a bandit samaritan, by considering him as a scapegoat of a corrupt legal and political system, and by emphasizing his vengeance motive and battles for a just cause, the Kid's creators formulated a justification for his violence. Along with justifying the Kid's violence, the emerging idea of the Kid as a good-badman is naturally revealed in descriptions of the outlaw's appearance and personal qualities. The Kid typically was described as "a nice looking a young fellow as you'd care to meet,"[53] instead of as a fiend with horns and a tail. The Kid's hair changed from an earlier coal black to light brown or blond tint; his eyes, once described as "glowing like coals," now were described as blue, or gray, or even once as "the mild blue eyes of a poet."[54] Whereas before the Kid's effeminate hands and tiny feet were cause for scorn, now such attributes were noted as merely a delicate part of an overall athletic, lithe, and sinewy physique. Previous descriptions of the Kid's clothing, furthermore, generally suggested contempt for the Kid by picturing him in outlandish, flamboyant, Mexican-inspired costumes or in totally grubby, worn out hand-me-downs; after 1925 a typical account of the kid's attire presented him in range garb. Neither an aristocrat nor a hobo, the Kid was a working person whose tailored, practical clothes reflected his creators' belief in the democratic ideals of the common man.

Perhaps the clearest instance of the Kid's evolving physical description can be found in attitudes toward his buck teeth. In earlier accounts his protruding teeth and fiendish smirk connoted the Kid's beastly nature, but observers in this period usually neglected to mention his teeth, or simply called them "slight projections," or even decided that "only when he was crossed did the protruding teeth look more like fangs than a grin, and [then] the deep blue eyes blaze balefully down a gun barrel."[55] Miguel Otero, one of the Kid's most ardent defenders in this period, took to task earlier accounts of the Kid's facial characteristics and provides an effective conclusion of this brief discussion of the Kid's transformed appearance:

> A light brown beard was beginning to show on his lip and cheeks; his hair was dark brown, glossy, heavy and luxuriant; his eyes were deep dark blue, bright, expressive and intelligent. The most noticeable features of his oval face were two projecting upper teeth, which some wild newspaper correspondents who never saw him describe as "fangs which gave to his features an intensely cruel and murderous expression." Nothing is farther from the truth. That his two teeth are prominent is quite true; that when engaged in conversation they were noticeable also true; but they did not give to his always-pleasant expression a cruel look, suggesting either murder or treachery.[56]

It is difficult to divorce discussions of the Kid's physical appearance from mention of his personal characteristics, for his interpreters consistently described both aspects in similar passages. Besides appearing now as a rather good-looking sort whom Dorothy Sayers' Lord Peter Wimsey might condescend to notice, the Kid was also endowed with gentlemanly qualities, which attracted legions of admirers. His athletic talents were in evidence upon the dance floor, where his additional "easy deference and considerate helpfulness" made him so popular "there wasn't enough of him to go around."[57] To accompany such ballroom talents, the Kid was labelled a "natural" gentleman because, for the first time, he was judged to be well-educated in books and music and was known rarely to drink or swear unseemly oaths. Besides being "as gentlemanly as a college-bred youth," the Kid was considered to be a natural-born leader whose toughness, coolness in danger, and personal magnetism attracted the sympathies of friends and strangers. Whereas before the outlaw significantly embodied a genteel world's fears of irrational violence, now the Kid was seen as a level-headed youth in control of his passions. "The average outlaw was a monster in human form with a sole mania for bloodshed and plunder," summarized one writer in 1935, "but not so the kid; when he created a stampede it was among his peers, and his sympathies were ever with the underdog. He was a mild-mannered youth, kind and companionable. Just such a type as any mother could have taken to her bosom, loved, and cherished."[58] That the Kid could be accepted as a mother's favorite who yet had no mother's guiding hand reveals the extent to which his audience was willing to see him in terms earlier reserved for Pat Garrett.

Along with the transformation of the Kid to a gentlemanly bandit who pursued a rightful cause and aided the underdog in a period when the law was ambiguous at best, it is clear that the Kid's significance was evolving from that of a cowardly devil's lieutenant to that of a man who "wasn't skeered of the devil with his horns on."[59] That there is a crucial change in perceiving the Kid during this period is further evident when we consider how he was increasingly seen as a romantic interest and as an important factor in the advance of civilization. Whatever else he may have been, however misdirected his energies were, the Kid was usually presented as a gallant ladies' favorite who had a señorita in every village. The Kid's romantic appeal is apparent in legends about cowboys leaving town after mistakenly dancing with the Kid's favorite girl, or how the Kid escaped jail because a lady had smuggled him a knife or a file. On several occasions observers voiced the notion that the Kid died *only* because he went to Fort Sumner to see his girlfriend before leaving for old Mexico. In addition, while he was alive the Kid was often reformed by his love of a woman. In the best formula, popular Western tradition, a 1926 ballad recounted what became a familiar theme:

> Thuh Kid was cold and arrogant
> He'd ride a good hawss lame,
> He played and sang, he shot tuh kill,
> He loved a poker game.
> But when Miz Maxwell smiled on him
> Thuh Kid grew limp and tame.[60]

Besides the fact that this ballad introduced the Kid's significant attraction for a "civilized" woman, other stories also tamed the Kid by discussing his marriage and his children or recounting his vow to lead a peaceful life in order to claim his love.

Just as the Kid's emergence as an eligible romantic interest reveals the major transformation of his image, so too does the fact that many observers agreed with George Coe and Otero that the Kid's exploits furthered civilization's advance instead of retarding its progress. Besides being justified by a revenge motive or persecuted by an unjust society, the Kid's conflict with Murphy, Dolan, and Jesse Evans was considered to have "formed an important step in the march of Western civilization."[61] Previously the general assumption was the Kid's death had likewise connoted the end of the reign of the revolver in New Mexico, but now the difference was that the Kid had advanced civilization by purging an impotent society of its truly evil elements before dying because of his love of a woman.

With this transformation in the Kid's role as a romantic interest and precursor of civilization's advance into New Mexico, whether the Kid was ultimately termed good or evil was beside the point. No matter what particulars a person might emphasize, few could believe that he was entirely vicious or totally virtuous; rather, observers customarily advanced the notion that his moral worth lay between such extremes of good and evil. The Kid in the 1920s, '30s, and '40s was regarded quite sympathetically—"a symbol of crude but nonetheless gallant frontier knight-errantry," "a David against the Goliaths of the law," a "Fairy Prince," or a "Robin Hood of the West."[62] The changing image of the Kid was made possible because a new formula, aligned with postwar cultural developments, noted the frontier's ambiguous definition of the law, created a justification for his violence, emphasized his noble qualities and deeds, and saw him as a factor hastening the advent of civilization. When this transformation of the formula for explaining the Kid included the further possibility that the Kid did not die in Pete Maxwell's bedroom, then the Kid emerged as a fully triumphant romance hero; when other accounts accepted the fact of the Kid's death and instead stressed the Kid's conflict of individual morality and social justice, then the Kid emerged as a figure of tragic import. Before turning to consider what purposes this new vision of the Kid served for its creators and audience, let us examine how the transformed image of the Kid appeared in the most significant narratives of this era to convey the Kid's possibilities as a romance hero or tragic figure.

Walter Noble Burns's *The Saga of Billy the Kid* reintroduced the Kid to a nationwide audience one year after Fergusson had questioned whether anyone remembered the Kid.[63] Mass circulation was aided by its selection as a primary offering in December 1926 for the Book-of-the-Month Club, which was in its first year. Club judges Dorothy Canfield, Heywood Broun, Henry Seidel Canby, and William Allen White selected the *Saga,* according to one of the judges, because it possessed "the vivid reality of the moving pictures without the infusion of false sentiment and the inevitable hoist of the story away from life toward melodrama. It is a chronicle such as the Elizabethans wrote and read."[64] While the *Saga* would be important to our study for no other reason than it has generated more controversy than any book in the Kid's bibliography, it remains a central document for its early presentation of what we have noticed are the basic elements of the new Kid formula. Instead of depicting the Kid as an outright villain in deeds and demeanor, the *Saga* portrays a noble, generous, daring, handsome, cool, and cavalier gentleman; instead of presenting the Kid's unjustifiable violence, the *Saga* presents the Kid as a persecuted youth forced to act violently in order to exist; and instead of fighting for an unprincipled, aristocratic greed, the Kid in the *Saga* confronts the corrupt machine politics of Murphy, Colonel Dudley, and the Santa Fe Ring. Whereas Chisum is called a Coronado, McSween a Galahad, and the Kid a Sir Henry Morgan, the *Saga* portrays their opponents as unlawful and greedy forces led by a "frontier Machiavelli" named Murphy. For Burns, "the boy who never grew old has become a sort of symbol of frontier knight-errantry, a figure of eternal youth riding for ever through a purple glamour of romance."[65] This is the basic theme of the book which provided the substance for the best-known Kid ballad and the 1930 and 1941 MGM films.

Although the Kid certainly rides on in the popular imagination, Burns accurately called his saga of the Southwest a "drama of Death and the Boy."[66] In true epic fashion, the author delays the Kid's entrance until he has completed an exposition of the conflict between Chisum and Murphy. Then, after halting the narrative to outline the genealogy of the Kid's legend and biography, Burns resumes the main course of action: during the Kid's rise to prominence in New Mexico the outlaw defeats Death twice by escaping from McSween's burning house and, later, from the Lincoln County courthouse-jail; however, at the moment the Kid appears safely ready to leave the country, Death reasserts its dominion and claims the Kid's life.

On several occasions throughout the *Saga,* Burns reminds us of the tragic nature of the conflict. While McSween's maintenance of religious ideals within a profane frontier setting made his story a "tragic personal drama," the Kid's conflicts were those of a boy born "to tragic victory and tragic defeat."[67] On the night of the Kid's death Garrett is introduced as "one of the four principals in the tragedy"; years later, when Burns visits the Kid's desolate gravesite he imagines "the old tragedy enacted over again almost within arm's reach."[68] And besides frequent allusions to Fate and Destiny, Burns's narrative contains chapter titles like "Child of the Dark Star," "The Lure of Black Eyes," and "The Rendezvous with Fate," phrases that suggest those irresistible larger forces that limited the Kid's freedom and mandated his death.

Although Burns's use of the word *tragedy* at times merely connotes a sadness at the taking of human life, and although at times his use of the terms *Fate* or *Destiny* appears to be a shorthand way of dissecting the narrative,[69] the *Saga* reveals larger meanings because Burns is able to depict the tragic drama of Death and the Boy both within the Kid's human personality and within the external flow of historical events. Whether in Burns's own phrases or those of Sallie Chisum and the others he interviewed, the significant factor about the Kid is that his personality combined both extremely savage and yet extremely gentle elements: the Kid's princely devotion to friends mated with his primitive, violent response to his real and imagined enemies; his compassionate generosity and good humor coupled with a "frozen egoism plus recklessness minus mercy."[70] While Burns claimed the Kid was not haunted by memories of the men he killed, he nevertheless was strangely obsessed with satisfying an oath of vengeance because he couldn't forget Tunstall's murder. While Burns was describing the Kid's internal conflict of savage and civilized drives, he also revealed the external conflict of lawlessness and law. Billy's own story is thus framed not only by the battle of Chisum and Murphy, but also by the larger context of the entire westering movement of civilization into territories. As larger historical forces were tightening the coils around the Kid's outlaw existence, the Kid's saga assumed tragic tones precisely because his inner desire for an Old Testament vengeance conflicted with a newly-emergent New Testament society. That the Kid was betrayed both within and without his person served to deepen the inexorable flow of the drama from life to death.

While others after Burns analyzed Billy's personality in much the same manner and yet found the Kid to be an abnormal psychotic, the significant point about Burns's description of Billy's desperado complex is that such traits are found not only in the outlaw but in the "businessman who plots the ruin of his rival; the minister who consigns to eternal damnation all who disbelieve in his personal creed; the love-pirate, who robs another person of her husband; the speed-mad automobilist who disregards life and limb. . . ."[71] If we place this linkage of the Kid and so-called contemporary desperadoes into the context of our earlier discussion of a postwar disillusionment with the corruption of traditional standards, I think we can move closer to the meaning of Burns's concept of the Kid. Within the closing circle of historical events which compelled men to perceive the Kid as an anachronism to be eliminated, Burns's *Saga* presents a jaunty and yet nervous Kid defying death for a brief moment when safety and love in old Mexico were yet possible.

However, as both George Coe and Otero would also suggest in the next few years, the resolution of the Kid's

> destructive and seemingly futile career served a constructive pur-
> pose; it drove home the lesson that New Mexico's prosperity could
> be built only upon a basis of stability and peace. After him came
> the great change for which he involuntarily cleared the way. Law
> and order came on in the flash and smoke of the six-shooter that
> with one bullet put an end to outlaw and outlawry.[72]

Although the Kid in this view was essentially a gunslinger doomed to extinction in a modernizing world that required the gifts of mercy and intellect,
the Kid yet paved the way for peace, stability, law, and order. In short, the
tragic pattern of the Kid's life revealed a constructive purpose, for without
his purgative violence more Galahad-like McSweens would have been sacri-
ficed to the altar of lawlessness and brutality.

Yet in Burns's apparent belief in the Kid's role as civilization's John the
Baptist the key word is *involuntary*. If we read the *Saga* closely and divorce
Burns's judgments from his presentation of the legend and his recitation of
the interviews with the Kid's survivors, we should see that the Kid's involuntary preparation for law and order is contrasted to Chisum, Wallace, and
Garrett's *voluntary* establishment of civilization through constructive actions.
If we also notice that the *Saga* opens with Chisum's role as civilization's ar-
chitect and closes with Garrett's role as a tragic hero, it is clear that the *Saga*,
far from being just a story of the Kid's tragic career, is actually a romance
story of civilization's triumph, a story which includes Billy's tragic conflict
within its pattern. Moreover, in the contrast between the treatment accorded
the Kid in the penultimate chapter, "Hell's Half-Acre," and the treatment of
Garrett in the last chapter, "Trail's End," we should observe how the Kid—"a
little cyclone of deadliness whirling furiously, purposelessly, vainly between
two eternities"—is not finally a tragic hero but is rather a tragic figure.

This distinction may seem arbitrary or even precious, but I believe it helps
us understand the conflicting response to the Kid revealed by the *Saga*. My
point is that the Kid's presence as an inarticulate, purposeless tragic figure
within a story that presents the arrival of civilization and law and order allows Burns to affirm the values of peace, strength, stability, courage, and
intellect that he discovers in Garrett, Chisum, and Wallace. Rather than existing as a truly tragic hero like Garrett, a man who furthered community
interests and yet was destroyed by those he helped establish, the Kid dies
suddenly and less meaningfully through Fate's intervention.

However, when we remember that Burns described the "desperado complex" as existing in such civilized figures as contemporary ministers and businessmen, and when we recall Burns's sentimental lamentations over the lack

of romance in his day, there clearly is for Burns an uncertainty—even a skeptical awareness—about the condition of the America which, after abusing the Kid and Garrett, continued to remove the individual's control over his own destiny. Where the Kid as a romance hero in the 1930s and 1940s preserved civilization and yet posed no threat of absolute power since he was not integrated into society, the Kid as a tragic figure in Burns's *Saga* likewise promotes civilization; but his death also reveals the author's sadness about a loss of the adventurous spirit in the modern world. Like Fergusson only a year earlier, Burns prefers the Kid to Jesse James, and invents him as an outlaw whose virtues balanced his vices; nevertheless, Burns's tone is unavoidable in the *Saga*'s final pages when he discusses the melancholy prospects for a postwar society that seemingly had lost touch with a vital past during its headlong search for pleasure. At the same time other writers during this period resurrected the Daltons, Earps, and Hickock, Burns's revival of the Kid revealed a divided response to the outlaw's meaning: although his prose argued for the Kid as a tragic figure, his plot argued for civilization's triumph over lawlessness, a triumph justified in the fact that no flowers grew on the Kid's blasted grave. Uneasy about the Kid and uneasy about the present state of civilization, Burns's divided aims in the *Saga,* present in the distinction we can make between his vision and the legend's vision of the Kid, were not noted by critics and a reading public eager to revive or criticize the romance.

This view of what is perhaps the most important book in the Kid's bibliography is possible because a close reading can proceed today without worry over how Burns's account has distorted history. Although some critics of the *Saga* quickly saw it had no pretensions to portray anything other than the Kid's legend and the few biographical facts available, most critics and reviewers were unable to notice the narrative's distinction of Burns's viewpoint and the perspectives offered by those he interviewed. Critics of the *Saga* typically ascribed all judgments of the Kid solely to the book's author because the book's critics were intent on exposing the *Saga*'s unhistorical evidence, on criticizing Burns's prose style, and on defending Pat Garrett.

When we turn to the 1938 ballet *Billy the Kid,* it is also clear that many of the Kid's observers, perhaps never having seen the ballet, immediately judged it harshly for romanticizing the legend simply because it was a ballet. But for those who have seen it performed, it is clear that far from presenting the Kid as a romance or even a tragic hero, the ballet Billy presents a tragic figure in a manner similar to that of the *Saga.*[73]

Similarities between Eugene Loring's choreography and Burns's *Saga* are inevitable because, like so many contributors to the Kid's bibliography, the ballet is based in part upon Loring's awareness of the Kid's legend as detailed in the *Saga.* Scored by Aaron Copland, Loring's *Billy the Kid* was first performed by Ballet Caravan in October 1938 in Chicago and since then has been revived by several different companies in various countries. *Billy the Kid* is often called one of the glories of American dance, and it frames the outlaw's episodic tragic conflict with society with a prologue and epilogue centering on Pat Garrett and a group of pioneers moving toward the setting sun. Thus, the basic structure of the ballet, like the narrative structure of Burns's *Saga,* presents Billy's story as one episode within the larger historical context of the westering experience. The ballet's Billy is an attractive, athletic, and vital character who begins his violent career at the age of twelve by immediately stabbing to death his mother's slayers; yet after this initia' street scene in a frontier town we see the fugitive Kid increasingly isolated from the community until, alone and hearing a noise near his campfire, the Kid strikes a match and is shot by the nearby Garrett.

The tragic nature of Billy's story emerges as his cold, calloused, deadly behavior is seen to be the accidental result of his early commission of violence. Yet like Burns's Kid, the ballet Billy is no tragic hero because his actions are cruel and ruthless, and because his only community is a group of corpses or an imaginary encounter with a Mexican sweetheart. Whether one believes the *pas de deux* is a dream (the sweetheart is usually played by the same dancer who earlier in the ballet was the Kid's mother) or is a real encounter for the Kid, even this final, lyrical moment in a score of great energy is marked by Billy's inability to merge with his partner and dance as one. Although a group of native women mourn for his fallen form in the brief "Pieta" scene, the restored community appears in the final scene's cyclic return to the pioneers advancing toward the now-setting sun. Hardened by the experience of the Kid's conflict with society, the pioneers' determined advance toward a bright yellow sun, accompanied by a striking use of tympani, has now become an uncertain, hesitant movement as the pioneers alternately face the sun and yet turn to gaze at the past they have travelled across. In this manner we understand how the muted nature of civilization's advance leads us to wonder whether this progress will liberate and regenerate the self and society or will—as in the Kid's example—destroy or hinder an individual's vital energy and self-expression. While the ballet's dramatic movement confirms the belief that a community could not exist with a Billy the Kid, it also asks whether a community can survive such things as a Depression or approaching war without Billy the Kid's dynamic energy and total commitment to survival.

The tragic pattern in the large romance story-form of the *Saga* and the Copland-Loring ballet details an irreconcilable tension between an individual's craving for the freedom of total self-expression and the inevitable surrender of this unrestrained individualism to the larger environmental forces which the individual can't resist, conquer, or understand. Although the Kid is never as intensely self-conscious or as articulate as a Hamlet or a Macbeth, the very inarticulateness of his character and the very purity of his vengeance motive, although serving to isolate him from the community, endow him with an attractive appeal—for who has not struggled to express one's concept of life, and who has not wished that one's actions followed so closely upon thought? Thus awful and yet attractive, the Kid as a tragic figure reveals pathos, not *anagnorisis* (recognition). In the most artistic examples of this use of tragedy within an overall romance plot, the sense of rightness felt by an audience at the main character's death is mingled with the sense that the inevitable narrowing of human options—the growing awareness of time and destiny's impact on the figure superior to other men—entails a diminution in life's possibilities. Unlike the *Saga* or the ballet, however, the least successful examples of this concept of the Kid, the 1941 MGM movie starring Robert Taylor and the 1950 Audie Murphy vehicle *The Kid from Texas,* offer flat, one-dimensional portraits of the Kid's resistance to the community's interest, thus preventing any recognition that the struggle to realize justice has intimated anything more transcendent than an empty grave to be filled.

Although the legend publicized in Burns's *Saga* inspired much of the material present in the cinematic invention of the Kid, the cinematic Kid was, except for the Murphy and Taylor movies, an embodiment of the noble bandit ideal, which was one strand of the revitalized formula for inventing the Kid during this era. The impact of the cinema version was considerable because the movies did the most to establish the Kid as a figure in popular culture. By examining the changing image of the Kid between 1930 and 1950 we can understand how the Kid as a romance hero was related, if only in fantasy, to the kind of cultural preoccupations we considered earlier in this chapter.

Several critics predicted the film Western's demise after the introduction of motion picture sound and after Lindbergh's flight had replaced the cowboy in the popular imagination with the aviator, but between 1930 and 1932 such films as *Cimarron, The Big Trail,* and *Billy the Kid* demonstrated both the continuing appeal of the epic western and Hollywood's solution to the problems associated with filming outdoor sound movies. Directed by King Vidor, who had recently been nominated for the Oscar for Best Director (for *Hallelujah*), MGM's 1930 *Billy the Kid* was not the box office success of that studio's other 1930 releases *The Big House* and *Min and Bill,* but it was an interesting film for several reasons: it was filmed simultaneously in widescreen and regular-screen film; it was endorsed in an open letter by then New Mexico governor R. C. Dillon; and it had William S. Hart as technical advisor.[74]

That a film starring the Kid was made at all at that time was perhaps due to the Depression's impact on traditional symbols of the state and law and order. More to the point, however, is a consideration of Vidor and screenwriter Laurence Stallings' efforts to convince Irving Thalberg that the film was not too violent and that the Kid could be a proper hero. When Thalberg expressed his reluctance to approve the project, Vidor convinced him that the Kid only killed in the first place in order to revenge an insult to his mother:

> This bit of historical half-truth was emphasized in the hope of convincing Thalberg that all of the Kid's murders were understandable. . . . Then I took Billy through scenes of murder in self-defense, and murders on the side of justice if not the law.[75]

As this statement reveals, Vidor perceptively realized that the Kid could be understood and approved only if he was shown killing in self-defense, revenging an insult, or upholding "the side of justice if not the law." In particular, the widespread belief that a discrepancy existed between the law and true justice not only allowed the Kid to exist in 1930, but created the atmosphere for the popular acceptance a few years later of such other good characters operating outside the law as the Lone Ranger and the Cisco Kid.

Vidor's completed *Billy the Kid* is essentially an adventure story that dramatizes the successful founding of a new world after a series of struggles with powerful antagonists who, in order to preserve their corrupt power, inhibit the opportunity of others. The film's opening scenes reveal how the basic conflict between true justice and law is embodied in two opposing groups who pursue contrasting visions of the future shape of society. An initial long shot introduces us to the McSwane/Tunston (McSween/Tunstall) emigrant wagon train traversing a grassy plain in search of a new start within the vast public domain.[76] While this group of hardy pioneers is framed by a natural landscape, the next few shots introduce us to the securely established world of Colonel Donovan (Murphy) by portraying the interior of his Lincoln saloon, a corrupt dark place where Donovan's squaw demands monetary tribute from McSwane/Tunston before they can enter Donovan's office. Although the two settlers learn that Donovan has usurped the law, they decide to settle in the area despite the Colonel's thinly-veiled threats of retaliation. As Lincoln's sheriff, justice of the peace, postmaster, and notary public, Donovan is analogous to a king, and his power over his subjects is revealed in the next few scenes which show his retainers, particularly a scruffy Balinger (Olinger), evicting and then murdering a small rancher and his wife, or rustling horses from other small ranchers in Donovan's domain.

Within the first few minutes of the film's beginning, then, Vidor established a visual and verbal contrast between the settlers' democratic ideals and the Colonel's aristocratic depravity: whereas the settlers are a community and address each other as "Mister," Donovan is "the Colonel" whose community is composed of paid killers; whereas the settlers have wives and children, Donovan possesses a squaw and is childless; whereas the settlers desire to live on the land, Donovan evicts people from the land and holds court in a saloon; and, finally, whereas the settlers feel they are in the right because the land is in the public domain, Donovan uses the law's shield to control and corrupt their admirable intentions. With the additional contrast of light and dark scenes, and with several low shots from the settlers' point of view looking up at the sneering faces of Donovan and Balinger, Vidor clearly establishes our sympathy for the powerless, unarmed community of settlers who only wish enough land to make a living on.

While in its outlines this basic conflict between good and evil or true justice and corrupt law appears no different from the conflicts described in the earlier dime novels, the fact that the Kid, not a detective like old King Brady, appears from outside the fledgling society's ranks to assume their burden indicates a major change since 1881. At the point in this conflict when the settlers are enumerating the outrages of Donovan's mob, are arguing among themselves and threatening to leave, and are being heckled by Balinger and others who want to provoke a gunfight, the Kid magically appears on the scene and dispatches the villains with a few well-placed volleys. "Killin' rats comes natural to me," Johnny Mack Brown's Kid advises his audience, and throughout the rest of the film the Kid corrects injustices, avenges Tunston's and McSwane's murders, and even falls in love with Tunston's ex-fiancée.

As we saw earlier in the quote from Zane Grey's *Nevada,* the Kid here fulfills the redeemer's role because only his deadly and courageous skills can meet the threats posed by such powerful antagonists as Donovan and Balinger. In 1930 society needs the Kid alive rather than dead, for such a traditional symbol of civilization as Pat Garrett is here unable, although willing, to defy Donovan's quasi-legal disruptive activities. After Teapot Dome and Capone's control of an entire city, it was far easier to create and accept a narrative that portrayed an instinctively right but woefully unprotected society held in thrall by powerful organized forces; similarly, after the publicity of the government's inability to control scheming finance capitalists and the police's inability to convict urban criminals, it was far easier to fantisize an avenging angel using extralegal means to ensure a quick and decisive justice.

To validate the Kid's role as an avenging protector-hero, the film emphasizes certain aspects of the Kid's appearance and exploits, and also subordinates or neglects exploits which would deny his heroic status. Vidor and Stallings' script, for instance, leaves out the Kid's dubious participation in the killing of Brady, Hindman, Carlyle, and Buckshot Roberts. Nor does the film show Billy's rustling activities or his killing of Mexicans or Chisum cowboys. Instead, we learn that the Kid's initial violence was not just to avenge an insult to his mother but to avenge the cold-blooded murders of both his parents; in addition, the Kid is portrayed in the film shooting Joe Grant only to protect Tunston, killing two men in order to avenge Tunston's death, killing Donovan for murdering McSwane in cold blood, and finally killing Balinger to satisfy his innate sense of justice. Significantly, the Kid's escape from jail occurs because Wallace Beery's Garrett, not a mere deputy, is surprised during a card game—but this only allows Billy to reassure Garrett that he wouldn't shoot him in the back. Besides this acceptable motivation for his violence, the Kid's appearance as a tall, athletic, gracefully attired figure who plays the piano and drinks lemonade favorably contrasts with Balinger's short, stocky, unkempt figure with rude manners.

Nevertheless, as much as Johnny Mack Brown's Kid is defined by his deadly skills and prepossessing appearance, he assumes heroic proportions only as the film stresses his selfless donation of talent to the community. Because of his good manners and gentle demeanor, the film's heroine tells Billy during the McSwane siege sequence that "somehow it's easier to imagine you calling on a young girl with posies in your hand—than with that rifle." Yet because of his oath of vengeance and society's need for protection, the Kid can only answer, "I'd like to do that too, someday." In the film's closing moments, when Billy attempts to deny his attraction to the heroine so that she won't risk her life for him, he defines himself as a killer—but Claire will have none of it: "You're not that. Every killing you've done has been needed. You've made this town a decent place to live in." Because Billy, in short, is only presented as killing to ensure justice's triumph over a corrupt law, and because his handsome appearance belies his deadly skills, the film asks us to identify with the favorable reactions of both the heroine and Lew Wallace to their first meetings with the Kid. When Wallace tells the Kid that he favorably succeeded his expectations, the Kid—in a response that turns the earlier stereotype on its head—responds that "I left my horns and forky tail back there in the hills."

Even though Wallace's entrance and Donovan's death at the Kid's hand had established the secure beginnings of the new society in which justice and law were not divorced, the Kid's final struggle is a purely personal one. And because Billy must refuse Wallace's amnesty offer to complete his personal quest for vengeance against Balinger, he is considered an exile while Balinger walks the Lincoln streets as a deputy. Billy's capture, escape from jail, and killing of Balinger thus finalize the dramatic confrontation of good and evil, and confirm the Kid's status as a romance hero who achieves an important mission and receives society's rewards. Yet unlike earlier good-badman figures like W. S. Hart's Draw Egan, the Kid's exploits do not serve to integrate him into society. Although the Kid is allowed to ride away from his hideout when Garrett purposely misses shooting him, the Kid and the film's heroine can only ride their horses across the border in order to settle down.

The Kid's role as a destroying angel with spurs who protects decent farmers and ranchers from exploitation by tyrannical figures of authority is extended to several other movies during this era. Eight years after the 1930 MGM movie Roy Rogers appeared as a singing Billy the Kid in Republic's *Billy the Kid Returns*. Though as the Kid he is killed by crooked ranchers in the movie's first part, Rogers returns as a cowboy who impersonates the Kid and who in this guise eventually captures the villains after tricking them into stealing U. S. Army horses. If nothing else, this movie demonstrates how a traditional cowboy hero disguised as an outlaw could act to correct injustices with the outlaw's freedom from legal restraint, and yet not actually be an outlaw. Between 1940 and 1943, furthermore, Producers Releasing Corporation produced a series of seventeen "B" Kid films starring either Buster Crabbe or Bob Steele as the Kid. Although not as artistically competent as Vidor's film, these "B" Billy movies do feature a Populist Kid who protects the simple, honorable common folk from exploitation by the law and politics. In these various films, evil is defined as such thinly-veiled current problems as crooked racketeers who swindle farmers or dominate towns like Santa Fe; organized gangs that rob bankers who are on their way to New Mexico to prevent a "bank run"; and corrupt politicians or bankers who hire thugs to keep farmers from paying off their mortgages.

Besides living again to fight another battle in the series' next episode, the Kid in these films also appears as a triumphant romance hero because the Kid is paired with an older sidekick (like Smiley Burnette or Al St. John) who assumes the comic burden of the film—thus freeing the Kid to sing songs, save society, and sling kisses at female admirers. In this manner the portrayal of a comic buffoon and a romance hero unified in their quest to destroy powerful forces that exploit rather than protect the common folk intensifies the narrative dramatization of a unified society emerging unscathed after a confrontation with external and internal divisive forces. The culmination of this vision of the Kid's role occurred in 1949 when Lash Larue starred as the Kid in *Son of Billy the Kid*. So sanitized has this image of the Kid become that in this movie the Kid is not a Lone Ranger-type but a banker who helps his son and the authorities capture the real villains.

When we consider that the so-called cult of the outlaw was basically established between the stock-market crash of 1929 and the onset of America's participation in World War II, it is not difficult to understand how a film like Vidor's 1930 *Billy the Kid* was a product of the Depression and played on the public's knowledge of social and economic inequality. After Roosevelt's New Deal had been in effect for a few years, however, the public's preference for the G-man instead of the gangster movie reflected a renewal of faith in the legal instruments of justice whose actions consolidated society. Thus, it might be expected that when Cagney played a G-man and not a gangster, or when Vidor directed *The Texas Rangers* (1936) rather than *Billy the Kid*—that is, when law and order were on the upswing—the outlaw hero would lose relevance. Yet what happens during the late Depression and early years of World War II is that more ominous threats to society are discovered than an outlaw in pursuit of vengeance. At the same time Gene Autry, the three Mesquiteers, and Hopalong Cassidy were reaffirming society's defeat of cinematic symbols of injustice, civilization's true enemies were not outlaws like the Kid or the Lone Ranger or Jesse James, but were rather the crooked shysters who defrauded innocent farmers, Indians, and townspeople. Significantly, at least in the Kid movies, it is not so much that the symbols of the state are evil as that evil men are in control of the state and threaten society's very existence. In effect, the Kid's outlaw status as a romance hero discloses a conservative impulse: that is, the Kid destroys evil bankers—not banks. When this domestication of the Kid's violence is allied with an audience's psychological yearning for an immediate and decisive deliverance from the anxieties of reality, the outlaw's special status as a skilled enforcer unrestrained by an inefficient or exploited legal system sustained its relevance: here was a transcendent figure of justice—not anarchy—whose virtues of toughness, courage, and self-reliance were necessary to conquer the threat of totalitarian power in the hands of a crooked banker. Although Vidor's movie supports the Kid's defense of a rural agrarian world while the later "B" movies reaffirm a settled society's traditional democratic values, both concepts of the Kid's relationship to society share the impulse to view him as the defender of a society in danger of capitulating to exploiters of laws and finances.

If the Kid's unrestrained quest for vengeance is not aligned with a social commitment, however, then his deadly skill could be considered as dangerous to society as the unscrupulousness of any of the era's demagogues and dictators. Although the early 1940s saw the "B" Billy movies duplicate the idealization of Populist Robin Hood outlaws in movies about Joaquin Murietta, Jesse and Frank James, or the Daltons, MGM's 1941 remake of *Billy the Kid* was influenced more, as John Lenihan has argued, by the possibility of war in Europe against Hitler than by the frustrations and inequalities of the Depression. Whereas the 1930 movie could be said to have popularized the romantic legend Burns resurrected in the *Saga,* the 1941 movie starring Robert Taylor could be said to have depicted the tragic side of the *Saga:* the Kid's fatal quest for vengeance amidst the inexorable advance of civilization. As the opening credits conclude, we read that "there rode a young outlaw who lived his violent life in defiance of an advancing civilization"; as the film ends, we read that "as the ways of law came to the last frontier, the last of the men of violence found his peace."

Although this comment suggests the film's main point is the satisfaction of the Kid's death after he achieves the "peace" of fulfilled revenge, the closing line rather simplifies matters. The film is not truly concerned with the Kid's last-violent-man status but with two other issues: community solidarity in the face of unbridled aggression, and the ideal of personal maturity. However tragic the Kid's quest to find the killer(s) of his father and Keating (Tunstall) might be, it is, as the movie's real hero tells him, "the last step to where there can be no friends. Where every man will be against you." Although the movie recognizes the fickle application of justice by telling us the Kid's father's murderer was acquitted, and by showing us the Kid is framed for murder, his unwillingness to let the democratic process take its course is to be considered a dangerous usurpation of power. As Keating warns the Kid early in the movie,

> You know, things are going to happen in this country. Guns and shooting are going out. Law and order is on the march. You better look out, or they'll run you over. . . . And when they [the people] get together, there isn't a man fast enough on the draw or tough enough to stand against them. Not even Hannibal, Napoleon, or Billy the Kid.

By identifying the Kid with Napoleon rather than Robin Hood, and by stressing the Kid's quest for excitement and adventure rather than for mature social commitment, the film suggests on the eve of America's entry into the war with the Axis that progress will result when the people unite to withstand the threats of those who—like Napoleon or Hannibal or the Kid—employ violent means to further purely selfish interests. In the one truly interesting long shot in the entire film, for instance, the large posse distantly pursuing the Kid is framed by awesome rock and cloud formations. As in the manner of the nineteenth-century Hudson River school of painters or in the Western films of John Ford, the shot contrasts a small, but purposeful human group in the foreground with an imposing natural setting, and thus thematically places the drama of individual humans within the larger perspective of historical change. In this film, just as the posse will shortly end the outlaw's defiant rebellion, so too in the physical landscape the ominous clouds approach and begin to close off the open spaces and to cover the monolithic rock formations. The crucial point is that such cinematography and such dialogue as

quoted above suggest that society's pursuit of the Kid is not morally repre-
hensible like the mob hysteria indicted in director William Wellman's *The
Ox-Bow Incident* (1943). If one interpretation of *The Ox-Bow Incident* stresses
how the movie's indictment of mob rule reflects concern for the contemporary threat of Nazi terror,[77] then we might similarly conclude that the 1941
Billy the Kid reveals concern over the totalitarian power wielded by such unrestrained and apparently immoral individuals as Hitler and Mussolini. Although corrupt law and illegal manipulation of army contracts are exposed
in the film, the Kid's isolated quest is considered more evil; he is more like
Quantrill than the Lone Ranger, more like an outlaw whose bloody quest for
vengeance, no matter how morally justified, seems fatally out of place in a
society requiring group commitment to survive.

While we might question the film's confident and perhaps arbitrary notion about what constitutes necessary and justified violence, any dramatic
complexity inherent in the issue of society's use of violence to end violence is
dismissed, for in the end the Kid desires death, not confrontation. Unlike
what will happen in the years after *The Left-Handed Gun* (1958) appeared,
here society does not bombard the Kid with a fusillade of bullets. Rather, society's chief representative—a combination of Garrett's gunfighter talents and
McSween's moral honor—politely accedes to the Kid's death wish by felling
him with one bullet as the Kid purposely draws with the wrong hand. With
this sentimental dramatization of the Kid's death, however, the Robert Taylor film develops a dramatic tension between its mode of emplotment (tragedy) and its mode of argument, which affirms the positive values of civilization's
triumph over both internal (the corrupt manipulator of beef contracts) and
external (the Kid as outlaw) threats. On one level of response, this black-
suited, glowering, narrow-eyed punk with razor stubble, this outlaw who
blurts out lines like "go chew on your lariat," deserves to be put out of his
misery so we can have peace. Yet on another level, this Kid devoted to avenging his parents' murders regardless of his own fate, and this outlaw played by
an actor known for his appealing roles in other movies—this Kid demands
audience sympathy. Similarly, the society depicted in the film that is too
weak and ignorant to recognize and destroy its internal corruption deserves
little audience identification; yet the society portrayed in the film as uniting
to withstand the Kid's anarchic terror is to be admired and emulated. Ultimately, the film's apparently divided aim—to argue for the Kid as an uncon-
trollable rabid dog and yet to cast a well-known romantic lead as a doomed
idealist—illustrates once again how the inventions of the Kid during this era
display an ambivalent response to the Kid's story.

If the Kid's legendary noble qualities and deeds had been more pronounced,
and if the Kid's character had been drawn with more complexity, the 1941

Billy the Kid might have anticipated the fully tragic Kid who would be the product of the 1950s' vision of the outlaw. As it stands, the film is now notable only for its introduction of the Kid's death wish, an idea which director Arthur Penn extends in *The Left-Handed Gun,* and for its presentation of an older actor as the Kid. Every other Kid film, except perhaps the Lash Larue *Son of Billy the Kid* (1949), has typically been a useful vehicle for introducing a "rising" young male performer to movie audiences.

Formulating the Kid as a romance hero or as a tragic figure depended basically upon his creators' willingness to dramatize the Kid's internal conflict between vengeance and mercy, his "pawn-like" status in the Lincoln County War, his death due to love or betrayal, and his noble qualities on behalf of a just social cause. By the 1940s and the early years of the Cold War, the sympathetic Kid was being challenged by those interpreters who were willing, for various reasons, to conceive him without the social commitment to prevent the exploitation of the poor and weak that defined the Depression-era Kid. While Taylor's portrayal of the Kid negated the idea of the Populist-protector Kid, it may be that it did not influence other interpreters of the Kid during the 1940s because the 1941 film's true hero played by Brian Donlevy spouted sanctimonious speeches about the inevitability of moral order, justice, and civilization at the same time that the world was witnessing a rather darker view of human nature.

Whatever the case, the "B" movie Billy continued envisioning the Kid as a romance hero at least through 1949, while the 1950 Audie Murphy *The Kid from Texas* resurrected the Kid as a tragic figure whose fatal willingness to fight injustice rather than to negotiate a peace seemed more in tune with the heated-up atmosphere of the Korean War years than either the arbitrate-and-wait-until-provoked attitude of Brian Donlevy's 1941 character, or the avenging protector image of the Depression era Kid. No simple one-to-one relationship of image and context is to be found whenever we view any of the Kid films years after their original appearance. Yet as we try to understand the currents of thought and feeling that were present when the film was created and viewed, we can speculate about which elements of the Kid's basic story would "speak" to a particular audience. What we discover in viewing the Murphy film is several interesting variations that suggest the Kid's changing importance. Unlike other cinematic inventions of the Kid, *The Kid from Texas* draws out the Kid-Wallace confrontation amid a high country setting so as to emphasize their contrasting dress and age and their utter inability to reach an accord. Along with this scene's disclosure of an emerging adversary culture opposing adult figures of authority, Murphy's Kid and the young female lead (Gail Storm) realize a common bond as each youth attempts to create an identity free from adult supervision. And for the first time in the

Kid films, Pat Garrett *betrays* the Kid and shoots the outlaw dead as the latter figure gazes through a window at his unattainable love interest, who symbolically stands beside a piano prior to leaving for the East. That the film emphasizes these kinds of narrative elements and character oppositions, and that the Kid is cast as a returning veteran of the border wars who defies Wallace's amnesty proclamation and pursues his own course of justice, indicate how such then-current preoccupations with the problems of returning World War II veterans, of increasing episodes of juvenile delinquency, and of international threats to American autonomy were displaced into the Kid's story.

In this view *The Kid from Texas* marks the approaching end of the vision of the Kid as a tragic figure, for after 1950 responses to the Cold War, the war in Korea, the natural counterreaction to the sympathetic or sentimental Kid, and the extension of the Kid's psychological complexity would combine by 1955 to present different Billy the Kids who might resemble the previous Kids, but who would perform different functions for their creators and audiences. At the same time, a fitting conclusion to the vision of the Kid as a romance hero occurred with "Brushy Bill" Roberts, the most famous claimant to the Kid's title as a man who lived long after 1881, died in Hico, Texas, on 27 December 1950. As long as in history or in the imagination it was thought plausible to believe that the Kid was mistakenly identified as the body on Pete Maxwell's bedroom floor, the Kid's noble deeds and protection of society's helpless would be triumphantly heroic—not tragic. One of the interesting occurrences during this era, of course, is that various rumors were circulated about the Kid's escape from Garrett's clutches and subsequent residence in rural Texas, Mexico, and Arizona; yet after "Brushy Bill's" death in 1950 and the 1955 publication of his story, no longer was it plausible to believe that the historical Kid was alive, and no longer did the invented Kid ride unscathed by Pat Garrett's bullets.

An interesting transition between visions of the Kid from the 1940s to the 1950s is Howard Hughes' *The Outlaw* (1943; released 1946). Regardless of its confused intentions, and its now tame eroticism, *The Outlaw* (starring Jack Beutel as the Kid) presents the Kid as a familiar romance hero who yet exists without social concerns. In contrast to the fatal seriousness of the 1941 *Billy the Kid,* Hughes' movie concludes with the Kid married and alive and riding a horse with Rio (Jane Russell) toward a new life; yet in contrast to the 1930 Vidor film, which also concludes with the Kid's survival and hints of his eventual married status, *The Outlaw* does not portray Billy saving the defenseless common folk from tyrannical capitalists or land-grappers. Rather, *the Outlaw* is concerned, as critics have written, with the relationship of men to men, women to men, and both sexes to horses. While its image of the Kid and its resolution thus recall Vidor's 1930 film, its presentation of the interrelationship of love and violence, its muted consideration of homosexuality, and its playful disregard of Western cliches anticipate the Kid who emerged in the late 1950s and 1960s.[78] And while this film can be and has been discussed in the history of American cinema as an example of sexist cinema or of the American penchant for mammary eroticism, in the history of the visions of the Kid *The Outlaw* is further important because its offscreen battle with censors and its producer's battles with directors introduce the creative artist as outlaw theme, which will dominate artistic conceptions of the Kid after 1955.

In general, the creation and acceptance of the Kid as either a romance hero or as a tragic figure suggest his creators' and consumers' ambivalent response to post-World War I and Depression era cultural developments. Disillusioned by judicial and legislative corruption, skeptical of America's urbanization, disgusted with the results of Prohibition, and hopeful that some portion of the nation's historical and cultural past would survive and shape the present, the Kid's most influential creators selected, omitted, and fabricated facts that meshed with their concept of the Kid, the West—and America. As we have seen, to validate the concept of the Kid as a preferable alternative to Capone, as a Populist Robin Hood, or as a defender of middle-class democracy, his creators selected or invented legends that stressed the Kid's persecution and revenge, romantic interests, samaritan deeds, and even his life after death. Omitted or placed in the background were his killings of Joe Grant and Chisum cowboys, his rustling activities after the conclusion of the Lincoln County War, and his alliance with Chisum. In a cultural context which seemed to deny the individual's control over his destiny, New Mexico's governor wrote an open letter for the 1930 MGM movie stating his belief that the Kid fought for personal liberty; at a time when gangsters seemed much more evil figures than the Kid, historical figures like Chisum, Wallace, and Robert Olinger were precursors of the mob in their use of unprincipled violence and exploitation. Seen within a specific cultural context, the Kid as a good-badman in the 1930s should use his skills to defend the helpless, just as in 1950 such skills as a defender should be down played in favor of his justified isolation in pursuing a violent course to achieve justice.

Having examined in the above pages how the visions of the Kid embodied specific concerns of a particular decade, we need to consider what purpose was served by the romance story-form. Regardless of how *The Kid from Texas* discloses Cold War anxieties or how the Kid's ballet illustrates Depression concerns, what does their similar narrative structure and their similar presentation of the Kid as a tragic figure tell us? In addition, what does the Kid's presence as a triumphant romance hero throughout this era tell us?

To answer such questions and arrive at the meaning which unites these portraits of the Kid in these few decades, we need to remember two points. First, even when the Kid is presented as a tragic figure, the general mode of emplotment is the same as we saw in the last chapter, and thus should perform similar functions. Thus, in a period of great stress on traditional values, the romance story reaffirmed the possibiity of the American dream of a classless, church-centered, participatory democracy created and enjoyed by self-reliant individuals. Whatever the magnitude of the problems besetting civilization, this story further affirmed that problems are not so large that an individual hero cannot solve them. The service this fantasy performed for those who saw trusts and monopolies in control of individual lives is obvious. When we ask what ideals the Kid's role as romance hero preserved, the answer is clear: those preindustrial American ideals threatened by Teapot Dome, Capone, and the Depression. The Kid's heroic actions in the *Saga*'s revitalized popular legends, in the movies (except Robert Taylor's effort), and in the Coe-Otero line of books reaffirmed the American Dream in a time of rootlessness and deprivation and, ultimately, war again.

Yet, and this is the second point, the obvious difference now is that the outlaw Kid—not Sheriff Pat Garrett—defends society by destroying the villains who subvert democratic ideals. Thus, while the visions of the Kid resolve internal and external threats to democracy and reaffirm the emergence of a utopian society close to nature's beneficent moral influence, the visions of the Kid during this era are statements of social criticism in that they depict justice achieved only through extralegal means. The image we come away with is of a society helpless to defend itself, strapped by slow-moving legal machinery, and unable to distinguish bad-goodmen who outwardly conform to social mores from good-badmen who inwardly believe in the right things—but who must exist as outlaws to flush out the bad guys and avoid persecution.

Thus, implied in the elevation of the outlaw to sympathetic status is a skeptical distrust of a system that protected villains and persecuted heroes or the common man. At the same time, in short, that the Kid's actions reaffirm basic democratic values and restore the community to decent folk, the fact that he is not integrated into society suggests an awareness of the unsettling disparity of law and justice. Thus criticizing and yet yearning for an ordered society, the creators of the Kid were ambivalent to the dominant forces of this period. The same culture that legislated Prohibition and yet reveled in the gangsters' exploits and went to gin joints on the sly, that established the Legion of Decency and yet was entranced by *The Outlaw*, that saw the failures of democracy and yet fought a war against Hitler—this culture's ambivalent response is mirrored in the creation of a Kid who furthers civilization and yet can have no part in it—dead or alive.

5 "Through a Glass Darkly"

The Cold War Visions of the Kid, 1955–1961

McSween to Billy: "When I was a child, I spake as a child, I understood as a child, I thought as a child: but when I became a man I put away childish things.

For now we see through a glass darkly; but then face to face: now I know in part; but then shall I know even as also I am known." (I Corinthians 13:11-12)

—from *The Left-Handed Gun*, 1958

When does one era end and another era begin? To answer this question in the wake of the vision of the Kid popularized by Walter Noble Burns and the Hollywood films discussed in the last chapter, we need to start with Jack Thorp's 1945 statement that the Kid, when all things were considered, was actually "short weight for a hero."[1] This kind of statement, coming as it did when World War II was drawing to a close and the atomic age was just beginning, foreshadowed other similar conclusions about the Kid that surfaced after World War II ended. In 1950, for instance, as Audie Murphy's Kid was being shot to death in theaters across the country, one observer called the Kid "a mean, no-account, low-life punk" who was much inferior to the full-blooded Texas teen-agers who—in Murphy's real-life role—"slugged it out with the toughest aggregation of fighters the world ever knew: the Axis."[2]

During the McCarthy years of witch-hunts and espionage trials, others who believed the Kid was "short weight for a hero" praised the fighting ability of such dubious characters as "Buckshot" Roberts (who stood off Dick Brewer, the Kid, and others at the Blazer's Mill battle) as they simultaneously derided the Kid's toughness, ruthlessness, and masculinity. Curiously, "real" badmen like Sam Bass and Dave Rudabaugh—men who were more likely to chew tobacco and toothpicks than chase señoritas across the dance floor— were occasionally preferred to the Kid, whose samaritanlike deeds in popular legend and whose predilection for women constituted a fatal chink in his defensive armor.

When we consider the widespread paranoia about real or imagined Communist threats to democatic ideals at home and abroad that characterized the postwar era, we find it understandable that for some observers the Kid's outlaw status, including of course his defense of alien Mexican communities, would be condemned in the same tones that were reserved for Alger Hiss and the Rosenbergs. Nevertheless, the idea of the Kid as popularized in Burns's tradition was so embedded in the popular imagination that such comments basically represented minor voices within the main tenor of response to Billy the Kid. Even discounting the exposure of the Kid as a cinematic hero of a quest romance or as a tragic figure in the Lash Larue 1949 film and the Murphy 1950 film, writers like Erna Fergusson continued to publicize the Kid as a loyal, gentlemanly, and victimized youth. Even though the concept of the Kid as an adenoidal moron was bandied about in postwar criticism of the Kid's anti-American beliefs, Maurice G. Fulton suggested that a close study of the Kid-Wallace correspondence revealed both "the intelligent mind of William Bonney" and the Kid's apparent role as a scapegoat because Wallace could not fulfill his promise of a pardon. The widely-distributed *Trail Driving Days* (1952) still recounted the Kid's life, death, and resurrection in the popular culture by means of prose culled from the Upson-Garrett and the Burns biographies.[3]

Regardless of the comments by Thorp and other less charitable demythologizers of the Kid's legend, then, the idea and image of the Kid as an admirable bandit was difficult to dislodge. Even forty years after Harvey Fergusson and Burns had inaugurated the Kid as romance hero and tragic figure, Kent Steckmesser concluded that the Kid was "the American Robin Hood," and as late as 1977 Gary L. Roberts wrote in *The Reader's Encyclopedia of the American West* that "as an American Robin Hood, Billy the Kid still moves through the literature of the West, defying all efforts to understand the historical figure hidden in the gunsmoke of the legend."[4]

Given such conclusions, it thus may seem irrelevant or even foolish to inquire when the Burns era concluded, for the sentiments of the past continue in the present. Older Billy the Kid material continues to be recirculated and reprinted; past visions of the Kid in the cinema periodically reappear on afternoon or late-night television. The popular legend of the Kid as a noble bandit, as an American Robin Hood, will surface after Burns's *Saga* is out of print, just as the Copland-Loring ballet will be restaged. In addition, the Reverend Andrew Jenkins' 1926 ballad of the Kid, written after his reading the flyer announcing the choice of the *Saga* as a Book-of-the-Month Club selection, will someday be rerecorded by a musician following the releases of Vernon Dalhart (1920s), Woody Guthrie (1930s), and Ry Cooder (1970s).

It is also plausible to suggest that the image of the Kid as a satanic killer as well as gentlemanly bandit will continue to demand our attention. After all, we have been and will be in the future concerned with popular concepts which by their formulaic nature tend to fall into basic categories of judgment. The conjunction of both the heroic and villainous Kid, for instance, was illustrated in 1949 when—at the end of the Fergusson-Burns-Vidor tradition—a physician intent on classifying the psychological types of Western gunmen and a social historian intent on classifying folk heroes offered opposing visions of the Kid. The physician-author in an unsurprising application of popular Freudianism classified the Kid as a member of the Western gunman group dominated by an inferiority complex; the historian revealed how the Kid's legend demonstrated his affinity to such heroes as Achilles, Ulysses, and—of course— Robin Hood.[5] This type of divided response to the Kid's general image no doubt led both William Keleher in 1950 and Kent Steckmesser in 1965 to suggest that there are basically *two* Billy the Kids in legend.[6]

Even though such notions about the Kid's famous or infamous significance will continue to appear, and even though critics will continue to question the accuracy of such conclusions, it is still important to explore the visions of the Kid in the postwar era to detect the emerging signs of another dominant story-form that revealed American preoccupations. Thus, even though a cursory glance at the brief sentences or single paragraphs that treat the Kid in the years after World War II may reveal a similarity to the earlier visions of the Kid present in Hough or Burns's work, the important fact is that at this time the Kid merits only a brief mention, whereas earlier he characteristically merited an entire chapter or article-length study.

However, I introduce the above example merely to suggest that our examination of the Kid bibliography since 1881 entails a recognition that history is not solely a linear development with clearly established beginnings and ends. Since we have been and will be primarily concerned with the evolution of human sensibilities—not material artifacts like revolvers or bridle bits—it is more useful to consider history as a wavelike flow of motion, and thus to consider our task as that of ascertaining the symbolic point at which a newly emerging wave of thought and feeling crests into a dominant shape just as an earlier wave recedes into the distance.[7] And if, as is surely the case, a newly-emerging wave is similar to previous ones, we are certainly witness to how, as in Shakespeare's sonnets, the study of the history of ideas reveals also the tyranny of time defeated by the human imagination, defeated by the presence of the old inheritance in the face of the new.

Granting this analogy, we can refine the question which opened this chapter. Instead of first asking when an era ends and begins, in short, we should rather explore this question: what circumstances would conspire to dislodge a previous era's dominant explanation of the Kid's story? Or, more specifically, what happenings would call into question the explanation of the Kid as a romance hero or tragic figure?

As we saw in the previous chapter, the initial concept of the Kid as a villain in romance story-form was transformed as the evidence of historical events and the formula devised by the Kid's creators questioned or revised inherited definitions of such terms as *hero, outlaw,* and *civilization.* Yet whether the Kid was perceived as a villain, hero, or tragic figure, it is important to realize that the results of his actions—at least according to his interpreters—maintained a balance between the self and society. Whether named Pat Garrett or Billy the Kid, the heroic protagonist in the story-forms we have examined opposed the savage forces conspiring to prevent the emergence of civilization, regardless of whether savagery was defined as the barren New Mexican wilderness or as the meretricious exploiters of the common folk. Although the conflict of good and evil ultimately required an anarchic use of violence, the hero's personal code was aligned with the best interests of the community. Thus, rather than existing as an anarchic threat to the newly-founded civilized society, the hero regenerated the community as well as redeemed his own self.[8]

Thus satisfying an audience's twin desire for the security of the ordered world of the community and the freedom of unrestrained self-reliant individualism, the Western hero as the Kid or Pat Garrett internalized the often contradictory cultural responses to the meaning of the West. Depending upon which moral standards one adopts, this type of hero, as John Cawelti has demonstrated, could be considered virtuous or vicious, altruistic or selfish, idealistic or pragmatic, and socially-committed or selfishly free. By the standards of the old frontier, the hero whose extralegal violence satisfies an inner moral code and yet preserves the community from extinction is a killer but no criminal, an abuser of the law and yet defender of justice, an outcast from society and yet committed to its defense. By the standards of a settled, middle-class society, however, the hero's extralegal violence constitutes a danger to the future order of society, and thus numerous resolutions to Western formula stories fantasize the solution of the good-badman who departs society after an act of legitimated violence.[9] Neither so totally pure as to refrain from a violent defense of his inner moral code nor so totally depraved as to relish wielding his destructive power, the Kid or Garrett as heroic protagonist has since 1881 mirrored the traditional status of the Western hero whose moment(s) of violent action resolved in fantasy the apparently insoluble conflict between self and society.

If this is a correct assessment of the functions previous visions of the Kid and Garrett served for previous audiences, then we can move closer toward answering our initial question by examining the Kid bibliography for instances where neither the hero nor society are redeemed and regenerated by a moment of violent action, where the thus insoluble conflict of the self and society is not imaginatively resolved at the conclusion of the Kid's story. We perhaps could say that a symbolic turning point in the idea and image of the Kid occurred in the 1950 Audie Murphy film when the narrator concludes by saying that *only* God could judge whether the Kid was an "El Chivato" or an "El Diablo," or when the J. C. Dykes bibliography of Kid material appeared in 1952, or even when Edwin Corle's fictional biography *Billy the Kid* was published in 1953. Certainly the Murphy film comment foreshadows the reluctance of 1950s and 1960s Kid historians to consider the Kid as either saint or satan; the Dykes bibliography marks a symbolic end to earlier concepts of the Kid in its summary of the influence of the Upson-Garrett, Siringo, Hough, and Burns books; and Corle's attempt to puncture the inflated notion of a romanticized bandit foreshadows later portraits of the Kid as an unreflective, inarticulate outlaw whose only outlet in self-expression is that of violence along the lines of filmmaker Sergio Leone's 1960s spaghetti-westerns' heroes.

Although these revisionist efforts point the way toward a consideration of the problems of discovering the historical Kid (Dykes), the problems of alienated youth (Murphy's film), and the problems of violence (Corle), they yet are not concerned with or do not sever the classic formula's balance of hero and society, and thus do not offer a vision of the Kid markedly different in either form or content from previous visions. In my own view, we do not reach a turning point in visions of the Kid until around 1955. In the first place, in this year appeared the most provocative account yet of a man who claimed to be Billy the Kid, a man who claimed that as the Kid he was never buried in old Fort Sumner in July 1881. As it turned out, "Brushy Bill" Roberts did die in December 1950, but his account—entitled *Alias Billy the Kid*—did not appear until 1955.[10] According to "Brushy Bill" a man named Billy Barlow accompanied him to Pete Maxwell's meatlocker on the evening of 14 July 1881, and it was Barlow who was shot that night by Garrett and was buried by the locals next morning. However one reacts to this account and its disturbing revelations (disturbing because Bill reconstructs certain events in the Kid's life in a manner familiar to only the most devoted Kid researchers), "Brushy Bill's" story is the last conceivable effort to confirm the legendary notion that the Kid lived long after July 1881. After *Alias Billy the Kid,* the characteristic focus was not on the Kid's potential for a life after death, but rather on the circumstances of the Kid's death and the destructiveness of violent force—a focus that seemingly revealed the Kid's creators' and consumers' anxiety about the lethal destructiveness of nuclear weaponry and other sophisticated armaments.

While in this perspective *Alias Billy the Kid* symbolizes the demise of the Kid as a crusading romance hero who saves the mortgages of little old ladies from foreclosure, another 1955 item marks the emerging invention of the Kid as a tragic protagonist alienated from a materialistic consumer society. In July 1955 NBC TV's *Philco Playhouse* dramatized Gore Vidal's three-act teleplay *The Death of Billy the Kid.* Starring Paul Newman as the Kid, the teleplay traces the declining pattern of Billy's life between the news of Wallace's amnesty offer and his death in 1881. Instead of devoting attention to the dashing Kid who escaped from the burning McSween house or the chivalric Kid who respected women and children, the teleplay explores the timeless conflict between the law and order necessary to preserve the community and the individual self desirous of making reality match dreams. In the opening lines of the teleplay we learn that Billy's activities during the Lincoln County War had made him a national celebrity, but that this status causes problems that ultimately lead to his death. Although the Kid, as he tells Wallace in the teleplay's second scene, desires merely to live the way he likes before he dies, gunfighters like Joe Grant come looking for him in order to make their own reputations. And because the Kid can't measure up to the Eastern storybook creations of his life and deeds, an unnamed drunk eventually betrays the Kid's presence for a few coins. Armed with this information, Garrett waits for and then kills the Kid in Pete Maxwell's darkened bedroom. Ironically, as the Kid first appears in the teleplay he is donating some loose coins to the drunk's outstretched hand. On this level of plot analysis the teleplay interestingly dramatizes the American public's paradoxical love-hate relationship with its glamorous public stars, and the fate of Vidal's Kid—bedazzled by the publicity surrounding his exploits and betrayed by a fickle public—recapitulates the tragic fate of a succession of American public figures in this century.

Although other publications previous to the teleplay's appearance had noted the classical tragic dimensions of the Kid's historical conflict with an unyielding and corrupt legal and political system, *The Death of Billy the Kid* explicitly identifies the Kid as a tragic hero by means of frequent allusions to familiar tragic themes and motifs. Besides the teleplay's gradual presentation of the fates which betray human ideals, it likens the Lincoln County War, for example, to a struggle between the Montagues and the Capulets, a conflict that is tragic because young men like Billy learned how to kill. At the same time the Kid assumes tragic proportions as a martyred Jesus-figure betrayed for money by the Judas figures of a local drunk and Pat Garrett, the Kid is thought by the Mexicans to be "a kind of God," and is called by the drunk "the golden boy marked for slaughter." Because the Kid's death is likened to the fall of a god from a temple, and because the Kid is marked as a sacrifical victim who is closely allied with Nature (not material wealth), Vidal's Kid emerges as an archetypal doomed Dionysus whose death connotes the triumph of Apollonian order, reason, and control over the elemental forces of the natural landscape.

Unlike the tragic romances of the previous era, however, the teleplay does not frame the death of the Kid with references to the irresistible progress of civilization. Although characters tell the Kid in the course of the teleplay that he was "born the wrong time" or that his way of life has had its day, the teleplay's final epiphany of law does not coincide with the founding of an ideal human community. The delicate balance between self and society and the balance between the old and the new orders of value forged by previous inventors of the Kid (and Garrett) are now severed: the Kid's often violent personal code is not aligned with society's interests, while the society's need for order dehumanizes the individual members. To use the teleplay's image, eliminating the "hawklike" Kid leaves a surviving society of "chickens" intent on conformity to mass opinion. Although Burns and others in the previous era were apprehensive about their society's present direction, they were yet hopeful that the ideals of the past would be incorporated in the new urban-industrial society. Here the Kid is at odds with a society not worth redeeming—if by that it is Garrett's coldly calculating acceptance of the sheriff's job, the drunk's inebriated, pretentious dialogue, and the Gutierrez's meek conformity to prevailing opinion that define the shape of the future society.

In addition to the teleplay's omission of a framing device and its foregrounding of the Kid's outdated pursuit of purely personal goals, a pursuit which moves the Kid toward the tragic hero's death or isolation from society, the teleplay also presents a different narrative movement from the previous inventions of the Kid. Whereas earlier narratives of the Kid's life and death progressively unfolded a linear sequence of action that inevitably proceeded to a moment of violent action (the Kid's death or his defeat of "real" badmen), here the narrative "progresses" in a circular manner as the Kid and Garrett return and depart and reappear in the claustrophobic interiors of Fort Sumner dwellings. Instead of a sequence of Promethean, awe-inspiring acts, the Kid—after he refuses Wallace's amnesty offer—pursues no morally justified quest but rather realizes how the circle of his day's life has been narrowed to a chance encounter he cannot resist or prepare for. Unlike the earlier conclusions to the *Saga,* the ballet, or *The Kid from Texas* film, *The Death of Billy the Kid* holds out little hope for the reconciliation of man and his society. Here there is change, but no progress; here the flights of angels, so to speak, carry the Kid away, but the remaining societal group has lost its identity and sense of moral purpose.

Although on one level *The Death of Billy the Kid* recapitulates the classic myth of a sacrificial youthful god dying to ensure nature's fertility and society's future existence, the teleplay questions whether such a sacrifice, such a destruction of youthful energy and innocence, will produce such dividends. On a specific sociocultural level the teleplay's presentation of a tragic Kid alienated from a hypocritical materialist society reveals a vision of an American Nightmare—not an optimistic belief in the American Dream—in postwar American society. As much as any cultural criticism of sociologists and intellectuals done in the 1950s, *The Death of Billy the Kid* indicts the dehumanization inherent in America's developing homogenized, middle-class white suburban society. What happens in the years after 1955 is that the earlier *Saga*'s Aeschylean sense of historical tragedy as a therapeutic aide to the achievement of self-confident action in the present is replaced by a more Sophoclean tragic sense that reminds us of the dangers involved whenever a society forecloses the human potential for independence and dignity. The discoveries and visions of the Kid in this era recognize on different levels of aesthetic brilliance that the world has grown old, that the age of heroes is past, that freedom and openness have evolved into conformity and limitation, and that alienation is a permanent element in the human condition.[11] Even those who pierce the legend to discover the historical Billy the Kid, and even those who as a result of their discoveries subordinate the Kid's presence in historical accounts of the Western experience—even these interpreters of the Kid, as we shall see, recapitulate a tragic story in their essays and their criticism of previous Kid publications.

That the Kid emerged in this manner at this time can be attributed to several factors besides Vidal's perceptive presentation of the Kid's story. In the first place, because by 1955 Korea and McCarthy were history, and the Hollywood Production Code had relaxed its standards, a more agreeable ambience existed for airing the problems critics felt were endemic to America's postwar corporate society. Second, the Kid as an outlaw youth familiar with the consequences of violence and in confict with established social values constituted an effective subject for displacing into the past any interpreter's concern with postwar problems of alienation, anxiety, and disillusionment. Within a year of the teleplay's production both a new biography and a new novel of the Kid extended the themes of Vidal's teleplay, and within six years two films—Arthur Penn's *The Left-Handed Gun* (1958), based on the teleplay, and Marlon Brando's *One-Eyed Jacks* (1961), based on Charles Neider's 1956 novelistic treatment of the Kid—further established the Kid as a more psychologically complex outlaw estranged from any commitment to a materialistic and conformist society.

The first significant biography of the Kid to appear since Burns's *Saga* (1926) and Miguel Otero's *The Real Billy the Kid* (1936) was Frazier Hunt's *The Tragic Days of Billy the Kid* (1956). Although the title alone indicates a transition from the structure of Burns's *Saga,* most reviewers of *The Tragic Days* either praised its use of Maurice Fulton's historical research or placed the biography squarely within the Garrett-Burns-Otero tradition. That the Kid emerges in the book as a quixotic romantic idealist along the lines of Harvey Fergusson's 1925 vision of the Kid is undeniable if we examine only some of the narrator's conclusions about the Kid. Like Fergusson's symbolic Kid, Hunt's Kid—unlike his Pat Garrett—"wasn't after money or power. He just wanted to be left alone," he "just wanted to be free as the wind, to race horses and play monte, and go to bailes, and once in a while slip off in some little adventure that paid off in a few head." That rustling could be called "some little adventure" of course lessens our revulsion at the Kid's crimes, just as at another point in the biography Hunt reminds us that the Kid "wasn't a cold-blooded calculating killer," but was "a bright figure, a symbol, an unforgettable and arresting character." Similarly, in the first chapter Hunt suggests that the death of the legendary Billy the Kid as a result of recent historical research leaves us with a historical "warm and friendly human being, authentic and accountable."[12]

By restating such typical notions about the Kid's dashing, likeable nature and by further recounting the Kid's noble defense of oppressed Mexicans, Hunt's biography apparently represents little divergence from the Kid as interpreted by Burns and others in the previous era. Yet regardless of the similarity of these conclusions to those reached in earlier accounts, *The Tragic Days* undercuts a simple thematic presentation of a noble bandit by presenting the Kid inextricably caught in a web spun by himself, by powerful *ricos* who wish to rid the area of this symbolic figure of fugitive freedom, and by fate. In addition to the book's presentation of the Kid as "a poor little mortal fighting the tides of his fate," the Kid's story for Hunt occurs unfortunately in a time when the twin values of idealism and materialism could not coexist on "this silly, spinning globe."[13] Thus, as in Vidal's teleplay, there is no reconciliation of the self and society, no balance of the heroic and prosaic; the Kid heroically migrates towards a rendezvous with Death because he chooses not to go to old Mexico, but rather to conform to "his own projected vision of himself as a valiant boy on horseback, fighting his lone battles seemingly against insurmountable odds."[14]

His freedom thus curtailed by a self-concept he won't deny and by the ambitious designs of others, his destiny shaped by the deaths of his mother and Tunstall, the Kid in *The Tragic Days* emerges as a romantic figure enmeshed in a tragic flow of events—whereas in Burns's *Saga* the Kid was a tragic figure enmeshed in a romance narrative structure. The difference is subtle, yet decisive, and it indicates a more pessimistic conclusion about the prospects for an autonomous individual's existence. As in the teleplay, in other words, the biography omits a romance framework, for the relevant focus in the 1950s is not on the triumph of civilization over savagery, but rather on the vain strivings of an embattled individual endeavoring to preserve his integrity in a materialistic society. And as also is the case in the teleplay, Hunt's biography conveys a muted sense of the Kid's Promethean defiance of the fates, because just as society is characterized by its impersonality and betrayal, so too is the Kid ironically betrayed by *his* conformity to a fatal "projected vision of himself." In this sense we can see how the cycle of betrayals in the Kid's story radiates outward from the Kid in a series of concentric circles: the individual betrays and is betrayed by himself and society; society betrays and is betrayed by itself and the individual. Just as there is no escape from this eternal round, there is no final reconciliation of the idealistic Kid and materialistic Garrett, the individual and the organization man.

A similar preoccupation with the idea of the Kid as a hunted, isolated social outcast is demonstrated in Charles Neider's novel *The Authentic Death of Hendry Jones* (1956).[15] Narrated by a fictitious surviving friend of the Kid, one Doc Baker, Neider's novel details the Kid's capture by Dad Longworth (Pat Garrett), his confinement and escape from jail, his reunion with the rest of his gang, and their movements from the Monterey coast south to Ensenada and back north again, at which point the Kid is shot by Longworth and buried by the locals on a barren point called Punto del Diablo. In its bare outlines, *The Authentic Death* seemingly deserves the negative reviews it got because of its tired rehash of familiar Western themes of the romantic outlaw and its lingering stream-of-consciousness style devoted to portraying acts of violence.[16]

Despite these criticisms, the novel is noteworthy for its sophisticated presentation of both the human confrontations with death and the human consequences of violence. On the most basic level, of course, the novel's title is intended to contrast with the 1881 Upson-Garrett *Authentic Life,* and perhaps this simple recognition of the transition from *The Authentic Life* to *The Authentic Death's* tragic story is enough to substantiate the mid-1950s emergence of the Kid as a tragic hero isolated from the human community. Nevertheless, we should recognize how the novel's imagery, structure, and theme intensify the changed emphasis noticeable in its title. As in the last section of Hunt's *Tragic Days,* Neider's novel focuses on the Kid as a weary, prematurely-aging outlaw who fatalistically sees his "luck" change as a catastrophic series of events brings him closer to his rendezvous with Longworth in Hijinio Gonzalez's (Pete Maxwell's) darkened bedroom. The image of the carefree, humorous, defiant Kid is replaced by Baker's account of the Kid's troubled state of mind. Worried about a rising young gunslinger in another town, about his relationship with his mistress, about the jinx another member of his gang has put on him, and sensing that Longworth is pursuing his dreaming as well as his waking moments, the Kid, near the novel's end, draws upon Baker in a trance. Noticing the faraway look in his eyes, Baker realizes that

> He was rolling down that well-known street all right. He was tired, deathly tired. When I had first met him he was like a boy, believing that the bullet hadn't been made that had his number on it. His face was tight and clean, his whoops loud and frequent. But that seemed very long ago. [17]

So long ago, in fact, that Baker can only vaguely remember the events of the Kid's life before his capture sent him rolling downhill toward death. Whereas an earlier novel like E. B. Mann's *Gamblin' Man* (1934) employed a gambling metaphor to illustrate the Kid's triumph over insurmountable odds, Neider's use of a metaphor—which likens life to a card game—is rather to suggest that the Kid, throughout the course of the narrative, has drawn a bad hand and cannot be a winner.

Yet the novel is not only organized in the tragic manner because Baker tells the story of the Kid's ultimate death and isolation. Doc Baker himself is a tragic hero, for in his interweaving of past events and present reflections we learn how Doc Baker also is isolated from the present community of idealizers who believe the Kid never died, or who pay to see a trigger finger preserved in alcohol. Whereas the previous vision of the Kid as a noble bandit affirmed a hopeful reconciliation of the individualistic frontier ethic and the values of an urban-industrial society, here Doc Baker talks—but nobody listens. This isolation of the novel's two protagonists is further reflected in its dual circular structure: the circular movement of Doc Baker's reflections from present to past—from an opening announcement of the Kid's death to a closing description of its occurrence—is paralleled by the Kid's circular movement psychologically from life to death and geographically from Monterey to Ensenada and back to Monterey.

Recognizing the novel's structural and thematic unity in presenting both the Kid's and Baker's stories in a tragic pattern enables us to appreciate the intensity of Doc Baker's apprehension of the meaning of an *authentic* death.

To criticize the novel, as some have, for its graphic and leisurely depiction of bloodshed is to miss the point that Neider, like filmmaker Sam Peckinpah and poet Michael Ondaatje, is concerned with relaying the existential quality of violence in a manner more humanly felt than an antiseptic body count or external photograph. In this sense, the authentic death of the Kid is not precisely the Kid's physical death from a gunshot wound, but is rather the imaginative experience of death which constitutes the entire narration. While the Kid's physical death is announced in the novel's first sentence, in other words, the meaning of the Kid's authentic death is not apparent until Doc Baker (and we as his audience) experience the entire narrative process, its stops and starts, its digressions and repetitions as Baker examines the human encounter with death from as many angles as possible. An *authentic* death occurs only when the imagination can probe the personal meanings that exist beyond what the visual eye records.

This emphasis on Baker's imaginative ability to recreate the Kid's authentic death is important for several reasons. In the first place, it represents a fictional attempt to explore the Kid in a manner entirely different from the Kid's legend; this attempt parallels the efforts of historical researchers in the 1950s also to discover a Kid different from the legend. In the second place, the emphasis on the Kid's psychological confrontation with the closing cycles of events in his life defines this period's interest in the internal Kid. And finally, Neider's presentation of Baker's active imagination isolated from society either by choice or circumstance anticipates the artist as outlaw motif that dominates the poetic conceptions of the Kid during this era.

To quote Hayden White writing in another context, the tragic *agon* or conflict that we discover in works like Neider's novel, Vidal's teleplay, and Hunt's biography reveals "that the secret of history is nothing but man's eternal conquest with, and return to, himself."[18] This quotation is useful for our purposes because it suggests the turn inward that characterizes the vision of the Kid as a tragic hero in the novel, teleplay, and biography. Except for Burns's brief analysis of the "desperado complex," earlier visions of the Kid primarily dealt with his physical exploits in a vast Western landscape. As we move from romance to tragedy (and eventually to irony), as we move from a sense of limitless freedom to a knowledge of the forces that inhibit freedom, visions of the Kid correspondingly become preoccupied with the inner, psychological Kid who confronts death and the consequences of violence as he travels through a constricted, more claustrophobic landscape. The thematic image of the closed circle which is suggested by White's description of the tragic *agon* is also reinforced when, as in Neider's novel and Vidal's teleplay, the narrative structure is more static than kinetic, more devoted to the Kid's state of mind than to the actions resulting from the readiness of his trigger finger.

The circular narrative thus serves to intensify the tragic isolation of the hero alienated from society due to his inability or unwillingness to escape the eternal round of self-examination. This thematic preoccupation with the narrowing of life's options as a result of a catastrophic series of events is at times also visually reinforced, as in Arthur Penn's careful framing of the Kid's image in *The Left-Handed Gun* with the necks of horses, the shadows of windowpanes, the adobe buildings and arches of Madero (Fort Sumner), and a traveling frontier photographer's photograph of the Kid.

It is in this context of the Kid's emergence in the mid-1950s as a psychologically complex, tragic protagonist that we can understand why Penn's vision of the Kid, although representing in some respects a radical departure from the formulaic Western movies, is entirely in line with the Kid we have discovered in the earlier Vidal teleplay, Neider novel, and Hunt biography. This is not entirely surprising, of course, since the movie's screenplay, written by Leslie Stevens, is based on Vidal's teleplay, and since both the movie and the teleplay starred Paul Newman as the Kid.[19] In its basic outline *The Left-Handed Gun* presents the familiar story of the Kid's entry into Tunstall's employ, his quest for vengeance after Tunstall's death, and his ultimate death at the hand of Pat Garrett. Unlike the Vidor film, however, the plot invents no ingenious explanation for the Kid to live happily-ever-after with the woman of his dreams. Unlike in the Audie Murphy movie, the Kid's death does not inaugurate the reign of an enlightened, regenerated community. And unlike the Robert Taylor film, the Kid's death attracts our sympathies, for Newman's Kid emerges as a martyred Jesus-figure.

Yet the situation in *The Left-Handed Gun* is not quite as simple as either a summary of its plot or a contrast to the earlier movies would suggest. As I suggested in this chapter's first section, the emergence of the Kid in a tragic story-form occurred as his interpreters discarded the finely-wrought classic formula's balance between self and society. As part of this revision of the formula, the meaning of existence in society or in the isolated self is scrutinized, and the Kid interpreters' task is not simply a matter of creating a noble Kid or a demonic Kid. What Penn does in *The Left-Handed Gun* is to explore the irreconcilable split between private morality and public violence. Penn finds that in his films about social outcasts like the Kid and Bonnie and Clyde, he can force his audience to recognize that "we find ourselves confronted with the terrible irony that we root for somebody for a relatively good cause who, in the course of that good cause, is called upon to commit acts of violence which repel us."[20] This of course sounds like a restatement of the tension in films about the good-badman, but the difference here is that no transcendent act of violence resolves the conflict between admiration and abhorrence. The Kid, as the movie's opening ballad states, is "death's child," and is admirable in his desire for justice. He is identified as a Christlike figure when he emerges from the deserted hideout with his arms extended, his posture forming a cross; when he sits on his cot while in jail and the windowpane's shadow forms a cross on the wall behind him; and when he dies after drawing from an empty holster, his body completes a cross as it falls vertically across the horizontal poles of a haywagon. Furthermore, as in the teleplay he is betrayed by a person disappointed by the Kid's inability to live up to the myth created by the popular press.

Yet our sympathetic admiration for this martyred social outcast is tempered by the Kid's harsh fulfillment of what Penn has called the Kid's "psychopathic sense of what was just and unjust,"[21] by the Kid's betrayal of his Mexican friends, and by his forced invasion of McSween's house (which is burnt down by an irate mob in search of the Kid). The fact is, as one character says, wherever the Kid goes he brings "pain." The fact that the McSween house incident is staged not to reveal the Kid's daring, heroic escape against insurmountable odds indicates the changing focus of the movie's vision of the Kid's problematic course of vengeance. In the same manner, Newman's Kid who first appears as a shuffling, squinting, inarticulate figure carting his saddle across the open range separates this film's examination of the Kid from Johnny Mack Brown's stately, athletic movements and open countenance.

In this sophisticated symbolic version of the Kid's vengeance quest, the conflict between the Kid's need for a violent fulfillment of his personal code of justice, and society's need for the rule of law, for restraint in the use of violence, and for commitment to democracy, family, and religion—this conflict is irreconcilable. Ultimately, the conflict between the Kid's extreme individualism and society's laws and moral values is transferred to the film's audience. For just as the film's conclusion indicates that Garrett's killing of the Kid has resolved none of the problems raised by the Kid's presence as a troubled, delinquent youth, so too are we completely unable to commit ourselves to either extreme of the social contract. Thus, even though the Kid's death—literally caused by his drawing on an empty holster—reminds us of Robert Taylor's Kid's death wish in the 1941 MGM movie, here we cannot resign ourselves to either a life with the Kid or a life without him. Just as any imaginative identification with the Kid's primitive individualism must be tempered by an awareness of the terrible consequences of his defiant rebellion, so too any identification with a restored society as a result of the Kid's death must be tempered by a knowledge of society's own sadistic tendencies and hard instincts. The moral certitude that animated the killer of Robert Taylor's Kid is lacking here, for the admirable, yet unyielding Pat Garrett is admonished by his wife at film's end to come "home," a prospect we must relish with as little enthusiasm as we felt for the Kid's ease in adopting the role of judge, jury, and executioner.

The recognition that moral values are complex and the suggestion that Garrett and the Kid maintain a symbiotic relationship is extended in Marlon Brando's *One-Eyed Jacks* (1961), a film loosely based on Charles Neider's novel discussed above. Although Brando's Rio (the Kid) is not the marionettelike, manic-depressive Kid created by Newman, Rio is a troubled, brooding outlaw alienated from the good society, choosing instead to depart into the sunset after killing the sheriff who once was his partner and making a vague promise to return later to retrieve the sheriff's daughter (who is pregnant by Rio). Although the sheriff's hypocritical betrayal of Rio during their early outlaw days together directly contrasts with Rio's justified vengeance quest and sincere personal relationships, both men are "one-eyed jacks." That is, just as the jack's full nature is hidden because we only glimpse one side of his face, so too are the true natures of the sheriff and outlaw veiled by their visible, social positions. That "one-eyed jacks" are often used as "wild cards" in poker games, as cards having no certain value, endows the film's main metaphor with added appropriateness, for both Rio and Longworth are untamed men indifferent to fixed value systems. This realization that appearances are deceptive, that a sheriff may be treacherous and an outlaw noble, is of course a recasting of the familiar motif of the whore-with-a-heart-of-gold. After all, implicit in the good-badman formula was the recognition that a weak society could not recognize the bad-badman whose veneer of social conformity concealed a hard layer of evil. Yet in *One-Eyed Jacks* and, for that matter, *The Left-Handed Gun,* the outlaw is committed to no social values, founds no civilized world, and protects no oppressed peoples. Unlike Johnny Mack Brown's or Audie Murphy's Kid, these Kids do not recognize any predominant social values, but rather die or head back to isolated, sublime landscapes like that of the Monterey coast.[22]

The evidence of these significant interpretations of the Kid in these various genres suggests that far from reinforcing or reflecting postwar American society's complacency and conformity, the invention of the Kid as an alienated, psychologically-troubled youth betrayed both from within and without reveals cultural criticism as serious and strident as the social criticism of the decade's intellectuals.[23] Sociologists and cultural historians like David Riesman, Vance Packard, William Whyte, Paul Goodman, and C. Wright Mills lamented the postwar developments of a homogenized, standardized, regimented middle-class society. Regardless of the critic's philosophical or political viewpoint, all shared an immediate concern over the replacement of the independent, self-reliant, industrious entrepeneur of the last century by, to use these critics' most popular phrases, "the organization man," that "other-directed individual" manipulated by Madison Avenue's "hidden persuaders." Such criticism of a growing conformist society devoted to Cold War politics and the consumer ethic was founded on fears of dehumanization and the imminent prospects for destruction. After the experience of a great economic depression, two world wars, the advent of nuclear weaponry, and the paranoia of McCarthyism, it was clear at least to the critics of American society that inevitable social progress was an illusion, that the world was rather a chaotic, turbulent domain of alien forces unable to be fully comprehended and controlled.

Popular culture developments, representing as they do artistic creations cued to prevailing attitudes, unsurprisingly demonstrated a similar critique of mass society. Themes of alienation, loss of identity, disillusionment, and anxiety surfaced in comic books, science fiction films, and—of course—Western stories and movies. Science fiction films like *The Invasion of the Body Snatchers* (1956) and *The Incredible Shrinking Man* (1957) depicted humans as the prey of large, conspiratorial forces which depersonalized individuals or constantly posed a threat of destruction. The Western movie, as Thomas H. Pauly has superbly demonstrated in a recent article, transformed the image of the Western hero and his society. In such Westerns as *The Gunfighter* (1950) and *High Noon* (1952), for instance, audiences, Pauly writes, discovered a different image of life in the West:

> Gone was the conventional pre-war image of life in the West as one of vigorous activity, noble enterprise, shared purpose, and understood responsibilities. The panoramic stretches of landscape that formerly inspired a sense of freedom and opportunity became treacherous wastelands fraught with danger. Instead of protection, the precariously constructed settlements, which now became a more common setting, turned claustrophobic and sparked unwanted confrontations. Amidst these conditions, the previously enlightened leadership of the Western hero was found wanting. The antagonism and opposed outlook he had always expected from his enemies now surfaced within his own ranks. He even found a large measure of the problem lay in his own strong convictions and deadly skills. [24]

Just as the Western hero along the lines of Will Kane, Jimmy Ringo, and Shane were portrayed as men who strode the streets of towns far more than they rode horses across open landscapes, so too the frontier community, under its members' masks of amiability, became a treacherous place filled with opportunists and betrayers. As John H. Lenihan has stated in regard to the critical response to the controversial *High Noon,* both those who saw it as a primer of anti-McCarthy-like sentiment, and those who saw it as a support for the strong McCarthy-like individual opposed to invasion from without and subversion from within, sought "to define America's apparent malaise in coping with domestic and international exigencies in terms of *some concrete evil within itself.*"[25] That evil, furthermore, might be implicitly or explicitly defined as society's penchant for racism, imperialism, materialism, and conformism, but the overriding problem was that a meretricious, sometimes cowardly society endangered the Westerner's sense of individualism. As with the intellectuals' criticism of society's passive conformity to prevailing mass opinion, the popular Western film's presentation of an ambiguous gunfighter-hero torn between institutional tyranny and individual anarchy dramatized a problem immediately relevant to the concerns of its adult audience.

Whether in the two Kid films, the teleplay, the biography, or the novel, thematic preoccupations with the individual alienated from society, the irrelevance of simple moral definitions and choices, and the anxieties associated with senseless violence—all these concerns suggest that the Kid's interpreters in the 1950s were cynical about the prospects for a successful human transition from the Kid's unrestrained, self-fulfilling adolescent world to Garrett's mature world of social responsibility. Unable to express his deepest emotions, weary of being pursued by the furies who assailed him from within and without, and betrayed by his own personal code as well as the monetary desires of others, the Kid emerges at this time as another 1950s misfit rebelling against the placid conformity and the avaricious tendencies of a settled middle-class society.

Instead of the outlaw-hero who seeks redemption for his sins by means of an honorable social commitment, the Kid resembles a Southwestern rebel without a cause, a James Dean figure shuffling through Fort Sumner and learning the bitter lesson that society is weak, deceitful, treacherous, and tyrannous, ultimately desirous of denying his existence by capturing him in handcuffs or in dime novels. Whereas earlier the Kid's juvenile delinquency was attributed to his savage frontier environment, now the Kid as an alienated youth is not explained as a frontier slum-kid but is placed directly into a confrontation with an alternative social order which restricted the individual. Whether portrayed as a leather-clad Brando eyeing the locals in *The Wild Ones* (1954) or as Newman's Kid gazing at the world through a steamed-over hotel bathroom window, the complexity of the character and the uncertainty of his moral worth presage the ideological fragmentation that would characterize America in the 1960s and early 1970s. Significantly, whereas the previous era's visions of the Kid customarily raised the hopeful reconciliation of both the old and new values and generations by highlighting the respectful exchange of Wallace and the Kid, after the teleplay and the biography this event was usually missing, for negotiation seemed impossible in a polarized world.

Eventually, when the Kid's creators believed that the outlaw's death or isolation revealed the meaninglessness of life, the formula for inventing the Kid—as in Sam Peckinpah's 1973 film *Pat Garrett and Billy the Kid*—fully approaches an ironic vision. Imagistically, this transition from tragedy to irony can be likened to the transition from the Kid's inability in *The Left-Handed Gun* to understand Paul's lesson of charity as embodied in the "through a glass darkly" quotation, to Pat Garrett's shooting his mirror image only moments after he has killed the Kid in the conclusion to Peckinpah's film.

6   Into the Shattered Mirror

Visions of the Kid
from the Cold War
through Watergate

Essentially all western figures, whether historical or fictional, can be used
to dramatize the relationship of the self and society, or the ambiguous consequences of violent action. Wyatt Earp, for example, also the subject of
numerous films and books at this time, was a relevant figure for dramatizing the problems of leadership and social unity in the face of threats to the
community. By contrast, Custer's relationship with the Sioux has always been a
useful vehicle for dramatizing the problems of race relations, and in a 1958
Walt Disney production the general was portrayed as a racist instead of a
heroic leader of manifest destiny. Given the Kid's youth and outlaw status, it
is perhaps not surprising that he was revitalized during the late 1950s and
early 1960s as a frontier precursor of this era's alienated Beats, bikers, and
hipsters. Of course, not all Western films and literary works at this time that

included youthful leading roles portrayed troubled youths like the Newman Kid or the Brando Rio. Even Nicholas Ray's *The True Story of Jesse James* (1957), a Western version of his earlier *Rebel Without a Cause* (1955), presented the James gang's rebellious activities as hardly an anarchic threat to the established social structure. Still, this James movie—like the Kid films we discussed in the last chapter—did dramatize a similar disenchantment with an older generation, which appeared to have lost direction in a time of crisis because of its hypocritical pursuit of material success.

While we recognize how the Kid's emergence as a troubled youth in a tragic story is related to the era's cultural criticism of a society that seemingly constrained individual freedom and promoted mass conformity, we nevertheless should remember that this vision of the Kid was offered as a corrective to the received Kid of the popular legend. The transition from a presentation of the Kid's physical exploits in defense of dispossessed frontier folk to an exploration of his psychological state as a hunted outlaw or obsessed avenger was founded on the belief that hidden in the legend was an interesting outlaw who could be explained in human—not legendary or mythological—terms.

This skeptical attitude toward the received interpretations of the Kid is but one change in the image of the Kid after 1950. I am referring here not only to the serious attention given the Kid by artists like Penn and Brando, but also to this era's notable discoveries about the historical Kid's life. Just as the creative artists discovered a Kid at this time who bore faint resemblance to the romantic image, so too the researchers of this era unearthed and popularized a historical Kid who little resembled the Kid of Burns's *Saga*. As Gary L. Roberts has written in his study of the gunman's historiography, throughout the 1950s "Billy the Kid remained the most written about character in the American West"[1] because the Kid's bibliography was filled with essays, articles, and also short entries on more general accounts of the Western historical experience. Researchers like Maurice G. Fulton, William Keleher, Philip J. Rasch, R. N. Mullin, and W. E. Koop pursued the Kid with more responsible research methods and more accurate materials. Their discoveries, although usually published in small-circulation journals and *Brand Books,* were later repeated and sometimes distorted by more commercially-oriented authors like Harry S. Drago and James D. Horan, and by larger presses like Time-Life or Reader's Digest.

Basically, there were two results to this activity. In the first place, the Kid (as well as other Western figures) was placed more accurately in his historical period. Second, a more complete understanding of the Kid's role in history occasioned less attention to his individual exploits. Keleher's study of the Lincoln County War presented the Kid as a minor figure on the scene; Amelia Bean's historical novel *Time for Outrage* (1967), while portraying the Kid

as described in the work of Keleher, Mullin, and others, had as its main character a man primarily based on Sam Corbet, historical friend of the Kid's and
employee in the Tunstall store. Books by Leon Claire Metz, Horan, Drago,
and Joseph Rosa only included the Kid as he related to larger focuses on Western outlaws and gunfighters.[2] And except for Hunt's biography of the Kid in
1955, the most significant later biography of this era was not of the Kid, but
was Metz's biography of Pat Garrett.[3] Demythologizing the Kid, in short,
was accomplished not only by portraying him on film as a repressed homosexual (one view of *The Left-Handed Gun* Kid), but also by discovering the
Kid's minimal role in the Lincoln County War, his less than awesome murder total, and the prosaic facts of his boyhood.

Although in these historical works the Kid no longer dominated accounts
of Western outlaws and violence, there were nevertheless frequent complaints
raised against those interpreters of previous eras who, like Ash Upson and
Walter Noble Burns, created the Kid as "a demigod of the Wild West myth."
The characteristic motivation for these researchers, of course, was to set the
record straight about "the overpublicized outlaw."[4] As a result, frequent
protests about the public's acceptance of the romanticized Kid were lodged,
and those who couldn't distinguish between history and legend—those who
couldn't, to paraphrase one observer, recognize a fact unless it came up and
kicked them in the head—were ridiculed. Drago was moved to state that
"for half a century or more I have been trying to tell that story, presenting
what I found to be the truth, even though it has meant contradicting many
of my peers."[5] In *A Fitting Death for Billy the Kid,* Ramon Adams, the most
vociferous opponent of the legend-makers, likewise anticipated that for his
efforts he would "be criticized for taking the glamour from a folk-hero, for
denying people the right to satisfy appetites greedy for thrills and blood." As
Adams continues explaining his point, we learn that

> the real historian wants the truth. Too many historians are of the
> rockingchair variety, too willing to take someone else's word for
> what has happened in the past. When we see these so-called histo-
> rians, through the second and third generations, repeating legends
> which originated in the mind of some dime novelists and record-
> ing them as fact, it fills a lover of truth with resentment. It is not
> pleasant for him to see truth smothered by legend until that truth
> is no longer believable.[6]

It is not my intention here to doubt these researchers' intentions, nor to
discuss the historiographical problems associated with this stance. Instead, I
think it important here to realize that what develops in these authors' prefa-
tory and concluding statements is a portrait of the "real" historian alienated
from the great numbers of his peers and audience. Separated by their superior

knowledge of truth, Adams, Drago, Horan, and others who dredge the Kid material characteristically emphasize the distinctness of their visions of truth, its opposition to the established tradition of thinking about the Kid and other Western figures and events. Adams in particular restates in his several publications a Southwestern version of the American jeremiad tradition, and thus emerges as a latter-day Jonathan Edwards exhorting his unreliable flock during this era's Great Awakening.

The point is that the historical investigators of the Kid during this era characteristically create, as a way of defining their stance toward their tasks, the fiction of the isolated truthsayer. The resulting frequency of the moods of complaint, protest, and ridicule; the rejection of rhetoric, moral judgments and ideology; and the feeling of loneliness in the course of their quest for objective, verifiable truth—all these currents of thought and feeling, whether appearing in Western pulp magazines or in scholarly journals, ultimately reveal the Kid historian as his narrative's underlying heroic protagonist. And it is in this transition from the Kid as alienated hero to the historian as a heroic protagonist whose pursuit of truth isolates him from common humanity that we again discover the tendency toward the tragic mode during this era. Furthermore, if from one perspective an outlaw becomes an outlaw precisely when his violent vision of experience shatters cherished beliefs and becomes too terrible for society to behold, then we can extend our discussion to suggest that the Kid historian is a symbolic "outlaw" when he delivers truthful visions that invalidate current beliefs, and when he complains that his vision is unacknowledged.

Since throughout this study we have been considering the historian, biographer, and essayist as authors who are as involved in inventing fictions as are the poet or novelist, this mention of the writer as symbolic outlaw enables us to consider another dimension to this era's repudiation of previous visions of the Kid. As cultural historians of the 1950s and early 1960s have noted, the American experience with Fascism in World War II and with Communism in the Cold War led many to distrust or reject explicit ideological positions and instead—in a kind of intellectual patriotism—to embrace the American tradition of pragmatism. As one outgrowth of the rejection of overt ideological claims, American academic historians of this era popularized a "consensus" view of American history, which diluted the historical importance of conflict and dissent in American life. At the same time, American literary critics advocated the so-called New Critical position which closely analyzed the literary text to determine its intrinsic worth as art—not its extrinsic relationship with politics, philosophy, and psychology. The point is that while the Kid's researchers believed they were, like the outlaw, alienated from society in that academic historians ignored the Kid and the general public embraced the legendary Kid, these so-called amateur historians were yet closely aligned with the era's predominant intellectual developments. Thus, while on one level the Kid historian's emergence as an isolated heroic protagonist indicates extreme dissatisfaction with postwar society's inability to recognize the truth, on another level this emerging pose embodies the era's larger disenchantment with theoretical speculation. Just as historians were criticizing the ideological differences suggested by, say, the labels *liberalism* and *conservatism,* the Kid's researchers were criticizing the distorted "romanticism" of the popular legend.

In this context I think it appropriate to remark here that as much as the consensus historians softened the rough edges of American history by minimizing the conflicts of, say, the 1890s, the Western historians of this era in their own way lessened any audience identification with radical figures in the process of discovering the Kid's minimal importance in Western history. As is often the case, whether we are dealing with the Kid or the history of the American labor movement, to call for objectivity, detachment, neutrality, and unideological beliefs is in effect to argue for the preservation of the *status quo.* Essentially, to capture the Kid in history—to provide for his fitting death—is to eliminate dissent, to control the imagination which would invent or exaggerate the Kid, in effect to master the chaos of Nature. To remove the Kid from legend, in short, is not only an honorable attempt to discover a historical truth, it is also to reveal the futility of the Kid's outlaw activities. The ironic fact is that the legendary Kid as well as the historical Kid posed no revolutionary threat to established social institutions.

The above discussion offers a perspective by which to understand more precisely the context in which our present knowledge of the historical Kid was established. While it may appear to refute my emphasis on how the era's major Kid historians duplicated the tendency of writers and filmmakers to isolate a hero from society, I believe the discussion rather brings to light the dialectical tension existing between many of these historians' ideological values and their mode of argument. That is to say, an investigator like Ramon Adams basically creates the fiction of an honorable-man-turned-symbolic-outlaw in order to accomplish his quest for truth (*the* truth, as Adams would state the case). What Adams and others who share his quest desire is a finished product (the historical work in print), which can be used to correct society's failure to recognize and adopt the truth. Thus, any final criticism is not of society, but of society's failures—which are correctable. The Kid historian as outlaw, in short, is a temporary stance, for the boon of truth is returned to society. When we turn from the historian as outlaw to the artist as outlaw, however, no such tension exists, for the idea of the artist as outlaw isolated from society's forms and values is not a temporary stance but a permanent repudiation of inherited traditions.

Socrates suggested in Book X of Plato's *Republic* that poets be banished from the ideal human community because of their debilitating moral influence, and since that time the idea of the poet as outlaw alienated from society has persisted. Since the Romantic era in Europe and America, however, increasingly greater numbers of poets have chosen to begin and remain outside the city's gates. Originating as a Romantic conception along the lines of Goethe's Werther, the idea of the poet as exile, outlaw, or Ishmael became even more entrenched in our present century as the poet's forms, themes, and subjects became increasingly inaccessible to the common reader. In terms of the Kid's bibliography, we can discover the increasing distance of the artist from society and its conventional themes and forms by contrasting the traditional verse stanzas of Omar Barker with the open-form poetry of Michael McClure. What happens is that poets who imagine the Kid during this era adopt the artist-as-outlaw stance as a means of symbolically preserving the integrity of their artistic vision, and, ultimately, their social criticism. Poets like Jack Spicer, McClure, and Michael Ondaatje also deny that the Kid can be captured and understood by either history or legend, and in that denial they subvert traditional beliefs about knowledge and truth.

What these poets do share with all interpreters of the Kid at this time is the impulse to discover a total idea of the Kid denied by previous approaches. As Charles Olson—founder of the dissident Black Mountain "school" of poets and advocate of what he terms "projective verse"—states in conjunction with his essay on Burns's *Saga,* the problem with history is first that it, like most poetry, is overly influenced by forms that are alien to American experience. Along with an allegiance to false forms, Olson further argues that

> you have to add these false premises: either that s[ai]d Americans are more than they are (still waters, like the Indians or Wyatt Earp, who was also . . . nothing but a company cop); or less (mere killers, like we are taken, as Billy has been taken by those who do not hear, as one can say for Walter Noble Burns that does hear even if he overhears, the Kid's question 'Quien es?') . . . why El Chivato asked anything, this once, instead of barking, with his gun. [7]

Because of such shortcomings in form and presence, Olson concludes, "you better figure on man's interiors," not external descriptions of appearance and geography. Olson's belief is that typically the historian does not expend in discovering an event and writing it an amount of energy equal to that in the original event. In this argument, in short, Olson advocates that the historian invent a form which can obliterate a past-present time distinction and avoid the loss of energy in the present, "which is the only place where history has context."[8] It is the historian who in effect achieves a poetic vocation that demands Olson's attention, one who (we suspect) writes history as Olson does or who, like Burns, can hear and overhear what happened in the past and thus make it happen in the present.

It is this rejection of traditional history's external truths that animates contemporary poetic conceptions of the Kid. As the Canadian poet bp Nichol says in *The True Eventual Story of Billy the Kid,* "history always stands back calling people cowards or failures."[9] Michael McClure's two dramas about the Kid, *The Blossom* (1959) and *The Beard* (1965), remove the Kid entirely from history and place him somewhere in eternity.[10] Jack Spicer's *Billy the Kid* (1958) and Michael Ondaatje's *The Collected Works of Billy the Kid* (1970) subvert the externals of historical investigation by creating a Billy who exists within the poet's mind.[11] Furthermore, while all of these works play with the Kid's history or comment on the Kid's history, they ultimately affirm that the story of the Kid is beyond history because, as Olson implies above, there is no objective truth in history, because language creates reality rather than records it. Nichol in particular spoofs those earlier accounts which purport to offer the *true* story of the Kid:

> this is the true eventual story of billy the kid. it is not the story as he told it for he did not tell it to me. he told it to others who wrote it down, but not correctly. there is no true eventual story but this one. had he told it to me i would have written a different one. i could not write the true one had he told it to me.

Of course, anytime we read poetry we hardly require an accuracy to historical facts, yet all these works announce the death of the Kid in the opening pages as a preliminary to the task of creating the Kid. For these writers the Kid's "life" only begins with his death in history and in historical accounts.

In addition to denying history's traditional approach to the Kid, which is understandable for a poet, these works also subvert the traditional legendary formula of the Kid. Ondaatje's Kid, no saint or satan, kills plants with his urine, fornicates on an outhouse floor, vomits in the desert during a hangover, hallucinates a sexual encounter with Jesus Christ, and numbers among his dead a rabid cat. McClure's Kid seduces Jean Harlow in *The Beard,* and kills Tunstall and the McSweens in *The Blossom.* Nichol's Kid is a loser who was "called the Kid because he was younger & meaner & had a shorter dick." Spicer's Kid only "rides" when his poem's narrator hears a *radio* announce the Kid's death to him one fine hot summer day. All these poets are in a sense similar to Nichol's Kid who would "probably take legend out for a drink, match off in the bathroom, then blow him full of holes."

These poetic interpretations of the Kid are thus outlaw poems in the sense that they reject both history and legend, asserting instead that the "true" story of the Kid is the internal one which has little to do with the past events of his life and death. The fact is, as Jack Spicer says in poetic terms, that

> Delicate
>   as perception is
> No one will get his gun or obliterate
> their shadows.

These are also outlaw poems in the further sense that they reject traditional notions of appropriate subject matter and poetic form. Not only are the boundaries between past and present obliterated, but also demolished is the arbitrary distinction between "high" culture and "popular" culture subjects. Similarly, all these efforts reject what Olson calls the "non-projective verse," which demands that the poet manipulate his content to conform to the formal requirements of inherited poetic structures like the sonnet. By now, of course, the demand for and the acceptance of an open verse are as much a tradition as that of the rhymed couplet. Although Olson's sense of form following content is as much characteristic of Whitman's aesthetic as it is of contemporary poetry, the point is that in the 1950s and 1960s the Kid poets who in various ways adopted Olson's poetics were outlaws in the context of the Kid tradition and in the larger context of the poets and New Critics of the T. S. Eliot tradition. Yet having liberated themselves from an allegiance to formal verse forms, external history, and popular legend, these poets still confronted the problem of creating a form by which both to contain and release the Kid—to overhear him in that darkened bedroom as he excitedly asks "Quién es?" without allowing one's shadow to destroy the scene.

This is not a simple problem, for the structure of poetry and drama inevitably moves toward a stasis, a conclusion, which denies the constant movement of nature. For these poets the essential difference is that in a closed world with closed verse forms art is *not* life but is rather man's ordered reply to life's chaos; in the open universe we inhabit in this century, poetic forms—at least according to one contemporary aesthetic—while never equalling nature, should at least *parallel* nature's ceaseless movement.[11] The difficulty, then, is to be true to one's awareness of nature and also to be true to art and its demand for order. In Jack Spicer's *Billy the Kid,* the problem of devising an appropriate form is stated this way by the poem's narrator as he examines the external objects present in a room with him:

> A sprinkling of gold leaf looking like hell flowers
> A flat piece of wrapping paper, already wrinkled, but wrinkled
>   again by hand, smoothed into shape by an electric iron
> A painting

Which told me about the death of Billy the Kid.
Collage a binding together
of the real
Which flat colors
Tell us what heroes
                    really come by.
No, it is not a collage. Hell flowers
Fall from the hands of heroes
                    fall from all our hands flat
As if we were not ever able quite to include them.

Spicer's narrator at first believes he can be "told" about the Kid's death by constructing a collage of materials that symbolically represent the historical facts of the Kid's life. Yet he realizes that these facts—this collage—cannot accomplish the task, for they are "not ever able quite" to apprehend the Kid's death. Such a collage of material, he realizes in the next few lines after this quotation, is not the Kid—it is "Memory."

Ondaatje considers the identical problem by referring to photography. The first entry in his *The Collected Works* is a short note by frontier photographer L. A. Huffman on the difficulties of taking photographs of objects in motion, "passing horses at a lively trot square across the line of fire—bits of snow in the air—spokes well defined—some blur on the top of the wheel but sharp in the main." A few pages later Ondaatje quotes Paulita Maxwell from the *Saga* at the point she is complaining that the most famous photograph of the Kid "doesn't do him justice." Ondaatje's problem—like the photographer's, like Spicer's—is to capture a moving object, in this case the Kid. He acknowledges the difficulty by leaving the blank squares above each quotation empty, for no picture of the Kid has been developed. The task of creating the Kid is in a sense to fill in the blank area, but—as Olson suggested about history's next step—that blank space must be filled with a "man's interiors"—not a photograph. Instead of pretending to capture the essence of the Kid in a photograph, Ondaatje offers us the multiple exposures of prose, prose poems, poetry, dime novels, and interviews. While the Kid is none of these, he is all of these; it is only by experiencing the Kid from all these angles that we can return to the blank where the photograph should be and begin to fill it in.

By understanding the contemporary poet's problem of reconciling the creativity of the imagination and its accompanying destructiveness in ordering evanescent experiences into language, I think we can understand a major attraction of the outlaw figure—and the Kid—for a major poet wishing to confront any so-called open universe.[12] Just as the Kid is dead in the historical field and yet is resurrected in the legendary tradition, so too the poet's ability to create the illusion of continual process within a poetic drama which moves inexorably toward the closure of an ending reveals a life after death. In other words, one solution to the poet's dilemma is to create the persona of the outlaw as artist or the artist as outlaw, to employ the outlaw's mythic vitality after his historical death as a trope for the poet's attempt to guarantee an authentic life within the confines of an authentic death.

The first section of Jack Spicer's poem outlines the process by which we are to be told the Kid's story:

> the radio that told me about the death of Billy the Kid
> (And the day, a hot summer day, with birds in the sky)
> Let us fake out a frontier—a poem somebody could hide in with a
> sheriff's posse after him—a thousand miles of it if it is necessary
> for him to go a thousand miles—a poem with no hard corners, no
> houses to get lost in, no underwebbing of customary magic, no
> New York Jew salesmen of amethyst pajamas, only a place Billy
> the Kid can hide when he shoots people.

As in the first sentences of Neider's novel, the poem immediately introduces the fact of the Kid's death. Since it is a radio that announces this event, we know that we are within the narrator's mind, and, as the rest of the selection makes clear, the Kid's death is not the poem's subject. Rather, as Frank Sadler has argued, the poem is about creating a poem, about "faking out a frontier" in which the Kid can hide. The poem as an outlaw's sanctuary seems an appropriate trope, since in our act of "faking out a frontier" we are isolating ourselves from an external world (suggested by the radio), which would corrupt our ability to create. In addition, since our poem as frontier will be a place where "no hard corners" or "New York Jew salesmen" can intrude, we realize how Spicer's vision will be liberated from what he considers the restrictive poetic and intellectual traditions of the East.

The problem he sets up in this first section, then, is the problem of creation, and the rest of the poem presents the process of fulfilling the intent to "fake out a frontier," which eventually becomes the intent to know the Kid in opposition to the radio. Just as Ondaatje includes blank spaces for us to fill in, Spicer here suggests that the creative process of knowing the Kid will be undertaken together by "us," the narrator and the audience. The poem proceeds to the point where the narrator gradually submerges himself in Billy's point of view. The significance of this internal movement is that the narrator's pain at nearing the completion of the poem is analogous to Billy's pain as he moves toward the painful death which was announced in the opening line. In confronting the Kid, the narrator in short confronts both the pleasure and the pain of the creative act. In the poem's last section, however, the pain turns to joy as the narrator reflects on how the exploration of the frontier has opened up new possibilities even as the poem ends and Billy dies:

> Billy the Kid
> I love you
> Billy the Kid
> I back anything you say
> And there was the desert
> And the mouth of the river
> Billy the Kid
> (In spite of your death notices)
> There is honey in the groin
> Billy

Even as the poem concludes Spicer affirms both the vitality of the Kid and the poet. The Kid's earlier pain at having bullets in the groin is here transformed into the fertility of "honey in the groin," and the sexual suggestion appropriately symbolizes the fertility of the Kid and the creative process "In spite of your death notices." Thus ending and yet beginning, dead and yet alive, the poet intimates future possibilities for "faking out a frontier" by leaving the final lines incomplete, thus suggesting the illusion of the poem's being regenerated at any time. This device serves the same purpose as the famous closing freeze-frame of Butch Cassidy and the Sundance Kid in George Roy Hill's 1969 film starring Paul Newman and Robert Redford.

Besides the fact that Spicer and Michael McClure share an identification with the San Francisco Beat movement in the late 1950s and early 1960s, McClure's two verse dramas about the Kid further the sexual connotations that periodically surface in Spicer's poem. McClure himself has called his plays "outlaw dramas" in the sense that they have both displeased the critics and infuriated the "Establishment." *The Blossom,* a projective verse drama written at one sitting in 1959 in the manner of Kerouac's "automatic writing," was performed first in 1963 in a New York theater club, in 1967 on the University of Wisconsin-Milwaukee campus (it closed after one performance), and in 1968 in San Francisco. *The Beard* has a more spectacular history in the sense that its obscene dialogue and sexual explicitness led to a nightly arrest of actors during its run in a San Francisco North Beach night club and, later, to an obscenity trial.

In his program notes to *The Blossom,* McClure indicates his inspirational debts to both Charles Olson and Antonin Artaud. Given McClure's primal celebration of a "deep Reason," which is opposed to rational cognition, and his idea of drama as a form of sexual congress in which mammalian energy is transferred from actor to audience, it may appear strange that McClure would name Artaud as an influence, for this French artist is commonly associated with the Theater of the Absurd and a Theater of Cruelty. Yet what attracts McClure to Artaud's thought is not any dark vision of a dead, mechanical world but rather Artaud's notion of a magical "Alchemical" theater which, like alchemy, transforms the dross of nature into spiritual illumination.

This transformation is necessarily a painful process for both artist and audience, for it is a process by which all illusions are stripped away and, in McClure's terms, a man and woman are revealed as "bags of meat" or "spirit containers." Spiritual illumination does not occur, in short, by rational cognition or logical analysis but through a total eroticizing of man's relationship with the world. It is in this impulse for a magical, even painful, liberation of the flesh that we can fruitfully place McClure's plays in the context of Norman O. Brown's *Life Against Death* (1959), Herbert Marcuse's *Eros and Civilization* (1955), and Wilhelm Reich's criticism of contemporary culture's organized repression of the human instinctual life. As it is clear by now, we are on much more ambitious intellectual grounds than with the mammary eroticism in Howard Hughes's *The Outlaw*.

In any case, McClure's Kid as he appears in the dramas is, like the artist, "a seer" whose "senses are smashed by the sights he saw / IN SPACE / and the murders he performed."[13] As in Spicer's poem, a dialectic of pain and pleasure, murder and creation, is explored before an ecstasy of release is experienced psychologically and sexually. *The Blossom* is a difficult play to understand because of McClure's spontaneous composition and own periodic incoherence, but in general it dramatizes the conflict between, in Freudian terms, a repressive superego and an instinctual id. This conflict unwinds on several levels, and the "blossom" serves as an appropriate metaphor. Since there is in the play an explicit metaphorical union of a flower, the Kid's phallus, and the Kid's gun, the blossom which the play describes is at once the process of a flower erupting from the earth to daylight, the phallus swelling to an erection, and the gun exploding in violence. The outlaw as artist motif for McClure depends upon this sense of purgative violence breaking apart stereotyped preconceptions. As in Spicer's poem, the Kid's creativity causes pain, but it leads to new visions. In *The Beard,* the Kid and Jean Harlow indulge in a repetitive dialogue which seems to reveal an obscene dance with death as each figure strips off both clothes and ego defenses until the male and female are joined. McClure's new Adam and Eve, the Kid and Harlow, create a new Eden in which, like the conclusion of *The Blossom,* the flesh is resurrected, and the human is at one with Nature.

We have, of course, traveled a great distance from Billy's chaste courtship in Vidor's film to his oral sex with Harlow in McClure's play, just as Michael Ondaatje's description of a hen straddling a man shot by the Kid and heaving a "red and blue vein" out of his neck is very different from the polite deaths recorded in earlier films and poems. As we have seen, Spicer's poem created the poet as outlaw persona in order to explore the process of creating a poem,

where McClure's Kid—however much he personifies an instinctual id, a visionary seer, or a killer—was an avatar of the artist whose vision would regenerate society by "murdering" its repressive aspects to allow freedom in all forms
to exist.

In Ondaatje's *Collected Works,* however, we experience both the outlaw as
artist and the artist as outlaw in the process of discovering what is to my
mind the most significant publication in the Kid's bibliography. The title of
Ondaatje's work indicates the outlaw as artist motif, for it is Billy's creative
efforts that we read as we proceed through the narrative as it moves from his
capture at Stinking Springs to his death in Pete Maxwell's bedroom. The Kid
is an outlaw not only because he is a killer, but because he is a poet who
perceives reality in a manner different from those around him. As Ondaatje's
Kid says,

> the others, I know, did not see the wounds appearing in the sky,
> in the air. Sometimes a normal forehead in front of me leaked brain
> gasses. Once a nose clogged right before me, a lock of skin formed
> over the nostrils, and the shocked face had to start breathing through
> mouth, but then the mustache bound itself in the lower teeth and
> he began to gasp loud the hah! hah! going strong—churned onto
> the floor, collapsed out, seeming in the end to be breathing out
> his eye—tiny needle jets of air reaching into the throat. I told no
> one. [14]

The Kid is an artist and a killer, and here, as in Spicer's poem, the dialectic
of death and life, destruction and creation, defines the Kid's narrative. Ondaatje
solves the problem of both history's and photography's concentration on exte-
riors quite simply by creating the Kid from the inside out, by filtering experiences through the Kid's consciousness. We do not, finally, *overhear* the Kid
at the moment of his death, but *experience* the Kid's death in his own words.

The Collected Works is the longest and richest of the poetic treatments of the
Kid, and to do justice to it here is impossible. [15] Yet one way of understanding Ondaatje's creation is by considering it as a fuller treatment of the problem Spicer confronts in his poem. That is, *The Collected Works,* like Spicer's
poem, in its general outline moves from an announcement of the Kid's death
(in the second entry Ondaatje's Kid tells us "Pat Garrett / sliced off my head")
through an increasing sense of pain and loneliness as the Kid and the poem
approach an end. Yet like Spicer's poem, the tragic awareness of the Kid's
(and the poem's) inevitable end is tempered by the Kid's life after death in
legend, and by the poem's affirmation of the artist's continuing vitality. In
short, the fiction of the Kid as artist is controlled by the overarching fiction
of the artist Ondaatje as outlaw, as the poet whose works, like the Kid's collected works, live on in the present. Ondaatje suggests this reading because

on *The Collected Works'* last page that blank square for the Kid's photograph has been filled in with a photograph of the poet as a boy in a cowboy outfit.

All of the poems and dramas discussed here—to some degree—employ the Kid as an avatar of the poet-artist who murders reality in the process of creating poetic forms. All accept and begin with the fact of the Kid's death, and thus are outlaw poems not only because they contain explicit subject matter and experimental forms, but also because they reject the idea of a hypostasized Kid as discovered in history or legend. The Kid is only known in the present, immediate moment of creation, and the fact that he can continually be recreated in the imagination is less a cause for despair than one for celebration, because it validates the poetic process. Although the poetic Kid is dead or isolated, in short, he lives again in the imagination, and it is this sense of new life that, except for Nichol's playful poem, prevents this awareness of the Kid's tragic story from falling into an ironic conception of the meaninglessness of life.

Yet as in the historian's fiction of himself as outsider, we can again recognize the tragic mode in these creations. In Spicer's, Ondaatje's, and Nichol's works we are isolated in the poet's consciousness which is alienated from tradition, history, and legend. The poem as a frontier in which the Kid can hide is a paradigm for the tragic hero's isolation from society. Regardless of how meaningful is the Kid's quest in *The Beard* to discover the color of Harlow's pubic hair, McClure's Kid exists only in a fantasy of a New Eden in eternity, and in plays that are rarely performed. Yet the fictive Kid too, no matter how often he lives again in the poet's (and ours as audience) consciousness, has tragic proportions that reinforce his isolation from society. This is of course as it should be, for the Kid as poet *perceives* differently as well as acts differently, and he is caught—like the poet—in a tragic conflict of creation and destruction, love and death. The disparity between the Kid's youth and innocence and the violent results of his experience reveals a fruitful dramatic tension we discovered earlier in Neider's novel and *The Left-Handed Gun*. As the Kid's character unravels before our eyes in Ondaatje's *The Collected Works*, we experience the tragic awareness that life and death, love and violence, are inextricably woven together:

> She is brown and lovely, the sun rim blending into lighter colors at her neck and wrists. The edge of the pillow in her mouth, her hip a mountain further down the bed. Beautiful ladies in white rooms in the morning. How do I wake her? All the awkwardness of last night with the Chisums gone, like my head is empty, scoured open by acid. My head and body open to every new wind direction, every nerve new move and smell. I look up. On the nail above the bed the black holster and gun is coiled like a snake, glinting also in the early morning white.[16]

Here is the Western version of the Fall: demanding equal time, the shadow of the gun's reality cuts across the Kid's lyrical vision of love and new possibilities of sensitivity. It is precisely because Ondaatje and the others explore this conflict in a manner so as to reveal the Kid as a human being caught in a maelstrom of biological and political circumstances—it is precisely for this reason that they demand attention far greater than their obscurity would suggest we give to them, no matter how philosophically or aesthetically puerile some of their efforts are.

To discover Ondaatje's Kid displaying such sensitivity to sight and sound is to understand how far we have traveled since the early 1950s when the Bonney-Wallace correspondence was published, since we learned the Kid was a shrewd planner, but poor speller. Ondaatje's conception of the Kid as self-conscious artist and McClure's Kid as visionary seer cannot be summarily dismissed because they are not "history." Such a judgment misses the point that these poems equally argue that "history" is not "history" because it has sought to capture the Kid's spirit in the past instead of releasing it in the present. Similarly, to describe these poems' concept of the artist as outlaw as a Romantic concept in the manner of Burns's *Saga* and to leave it at that insight, would be to narrow any understanding of what specific meanings we can learn from discussing these obscure, noncommercial poets. Whether or not one believes all these poetic efforts are mere foolishness, we can and should examine whether there is any truth in Olson's statement that the new verse reveals a "stance towards reality outside a poem as well as a new stance towards the reality of a poem itself,"[17] or McClure's statement that his dramas are "spiritual autobiographies" of their time.

There is, of course, some difficulty in shifting from these works to the cultural context in which they were produced since there is little explicit social commentary. In this sense, these obviously experimental works share the impulse of more formulaic works to displace contemporary preoccupations into the legendary past. Yet these works do reveal a stance toward external reality, and by considering the *form* of these works we can illuminate postwar society's historical experience.

As it should be clear from the quotations I have introduced above, these poets, like many of their contemporaries who write on subjects other than the Kid, reject sequential narrative, traditional meters and syntax, and formal grammatical principles. Instead of presenting ideas in a time sequence as the narrative unfolds through a rational movement from opening resolution to final statement, these poets perceive ideas in terms of space, in terms of juxtaposition rather than sequence. As we have seen, for example, the opening line of Spicer's poem presents a juxtaposition of a radio and an announcement of the Kid's death, which is of course illogical; but it serves immediately to establish his contrast of the mythic and the prosaic. McClure's *The Beard* reveals a circular repetition of dialogue resembling the rhythm of jazz in the sense that the Kid and Harlow repeat the same motifs and exchange the same lines until a variation on their established theme allows them to depart in the manner of a solo instrument. Ondaatje's *Collected Works* disguises its linear movement from Billy's capture to his death and resurrection in legend by presenting the Kid's seemingly random perceptions about animals, people, sex, and violence.

The purpose of these approaches to form is, of course, to provide a new truth about the Kid by disrupting our expectations, by removing us from an ordered world and restoring a sense of wonder. Unrestrained by logic or formal requirements of meter and rhyme, the Kid poets blur past, present, and future time and produce a kinetic, violently shifting art that forces us as readers to be alert for the changes in point of view, tone, and scene. The most helpful analogy here, I think, is that the juxtaposition of, say, "New York Jew salesman with amethyst pajamas" and the image of the Kid hiding out in a poem accomplishes the same effect as fast cutting in time and space in the cinema or in television commercials. While the disruptive nature of this style is characteristic of all contemporary art forms from action painting to the cinema, this agile, kinetic style seems most appropriate for dealing with the outlaw, for its violent manipulations of time and ideas usefully parallel the violence in the outlaw's life (and death). Violent content, in other words, is more immediately experienced in a violent, anarchic form than it would be, say, in a heroic couplet.

By breaking up a linear sequence of ideas and images the poets force us to concentrate on the uniqueness of each moment during the experience of reading the poem since we can hardly be sure where we're going—or, as is the case in the least successful works—where we've been. Instead of looking for a meaning, in short, we experience a process of becoming, a process which is not complete until the reader participates in the poem's experience. In this way, as stated earlier, art is not life, but it can reflect life's change and movement by creating an illusion of endless creation. Thus, the Kid poets deny the Kid can be entirely captured in collage or photography or the poem, and instead create the Kid during the progress of the poem by presenting as many different viewpoints as possible.

As is the case with this century's developments in art, these poems' forms suggest a world which has lost an integrating principle, whether that principle be called God or a faith in social institutions. Violence in the form of the poems—the wrenching of syntax, avoidance of grammar, and blurring of temporal and spatial distinctions—appropriately parallels the outlaw's violent world, to be sure, but it just as appropriately reflects a violent society in which the harmony of man and his cosmos is lost, and in which traditional standards that have made society cohere are deficient. The fragmentation of the Kid into these personal artistic visions thus parallels the ideological fragmentation of American society during the Vietnam and Watergate years' political and social upheavals—the years of Goldwater and McGovern, Nixon and McCarthy, Martin Luther King and Malcolm X.

The poetic visions have subversive colorings, furthermore, for in these poems there is typically a repudiation of the occidental intellectual tradition, which has placed the highest value on abstract thought and rational cognition. The Kid poets reject the idea of him being discovered as a fixed entity as well as the human ego's presumption of transcendent control over nature and substitute for the rational man one willing to see himself as a part of nature. While the rejection of traditional poetic forms may originate an artistic act, it yet discloses an ideological content as well. Whether the Kid kneels before a nude Jean Harlow (McClure), shoots himself in the back (Nichol), or kills a rabid cat hiding out under Chisum's porch (Ondaatje), his creation as an artist by a Beat poet of the late 1950s and by a countercultural poet of the late 1960s reveals in both form and content the general era's alienation from mainstream American values and institutions.

The connection we need to make here is between these poetic conceptions of the Kid and the more formulaic conceptions of the Kid in popular film, history, and literature. What we discover—whether we move from Jack Spicer's 1958 "Billy the Kid" poem to Arthur Penn's 1958 *The Left-Handed Gun* movie or from McClure's *The Beard* to the 1966 *Billy the Kid versus Dracula* film—is that the shattering of traditional forms we witnessed in the poetic conceptions of the Kid is paralleled by a breaking of the formulaic interpretations of the Kid as a romance hero or villain, a development which began when the Kid was conceived as an alienated hero defying a conformist society. The further point is that in the 1960s, the viewer of the Kid, whether he disclosed a conservative, radical, or liberal position, found the Kid a useful tool for criticizing the established direction of American mainstream institutions and values.

During the 1960s and 1970s the Kid is on the one hand interpreted as a frontier progenitor of Sirhan Sirhan (the killer of Robert Kennedy), while in another account he is conceived to be a progenitor of the admirable "cool" associated with Ian Fleming's fictional James Bond. Popular Western author Will Henry creates a fantastical short story in which the "buck-toothed weasel" Kid is guided by an allegorical figure of death named Asaph.[18] Science-fiction author Samuel Delany creates the Kid as "Bonney William" in his novel *The Einstein Intersection,* while the Western and horror movie genres are mixed in the aforementioned Dracula movie in which the Kid appears as a clean-cut, mannerly youth who, it seems, could be at home in a beach-blanket movie starring Annette Funicello. Rock musician Billy Joel composes and sings his own ballad of Billy the Kid during these years, an effort which once again resurrects the artist as outlaw theme.

Admittedly, these selected examples of references to the Kid are with few exceptions interested in the Kid only as he relates to a larger subject. Thus, to deduce a formula's combination of story form and specific cultural materials is difficult. Yet the exploitation and manipulation of the Western formula are easily apparent in the Henry story or in the novel and film which fuse different genres. Basically, this plurality of Kids in different guises and genres reflects the 1960s realization that the previous decade's notion of a homogenous, middle-class white, suburban culture as *the* American culture disguised the pluralism in American culture. The title of William O'Neill's history of the 1960s, *Coming Apart,* applies equally well to the formulaic and poetic conceptions of the Kid as both arts repudiate, distort, and exploit the received legend of the Kid as populist Robin Hood or demonic villain. The only consensus about the Kid as we move forward from his emergence as a "hero" in a tragic story which functionally related to the 1950s social criticism of a conformist society is that there is no consensus about the Kid. He might appear as a romance hero who wards off Dracula, as a tragic, isolated figure whose life symbolizes a rock musician's career, or as a countercultural hero resurrected to combat the military-industrial complex as did Abbie Hoffman. However, we can most dramatically appreciate this shattering of the Kid's meaning as an index to a fragmented American society by examining the last items I shall discuss in this chapter, the three films that featured the Kid between 1970 and 1973: *Chisum (1970), Dirty Little Billy* (1973), and *Pat Garrett and Billy the Kid* (1973).

Director Andrew McLaglen's *Chisum,* starring John Wayne, basically recreates the traditional Western formula in which a hero's legitimate violence resolves the conflict between settled, middle-class society and anarchic individualism. The movie's basic conflict is between the frontier patriarch John Chisum (Wayne) and the scheming capitalist L. G. Murphy (Forrest Tucker), who in general rustles cattle and manipulates Lincoln's legal and financial orders to sustain his lust for power. Distinctions are important, if simplistically drawn, in this movie: whereas at one point Murphy says he "owns the law," Chisum declares that he "respects the law." The Kid (Geoffrey Deuel) is not a psychological misfit or an adenoidal moron in this film, but, though he works for Tunstall and helps Chisum capture rustlers, the Kid refuses to change with the times. Chisum, in fact, sees Billy as a younger version of himself, but after the epic conquest of the rangeland and the founding of Lincoln, Chisum realizes that "justice"—not the Kid's "revenge"—is the highest value.

It is precisely how *Chisum* shows justice being reestablished in the movie, however, that allows us to recognize the process by which *Chisum* fuses the traditional Western and contemporary cultural concerns. *Chisum* basically presents the conflict between Murphy and Chisum as occurring between the arrivals of Sallie Chisum and McSween in the territory and the climactic battle at the McSween store. Although the Kid's conflict with Jesse Evans and his romantic rivalry with Pat Garrett are subsidiary narrative developments, the battle at McSween's occurs because the Kid's vengeance quest to kill Tunstall's murderers has led him to McSween's to obtain dynamite to rob Murphy's bank. While in the store, the Kid and his small gang are surrounded by a posse led by Murphy, and a battle ensues. Just as the house is set on fire, Chisum—who had been summoned by Mrs. McSween—appears to save the day by driving a herd of cattle through the streets of Lincoln. Although McSween dies, Chisum kills Murphy during a fistfight, and the Kid defeats Jesse Evans in a shootout. As the film concludes, with order and "justice" restored, Chisum returns to the hilltop overlooking his domain and surveys a reestablished kingdom. Billy, on the other hand, is last seen leaving town alone after saying his goodbyes while the flames in the McSween house dance behind him, prophesying his future hell. We know the Kid's fate is to be killed by the Pat Garrett who was last seen in this movie washing dishes and wearing an apron.

Thus *Chisum* resolves the conflict between self and society by revealing how the strong, aggressive individual's ruthless violence can preserve the community. In outline the movie thus appears to recapitulate Vidor's 1930 MGM film. However, unlike the 1930 film, the major conflict here is between two frontier aristocrats, not between an aristocrat and a group of democratic frontier pioneers. In addition, whereas Billy was the protecting Robin Hood in the Vidor film, here Chisum—a powerful, violent, proud cattle baron—is instead called in to save and protect a weak society. Whereas the society in the Vidor film was similarly in need of a protector-avenger, however, it was yet a society in the process of being founded. In *Chisum*, the houses and streets of Lincoln have a permanent look about them, society is settled, and it is weak within, instead of being assailed from without. While on the one hand *Chisum* recapitulates the fantasy of the self-reliant individual entrepreneur contributing to the good of society in the manner suggested by Andrew Carnegie's *Gospel of Wealth* (1880), it also reveals the fantasy of a benevolent father-figure stepping in to protect the little man from both the Kid's unbridled aggression and Murphy's manipulation of the social order. This need for a protector and avenger to demonstrate temporarily his superior ruthlessness and violence in support of the helpless innocent has led John Cawelti to call Westerns of this sort *"Godfather*-westerns."[19] The appropriateness of this insight is demonstrated throughout the film during scenes in which

Chisum keeps an Indian chief from being ridiculed by soldiers, allows Mexican *vaqueros* to water cattle on his land, and starts his partnership in the McSween and Tunstall store and bank in order to help the small folk avoid Murphy's monopoly.

Given Wayne's announced conservative political position during the tumult of the late 1960s, and given the fact that Richard Nixon saw *Chisum* the night before he gave his famous speech about the Charlie Manson murder trial to the American Bar Association convention in Denver,[20] it is difficult to deny that for many audiences *Chisum* displaced contemporary problems about the generation gap, the use of violence, and the erosion of respect for law and order into this legendary New Mexican story. As the credits to the film appear in the first few minutes over the paintings that recall in the manner of Remington the epic odyssey of Chisum from Texas to the Pecos Valley, the accompanying ballad's last line is a question: "Can you still keep goin' on?" The question is directed toward the America of both Chisum and the viewing audience, for during this year of the Kent State and Jackson State student shootings and of the Cambodian invasion by American troops, many wondered whether America could keep moving on. *Chisum's* solution to a frontier society's internal dissent and corruption was for the father-figure to revert to the violent aggression he had employed twenty-five years earlier to establish justice and the good society. That Chisum could see a link, however faint, between his violent desires for immediate justice and the Kid's desire for immediate revenge suggests again how both conservatives and radicals were united in their disenchantment with America's lack of direction.

This same dissatisfaction with society, whether couched in a criticism of its dehumanizing tendencies or its weakness in facing external and internal threats, is what initially unites all these films from *The Left-Handed Gun* through Peckinpah's film, as indeed such disenchantment with mainstream American forms and values unites all the concepts of the Kid in this era. Yet in director Stan Dragoti's *Dirty Little Billy,* which appeared three years after *Chisum,* we move from the romance of the benevolent patriarch to the tragic isolation of a runty Kid experiencing the squalor of frontier Kansas. In the process we also travel from a traditional affirmation of the transcendent hero whose labors establish or preserve a New World garden to an ironic contempt for any such concept based on a naive faith in the perfectibility of human nature and society. Rather than society being regenerated by the hero's violence, both society and the hero are stained by its presence. In Dragoti's film, which stars Michael Pollard as the Kid, Billy is a seventeen year old who accompanies his mother and stepfather from the New York slums to the newly-founded town of Coffeeville, Kansas. The town's hypocritical mayor convinces the family to buy land in the area, but Billy revolts against the boring routine of the farmer's life and is thrown out by his stern stepfather. The Kid soon makes friends with the town's gunslinger and a saloon girl, who separately introduce him to the pleasures of firearms and flesh. However, all three are driven out of town by a conservative element fearing that their presence would scare off potential settlers, and in an ensuing ambush the saloon girl is killed by the citizens. Billy and the gunslinger-friend escape, and, after a climactic shoot-out with some evil outlaws, leave town. Meanwhile, after the Kid's stepfather dies, his mother takes up with the town's mayor, a despicable person intent on luring new settlers with false promises of fertile soil and friendly people.

In *Dirty Little Billy* neither the Kid nor the community is particularly appealing, but, despite its artistic problems, the movie does succeed in creating an antimyth of the golden West in theme, cinematography, dialogue, and casting. The golden tones of *Chisum's* opening Remington-like scenes are here replaced by a flat, sooty sky and a flimsy town populated with people who, in the words of one reviewer, look like coal-miners. Instead of Newman's handsome appearance or Wayne's Chisum who surveys from on high his vast domain, we see a short, snot-nosed Kid traipsing through the muddy streets of a dreary Coffeeville setting. Thematically, a savage world in which towns compete for settlers and exult when disasters befall other communities is paralleled by the bestial human nature present in the outlaw leader who threatens to sodomize an admittedly unglamorous Kid.

The cynical view of the Kid and his setting which pervades *Dirty Little Billy* reveals a tragic plotting of the Kid's eventual banishment from society, but this story is more accurately a drama of despair than it is of redemption, for the nightmare of social tyranny and hypocrisy that remains after the Kid leaves is accompanied by the continuing nightmare of the Kid's tyranny of casual violence. The Kid here is not only obviously an "antiheroic" parody of the gallant Kid invention, but his departure from society after a moment of violence reveals no reconciliation or reassurance that his struggle to exist has disclosed any meaning. As unattractive as Pollard's Kid is, he yet has no tragic flaw but rather appears to be an arbitrarily chosen victim of society's meretricious desires. *Dirty Little Billy* discloses a sodden world in which virtue is betrayed, power used for profit, and progress is an illusion. Instead of being regenerated on the frontier, these settlers resurrect their previous fears and prejudices. Whereas *Chisum* suggested that we could continue "goin' on" with a dose of that old frontier aggression that purges society of evil, Dragoti's film suggests that we never went anywhere in the first place—that there is nothing to choose between New York tenements and Coffeeville frame houses.

Director Sam Peckinpah's 1973 *Pat Garrett and Billy the Kid* similarly presents a world of closing options and lost individual freedom as his Kid (Kris

Kristofferson) is destroyed by a Pat Garrett hired by Chisum and the Santa Fe Ring. That film, like Vidal's teleplay and Neider's novel, focuses on the Kid's life between Garrett's election as sheriff in the fall of 1880 and the Kid's death in the summer of 1881 after his jailbreak and capture. Thus, we again enter a tragic pattern of events which by now we know full well, and the film's cinematography primarily depicts the Kid's fall in the autumnal colors of brown, gold, and red. "Times have changed," Pat Garrett (James Coburn) tells the Kid in the film's opening minutes, but Billy replies, "Times maybe, but not me." As in *Chisum,* Garrett and the Kid respectively represent the New and the Old West, but here Pat Garrett does not at film's end wash dishes with Sallie Chisum. Rather, after shooting the Kid in the heart Garrett turns to the mirror in Pete Maxwell's bedroom and shoots his own mirror image in the heart. As the Kid lies dead on the bedroom floor, arms outstretched in a crucifixion pose, Garrett stares into the shattered mirror and realizes that while he has killed the Kid physically, he has psychologically killed himself.

The Kid's decision to remain in New Mexico and be Billy the Kid, instead of leaving for the safety of Mexico where he would be just another gringo, recalls Harvey Fergusson's 1925 statement that the Kid's tragedy was caused by his desire to live up to a fatally anachronistic, yet heroic self-concept. Billy's refusal to leave the area or conform to the New West of finance capitalism inevitably results in his death; yet his decision to remain attracts our sympathy far more than does Garrett's decision to survive and grow old by complying with the powers in Santa Fe who usher in the standardized, regimented, corporate New West. By depicting the death of the Kid's West as a symbolic death of personal freedom in America, Peckinpah appears to be restating the familiar principle that epic turns to tragedy as the individual's personal values exist in immutable conflict with the human community. Indeed, if we only examined the conclusions of *The Left-Handed Gun* and Peckinpah's film, we would think initially that the repetition of Christ imagery in the two films indicates that little has changed since 1958.

Yet *Pat Garrett and Billy the Kid,* although less interested in exploiting the traditional Western formula than *Dirty Little Billy,* shares with the latter movie a plunge from tragedy into an ironic *mythos.* In Peckinpah's film humans are captives of their environment, freedom is an illusion, and sterility is a fact of life. Unlike *Chisum,* no father-figure rides in from the hilltop to save the day, for we are at a different point in the Kid's story—we are moving into winter, not summer. Like *Dirty Little Billy, Pat Garrett and Billy the Kid* thematically illustrates essentially paralyzed figures moving through a landscape of closed possibilities, figures who ritualistically act in accordance with codes of behavior that no longer have any meaning. In one of the film's more poignant moments, the Kid accidentally meets one of Garrett's deputies eating dinner in a settler's adobe house. The Kid and Alamosa Bill (Jack Elam) break bread together, cast about for a way to avoid a confrontation that neither wants, and yet realize—as Alamosa asks for a second helping of pie—that the game which has been set in motion from afar by invisible financial powers and distant historical events must be played out—that Alamosa must die after both act out a duel in which each participant cheats, while all the time the settler in the background sets about making a coffin for the loser.

So stagnant is this world of coercion, betrayal, and cowardice that not only is Garrett controlled by the faceless Santa Fe Ring and visually framed in several scenes by barbed wire, but the Kid too is a captive of a self-concept and is visually framed by such background items as corral poles and scaffolds. It is a decayed world perfectly revealed in a scene near the film's end: as the Kid sits alone at an outdoor table in front of a Fort Sumner adobe house, a swirling wind picks up, scatters dust through the air and flaps a white tablecloth, and as Garrett and Poe begin to make the final moves of the game off-screen, and as the bronze tones of the sunset start to fade to darkness, the camera pulls away until the film's resulting grainy texture creates the scene in the manner of a pointillist. The scene objectifies the film's dramatic and thematic presentation of a decayed world, for just as the Kid is killed by forces that would deny his freedom, this bleached-out scene denies any recognition that it is the Kid sitting at the table, for his image has been dissolved into a grainy relationship of colors.

The film's turn into irony is further evident in the lengths to which Peckinpah treats the symbiotic relationship between Pat Garrett and the Kid.[21] This is not surprising, since Peckinpah worked on the screenplay of Brando's *One-Eyed Jacks,* probably the first Kid item to suggest the symbiotic relationship between the outlaw and the sheriff. Unlike Brando's film, which presented this relationship in basically external terms of moral values, here Peckinpah and screenwriter Rudolph Wurlitzer portray the Kid-Garrett conflict in psychological terms as the symbolic conflict of a divided self. As the two act out their decisions between their opening and closing meetings in Fort Sumner, we first realize that their conflict assumes proportions as a quest for identity: the Kid, restless and bored after the Lincoln County War's conclusion, cannot truly exist as the famous Kid without Garrett's dangerous pursuit; Garrett, particularly after his deal with Chisum and the Santa Fe Ring, cannot truly exist without the Kid to chase after and give his life something more than a safe, domestic existence. And as the concluding mirror scene suggests, Garrett symbolically commits suicide by shooting his mirror image in the heart, for he has just moments earlier killed the Kid in order to be free of that part of himself and his past which prevented him from fully accepting his decision to conform to the financial world's vision of the future direction of New Mexico. In this manner, Peckinpah bypasses any emphasis on the moral conflict of such abstract values as good and evil or civilization and savagism, but instead offers the Kid-Garrett historical conflict as a projection of the violence the white Anglo-Saxon superego perpetrates against the wildness within itself, which refuses to submit to the demands of time and reality. Together and yet apart, alike and yet different, the Kid and Garrett personify a unified self; their fatal confrontation, however, dramatizes a timeless battle which every human being recapitulates.

The Kid's tragedy then appears also to be Garrett's, for the sheriff's pursuit of him is also a coming to terms with himself, with the losses he has incurred both within and without as he pursues the Kid. Seen in this way, the at times excruciatingly slow pace employed by Peckinpah to show Garrett's evasive, delaying tactics while in pursuit of the Kid makes abundant sense, for Garrett should of course be reluctant both to kill and to commit a suicide, symbolic or literal. To criticize the film for its static, incestuous movement is to criticize it for not being an action Western, but this is to miss the point that in this decayed world of browns and golds there is no meaningful action except a soul's slow pursuit of and dance with death.

Besides the irony involved in the contrast between the Kid's Mona Lisa-like smile at the moment of death and Garrett's troubled stare into the shattered mirror, the final irony is that in both history and the film Garrett is murdered by the political and financial forces that hired him to kill the Kid. Peckinpah's prologue and epilogue, omitted when MGM President James Aubrey ordered cuts in the film's final shape, show Garrett dying in 1908 after he was shot from behind while he was urinating besides a desolate New Mexican road. In the film's original vision, then, the internal story of the Kid and Garrett's circular movements in the Fort Sumner area is actually a flashback by Garrett, a narrative structure which reinforces the feeling that Peckinpah originally had created a Southwestern version of the circles of Dante's *Inferno*. Whereas at the end of *The Left-Handed Gun* Garrett is admonished by his wife to come home after finalizing the Kid's tragedy, here Garrett's death twenty-seven years after his killing of the Kid reinforces the film's nihilistic sense of the world. Burns's *Saga* also concluded with a discussion of Garrett's fate, but in 1925 Burns was yet hopeful that the romantic idealism he associated with the frontier past would constitute an integral part of modern American society. By 1973, the outlaw film wrested from the hands of the outlaw director explicitly asserts that freedom is impossible and that the law serves the powerful—not the just.

Thus, the Kid's tragedy here illustrates a shift into an ironic mode, which is not surprising since this obvious repudiation of traditional Western conventions promotes, to quote Northrop Frye on the themes of irony and satire, "the sense that heroism and effective action are absent, disorganized or foredoomed to defeat, and that confusion and anarchy reign over the world. . . ."[22] According to Frye, irony arises in a time of social breakdown and corruption, a time when the capacity to believe in heroes and heroic action is destroyed by the awareness of the fractured nature of society and the duplicity of politics. The ironic impulse also predominates during "wars" against superstition, whether that superstition be defined as naive religious faith or the privilege of aristocracy—to name just two familiar superstitions in our own intellectual tradition. In this war ideas are liberated from myth, and the separation of the two leaves room for skeptical distrust of any received tradition. And to illustrate this disbelief in the heroic, ironic imagery is characteristically that of the wheel or the closed circle.

Frye's description of these general characteristics of the ironic vision which dissolves any faith in humanity's ability to comprehend the world is an apt account of the entire period of the Kid bibliography discussed in this chapter. As we have seen, the effort to wage war on the romantic legend of the Kid was primarily an effort by historians, filmmakers, writers, and dramatists to liberate the Kid from earlier myths. In doing so, the Kid was characteristically shown pursuing a futile quest, betrayed by others, and foredoomed to defeat by death or isolation. The post-1955 Kid emerged as his creators recognized a fractured society, as well as—following McCarthy's antics—the duplicity of politics. Finally, as we discovered in Neider's novel, Vidal's teleplay, and Peckinpah's film, the image of the closed circle helps us understand each work's structural reinforcement of a change-without-progress theme.

Thus it would appear that Pollard's sleazy Kid is basically a forerunner (in cinematic time) of Newman's slightly older, psychologically troubled Kid who can't read and who walks more than he rides. Thus it would appear that a more appropriate way of characterizing this era's interpretation of the Kid would be to focus totally on the appearance of an ironic vision. There is truth in this characterization, of course, for as Frye further tells us, one form of irony is "the non-heroic residue of tragedy."[23] The previous era's inclusion of a tragic sense as in Burns's *Saga* or the ballet could thus be said to have evolved into this era's ironic interpretation of the Kid.

Except for *Chisum*, however, which as we have seen recapitulates the basic outlines of the traditional Western romance story, the major interpretations of the Kid prior to *Dirty Little Billy* and Peckinpah's film are more accurately characterized by the emergence of the tragic vision for one major reason. Although any tragedy which isolates the hero from society admits a recognition of a severed world that approaches the ironic mode, tragedy is yet a drama of redemption because it ultimately offers provisional release from this divided state which defines man in the cosmos. In terms of the interpretations of the Kid during this era prior to 1973, the tragic pattern of his life avoids the fall into irony simply because, as we have seen, a renewal of life was offered in the form of a redemptive artistic imagination or a partial reassurance that in the Kid's death the community gained in wisdom. In *The Left-Handed Gun,* Pat Garrett's shooting of the Kid does not lessen our disenchantment with the movie's human community, but at least Garrett's pursuit of honor (here importantly unconnected to financial gain) is opposed to the mob's violence. In the poet's concept of the outlaw as artist, the possibility exists for endless creation beyond the closing circle of the poem's structure.

If anything, then, the partial redemption granted in these works contrasts to the visions of *Dirty Little Billy* and Peckinpah's movie, visions which reveal an ironic awareness of life's meaninglessness. Besides the mere fact of casting a relatively "unattractive" actor as the Kid and of shooting the film in dreary colors, *Dirty Little Billy* is an ironic vision in another way. By presenting the Kid's early life prior to the Lincoln County War, no tragic obsession with vengeance is present, for there is no Tunstall to be murdered. A sense of meaningful revolt is thus lost, and the movie denies any escape from the closing circle of events. As if we are in a bad dream, we cannot—unlike Spicer's poetic persona—see any honey in Billy's groin or in society's future. Similarly, in structure, theme, and cinematography, Peckinpah's film depicts not just the hero's isolation from society, but his own ironic part in ensuring his own death.

The emergence of an ironic vision of course can be traced to several factors, not the least of which is the fact that an ironic treatment of the traditional formula was basically all that was left for the Kid creator desirous of advancing a different interpretation. Yet I think the presence here in 1973 of an ironic impulse to negate heroic action is due to more than a revolt against past superstitions. By 1973 events such as the Watergate coverup, the bombing of North Vietnam, and the invasions of Laos and Cambodia seemed to underline the vanished dream of sixties reform movements. That a law-and-order administration subverted the American political and legal process by engaging in unlawful acts, and that multinational corporations attempted to bribe foreign governments certainly revealed political duplicity. That reform groups had splintered into vocal and sometimes violent groups, and that we were fighting a war abroad at the same time we were wounded within certainly reflected a fractured society. That by 1973 Nixon's tactics reminded many of McCarthy only validated many audiences' pessimistic belief that we were returning to the same in the form of the different.

To be sure, all the conditions sufficient for a nihilistic viewpoint to appear had been present since the earlier tragic interpretations of the Kid anticipated the criticisms of an often repressive, certainly directionless American society that would surface in the turbulent 1960s. Yet by 1973 a tragic awareness of a severed world could be said to have shifted into irony, for the prophetic hopes for a better world had been dashed by the kind of overbearing ruthlessness that Wayne's Chisum demonstrated in responding to his era's corruption. By 1973, Michael McClure's prophetic hopes for a return to a Blakean sense of cosmic wonder, which had crystallized in his use of the Kid as visionary seer, relinquished the field, so to speak, to Nichol's ironic presentation of the Kid as a joke, as a disposable outlaw "born with a short dick" who died because he "snuck up on himself & shot himself from behind the grocery store." It is in this context that we can understand how Peckinpah's casting of Kristofferson and Bob Dylan (as Alias), two contemporary musicians and songwriters, invites us to draw explicit comparisons between the death of the Kid's West and the contemporary American scene. "The law's a funny thing," says Peckinpah's Kid as the 1881 world of finance capitalism and the 1973 world of the Watergate affair were confirming this very point.

The end of innocence, idealism, and optimistic hopes of eternal regeneration is an inevitable event in any person's as well as nation's life, perhaps, but the fact that this transition from the Kid's world of youthful freedom to Garrett's world of responsible maturity—the fact that this transition occurs at this time in the mode of irony rather than of romance or even a redemptive tragedy reveals how the dissolution of the Kid's heroic stance as victim or avenger parallels what Jack Nachbar has called the shattering of the basic Western formula, and—by extension—the shattering of the myth of a homogenous, unified American society.[24] As we travel in this era from the tragic opacity of the world in *The Left-Handed Gun* to the ironic, broken world of Peckinpah's film, we discover that it becomes increasingly harder to displace into the legendary past Garrett's troubled stare into Pete Maxwell's bedroom mirror, a stare that symbolically reveals the decline of a competitive culture whose century of violence against the Kid has become by 1973 disassociated from any ethical actions holding out hope for a future progressive society.

PART THREE

Understanding the Outlaw and His Interpreters

There was nothing at the edge of the river
But dry grass and cotton candy.
"Alias," I said to him. "Alias,
Somebody there makes us want to drink the river
Somebody wants to thirst us."
"Kid," he said. "No river
Wants to trap men. There ain't no malice in it. Try
to understand."

—Jack Spicer, *Billy the Kid,* 1958

7   Clio's Bastard Son

Understanding the
Kid's Interpreters,
1881–1981

The discovery of the West, then, has depended much on the
discoverer, who may only find what he looks for, or, failing that,
nothing at all. Few discoverers have come ready to respond to
whatever is there, or to what we now find there: most come with
some notion of what they want, and with very little interest in the
rest.
                         —Earl Pomeroy, "Rediscovering the West," 1960

. . . the gunman is Clio's bastard.
                    —Gary L. Roberts, "The West's Gunmen," 1971

The ironic vision, as Northrop Frye has suggested in his *Anatomy of Criticism*,
paradoxically and inevitably clears the way for a return to a mythopoeic vision
of experience. Since 1973, however, no major film, television show, novel,
or biography devoted to the Kid's life and death has appeared to offer any
vision of experience—ironic or otherwise. Although both the James-Younger
gang and the Dalton gang have been in recent years the subject of major
motion pictures and at least one serious novel, the Kid's only noteworthy
national publicity occurred in the early weeks of 1981 when a truckdriver
successfully stole the Kid's granite tombstone from Fort Sumner and transported it to California before he was arrested. While there have been two
recent plays written about the Kid, and while the Kid ballet has been revived
by such companies as Ballet West, interest in the Kid—at least until the

centennial summer of 1981—has been limited since 1973 to his brief appearances in books and anthologies dealing with such larger subjects as the Western outlaw, the westering experience in American history, and the American attitude toward violence. Still, even though the Kid has become in recent years subordinate to such comprehensive topics, the point is that since the ironic visions of the Kid which appeared in the 1973 films by Sam Peckinpah and Stan Dragoti, the Kid bibliography has been dominated by contributions that return again to a preoccupation with distinguishing history and legend.

One of the chief characteristics of the Kid's bibliography is the lack of attention given him by interpreters trained to discover, evaluate, and interpret evidence. Instead, the gunman, whether he be the Kid or Jesse James, has been interpreted by journalists, novelists, folklorists, friends, enemies, psychologists, and—to use a term popularized by Ramon Adams—"rocking-chair historians." As a result of such attention, the bibliography of an outlaw like the Kid has become notable for its other chief characteristics: its "monumental size," its frequent "grade school Grand Guignol" achievements, and its verbal in-fighting as generations of revisionists have challenged the Kid and his interpreters.[1] Just as Pat Garrett, for example, attempted in 1881 to revise the dime novels' visions of the Kid, and just as Walter Noble Burns in 1926 attempted to revise previous accounts by using previously-neglected sources, so too the general tenor of the works since 1973 which mention the Kid has been to revise our understanding of the Kid's historical record by revealing the false assumptions of previous interpreters and by viewing the Kid as an understandable phenomenon in the legend-making process. This development metaphorically resembles a hell of enclosing circles precisely because such books and anthologies have repeated old errors of fact, have contributed new errors of fact, and have passed off totally imagined incidents as authentic biography to an audience willing to trust the words *true, authentic,* and *real* in the title.

Published by such houses as Time-Life and Reader's Digest, and written by such authors as Harry Sinclair Drago, Richard Elman, Carl Breihan, and James D. Horan, these publications since 1973 attempt among other things to get at the "real" Billy the Kid and to reduce him from demigod to human being.[2] These authors concentrate on exposing the errors of past interpretations and on assuring us—sometimes in Olympian tones—that what we have before us is at long last the way it was in the past. While their efforts do not present the Kid's love affairs in the heated manner of the 1950s male adventure magazines, their efforts do at times lead us again toward a box canyon in our quest to understand the Kid as a real historical personage. Breihan, for example, reproduces Garrett's version of events and adds that the Kid dangled Morton and Baker's corpses from a tree as a warning to the Dolan crowd;

Drago, furthermore, adds a new number (eighteen) to the list of men killed by the Kid, and repeats the Garrett explanation of the Kid's jailbreak. *The Gunfighters,* one volume in Time-Life's widely publicized series on the old West, has the Kid killed on 13 July 1881, and resurrects the story of Mrs. McSween's playing the piano—accompanied by her black servant on violin—while her house burns to the ground. Finally, Elman briefly reproduces Koop and Mullin's research into the Kid's boyhood, but then offers the standard legendary treatment about such other events as the Kid's escape from the burning McSween house.[3]

While Horan's books are well-written and organized, and serve to publish documents and illustrations for audiences much larger and much less devoted than, say, the *aficionados* who read the small-circulation *Brand Books* and scholarly journals, his efforts concisely summarize the assumptions and problems implicit in the popular historiography of the Kid not only since 1973, but also since the end of World War II. When we examine a typical Horan production—*The Great American West* or *The Authentic Wild West: The Gunfighters*—we discover an attractive, well-intentioned package of photographs, actual correspondence between participants in the account, newspaper stories, and numerous government documents. In the Kid's case, for example, we are presented the text of the Lew Wallace-William Bonney correspondence, the text of Judge Frank Angel's report to Secretary of the Interior Carl Schurz, and the transcript of the Kid's testimony at Dudley's court-martial hearing. In Horan's introductory statements we probably feel patronized, perhaps guilty, for believing various legendary stories for so long, but we feel assured that at last we shall discover what the gunfighters, especially the Kid, *really were.* In these texts we discover a narrative thread that attempts to place the reader at the scene of events, and which moves entertainingly from scene to scene, and document to document. We also discover, given our wide reading in Bonneyana, that this same narrative commits occasional errors of fact—the siege at McSween's house, for instance, is said to have lasted *nine* days.

The serious reader could conceivably fault the author for such an error but the point of this, after all, is that we criticize and revise in order to understand, or at least point the way to understanding. Such factual errors aside, what we value in the pages of Horan's books—and also Ramon Adam's statements—is the documents, the collected evidence in photography and prose. The implied notion is that the historian's task is to get back to the documents and let them tell the story, which will then emerge only if and when the historian refuses to intrude his own presence and rhetoric. Yet the problem is that this notion asks us to believe that the mere accumulation of details will inevitably add up to history—as if letters produced letters, newspapers produced litters of little newspapers, and six-shooters spawned families of little derringers.[4] The problem remains that in attempts to pierce the fog of mythology and the armor of legend there is nevertheless little evidence of the historical imagination probing, assimilating, synthesizing, and reconstructing the Kid and his world. What is interesting about the Kid's bibliography, of course, is that such a problem is not solely the province of the Kid's interpreters since 1973. Given the explosion of Bonneyana in the popular culture media after the Kid's death, an explosion which immediately made him Clio's bastard, we understand why a mistrust of the human imagination and a faith in the documents became embedded in the Kid's bibliography.

Establishing a history of the Kid, and even a history of the Kid's images, is not easy because of the sway of the Kid's interpreters' major preoccupation: the separation of history from legend, reality from myth, and truth from fiction. Even though the task of defining reality is problematic at best, the Kid's interpreters have generally assumed that the "real" Kid as he "really was" in the historical field can be captured and defined, and that his legend can be put to death in the process of defining the true Kid. The assumptions underlying this endeavor are not troublesome in themselves—indeed, any interpreter of the past would find it difficult to proceed in his investigation without the faith that past reality can be reconstructed. Certainly in our own time Rasch, Mullin, Koop and others have proceeded with the faith and have successfully reconstructed portions of the Kid's biography.

Before mustering a chronological range of examples from the bibliography to illustrate the preoccupations with distinguishing history from myth, let me illustrate some common notions about the issue by quoting a passage from the foreword to William Brent's *The Complete and Factual Life of Billy the Kid:*

> Therefore, with this wealth of information at hand, as well as careful study made of Billy Bonney over the years, a painstaking and straightforward story, without bias or prejudice, will be attempted here, free from hokum, melodrama, or highly exaggerated scenes or situations, since the story of Billy Bonney needs none such. His own short life and events he was a part of, were dramatic enough, without any frills or window dressing at all. It will be as honest as the writer can possibly make it.[5]

Besides the characteristic declaration of honesty and the devotion to careful research, we notice here an insistence on the mutually exclusive nature of history and legend, of "life" and "window dressing." Whereas an authentic life reveals the presence of careful observation and the presentation of facts gleaned from research or actual experiences, legend reveals the presence of bias, melodrama, prejudice, and exaggeration. Besides Brent's patronizing tone toward those other interpreters who have been the prey of that wild beast "hokum," we also notice the Puritan-like mistrust of rhetoric ("frills"), and an insistence instead on a plain, straightforward, no-nonsense style: the altar of historical truth needs no polishing.

A wariness about reality and language pervades the Kid's bibliography, regardless of the image of the Kid or the work's publication date. Numerous prefaces and forewords invariably invoke the Muses. One early dime novel assured its audience that there was no need for melodrama in accounts of the Kid for his *true* history "eclipses any border romance, and dims by comparison the tales woven from the realms of fiction." Just as Garrett in his introduction distinguishes truth from fiction to justify his authority as an oracle of truth, so too does Charlie Siringo inform his audience that his is "a true and unvarnished history of 'Billy the Kid'." In *Pardner of the Wind* Jack Thorp acknowledges that "it is hard, maybe impossible, to separate the truth about him from the falsehood, the facts from the fiction. However, that is what I've tried to do." In 1960 Ramon Adams complains in his *A Fitting Death for Billy the Kid* that it is highly unpleasant for a "lover of truth" to witness "truth smothered by legend," because "after all is said and done, an ounce of truth is worth a pound of legend." A few years later in his study of the Western gunfighter, Joseph Rosa similarly declared that "when we seek the truth about the gunfighter as a man, myth must be distinguished from reality. . . . " And in recent years Marshall Fishwick and Kent Steckmesser have written books on the American hero and the Western hero concerned with distinguishing myth from reality or history from legend. Finally, as an indication of this preoccupation and the tone that invariably accompanies it, we should consider one recent author's statement lamenting truth's unfortunate demise: "She [truth] is, indeed, long since dead, shot down by the blazing guns of Wild Bill Hickock, Wyatt Earp, Bat Masterson, Billy the Kid, and a dozen others, and her corpse lies moldering somewhere on the Great Plains, in an unmarked grave."[6]

Throughout the bibliography interpreters have staunchly claimed truth and history were on their side, and these same interpreters have generally believed in one correct manner to relate their observations—although the discrepancy between thought and action has foiled many an author. Early in the bibliography the *Authentic Life* indicated the proper way to confront the task: " . . . make no pretension to literary ability, but propose to give to the public in intelligible English, 'round, unvarnished tale,' unadorned with superfluous verbiage."[7] A similar disclaimer to literary talent was offered in 1899 by Annie D. Tallent, who claimed her story was "a simple relation of facts expressed in plain, homely diction, without the slightest attempt at rhetorical embellishment."[8] A few years later in 1907 Nat Love, better known perhaps as "Deadwood Dick," affirmed his aim "to record events simply as they are, without attempting to varnish over the bad spots or draw on my imagination."[9]

The conventional assumptions about language and rhetoric made in these early accounts were repeated by later observers bent on distinguishing myth from reality and the fake Kid from the real Kid. Regardless of the image of the Kid offered, regardless of the literary talent displayed, and regardless of the "truth" value presented, observers appealed to their audience's trust by claiming to present *unvarnished* narratives that were *unencrusted* with tall tales and *unadorned* with literary embellishment. On the other hand, observers conveniently criticized other accounts of the Kid which were invariably marked by exaggerated events that disguised the truth which lay like the Sphinx behind, beneath, or below the observer's language. From Pat Garrett to the present we can trace the familiar notion that style or rhetoric is merely a surface decoration, a thin veneer or layer of varnish coating the solid wood of historical facts. The writer's supposed object was to keep this stylistic varnish clear and thin so the accumulated facts could reveal their story—as well as their transparent claims to historical truth.

The spatial metaphors employed in the above quotations encourage as well as reveal a firm distinction between the realms of history and legend, and of content and style. From Emerson Hough to James Horan a continual preoccupation is to keep these components on separate levels and erect a firm boundary fence between them. Such an effort, however well-intentioned, reveals the presence of what we can label a positivist view of human knowledge and the historian's enterprise, a view which aims to subdue the role of imagination and the role of language so that historical statements can move closer to the firm ground of actuality. In this view the only authentic basis for human knowledge is data apprehended by the senses, and the only possible meaningful statements are those that can be empirically verified. Historical accounts or scientific reports, then, are ideally inductive presentations of clearly-stated, logical positions, which are based on discovered facts. Truth in history is achieved when such statements correspond to the observable facts of the external world; historical untruth occurs when statements are not logical, or distort the self-evident facts, or do not correspond to any known facts.[10]

With this view of human knowledge it becomes highly important that our encounter with sensory data be presented in a "pure" language. If we as observers can prevent our language from becoming tainted by emotional concerns and stylistic considerations, then a clear and presumably more accurate view of the external world will be achieved; however, if our language is clouded with ideological concerns, ambiguous symbols, and rhetorical flourishes, then our polluted language will offer us an incomplete, frustrating, and inaccurate view of the external world. In this view language is analogous to a window-pane between the viewer and the external reality: if the pane is clear, so too will be what we see; if the pane is cloudy then so too will our perceptions be distorted. As Ramon Adams and others have stated, we must remove the window dressing so the real Billy the Kid will be available to our view.

Given these assumptions, the implications for the interpreter of the past are clear. Since facts are assumed to be independent entities lying around in the external world waiting to be found, the interpreter must discover these bundles of things labeled "facts" by striving to be free of the distortions that have troubled other observers of the same landscape. Just as the interpreter must cleanse himself of personal concerns in his search for facts, so he must also cleanse his language of figurative devices and faithfully transmit what the facts reveal. The investigator willing to learn the sense of the past, then, is a finder and a recorder, not a creator and an interpreter. Unlike the house of fiction, which according to Henry James has many windows to accommo-date its many viewers, the house of history in this view should ideally need only one, presumably large, window, since observers of the same external landscape who use an unvarnished language which corresponds to the observ-able facts of the landscape—these observers should all see the same view be-cause only one Billy the Kid is outside that window. One could conceivably discover the truth about him since that truth is independent of the observer and is only waiting to be discovered by the proper accumulation of facts and the neutral transmission of such facts. In this view, in short, Burns is easily dismissed for his stylistic flourishes, and the *Authentic Life* criticized for its fanciful elaboration of the Kid's early life.

It is only by discovering the pervasiveness of this view in the historiography and by pointing out the inherent problems of this rigidly dualistic separation of mind and reality that we can draw closer to our destination of a history of the Kid or a history of the Kid's meaning in America. If the assumption concerning the presuppositions of the Kid's interpreters is sound, then sev-eral difficulties immediately become apparent. In the first place, it becomes very difficult, as we have already seen, to distinguish history from legend— "hokum" from the "real" thing—when every contributor to the Kid bibliog-raphy customarily avows his love of truth and his efforts, finally, to present that truth. After all, it becomes difficult to define the truth when it has been anything but clear what the facts are and whom it is we are observing. Fur-thermore, what is a fact to one observer is often irrelevant to another: to say Burns's interviews with Sallie Chisum are not historical and that Rasch's use of census statistics is historical is basically to state an ideological preference for the solid statistics and to disregard that Burns's methodologies offer their own kinds of historical truths. After all, as I have stated above in conjunction with Horan's books, facts or documents or statistics may offer a view into history but they do not alone offer history.[11]

Another problem with the Kid's interpreters' chief preoccupation concerns the desire for a pure language uncluttered with emotions, symbols, or politics. How are we to design, much less agree on the fundamentals of such an observation language without throwing away words and yearning, like Bertrand Russell and Alfred North Whitehead, for the so-called certainty of mathematical logic? As others have stated, simply to say that one is plainly detailing reality or truth does not reveal reality or truth, but rather reveals an assertion about reality or truth.[12] This is a problem because the Kid's interpreters, regardless of their stated intentions, possess as human beings living in specific ambiences their own perspectives, which serve to distort the historical field in their own personal manner. No matter how plainly-written, no historical narrative duplicates reality. One may believe that the Kid was an adenoidal moron on the basis of one's discovery of facts and one's belief that he has narrated those facts in a plain style, but such statements actually reveal little about the Kid and more about the observer. One may impute the Kid's movements in real life to "Fate" or "Destiny," but such abstractions have little to do either with empirical facts or with an unvarnished style. And even when we make these obvious critical statements about journalists, hack-writers, and cowboy-authors, can we actually expect any interpreter—professional historian or otherwise—to efface his presence completely and to devise a language untainted by the tinge of personality or symbol?[13]

The most important problem associated with the major preoccupations of the Kid's interpreters, however, has to do with the role assigned to or adopted by the interpreters of the past. As we have seen, in this view the interpreter needs only to discover the facts that exist out there in the world and to transmit those facts in statements that correspond to empirical data. Such a view appears plausible, indeed harmless, but it is ultimately coercive, for the interpreter is required to submit himself to the facts, and to consider his language as an *ex post facto* expression of the facts. Such a role possesses a built-in disparagement of the interpreter and his task: it neglects the dynamic nature of the historical field in a search for a static, absolute truth. It further declares the interpreter to be irrelevant, and it ultimately shortchanges the subject of historical investigation due to its focus on finding the right language to present the facts. For when we ask what makes the Kid *real,* or when we seek to discover the truth about the Kid, can we discover those answers by amassing merely the facts about his kind of six-shooter? the number of men he has killed? his testimony in court? And, to extend the questions, does the constant preoccupation with revising inaccurate facts in others' accounts allow us to draw nearer to the Kid's reality? It would appear to be more to the point to recognize that the tallying of all the disparate facts might tell us something about the Kid but will not give us any explanation of the Kid's existence unless the framer of the facts draws out the implicit and explicit meanings of the welter of events and constructs a narrative that—however much it corresponds to the facts—possesses the flavor, the texture of actual persons, places, and events in a particular historical field. Can we not also add that as long as interpreters focus on cleaning the windowpane of others' grimy fingerprints, the Billy the Kid who existed in the historical record as a human being with thoughts and fears—this Billy the Kid will remain as elusive as ever, will remain Clio's bastard?

Agreement with the above assertions and questions does not necessitate a lapse into historical solipsism—the belief that one can never escape the mind and know the past—but rather entails a recognition of more recent thought concerning the nature of knowledge, language, and, for our purposes, the historian's role. An epistemology different from that of the positivists, one influenced by recent developments in cultural anthropology, cognitive psychology, and the philosophies of science and history, has pointed out the implausibility of viewing the human mind as ontologically distinct from any material reality existing in the external world.[14] Instead of distinguishing the external world from the viewer, this epistemology asserts that what we know as reality is created and maintained in a complex interplay of mind, environment, and community; in other words, instead of a distinction between internal and external worlds, we should consider this relationship as a transaction. Reality in this view is not a constant given but is a dynamic human construction conditioned by the individual's habits, expectations, culture, and education.

What is important for our purposes is that the emphasis on a transactional interplay of mind, environment, and community allows us to view myth and legend not as distortions or perversions of the truth—but rather as in fact different forms of reality and different forms of truth. As E. H. Gombrich, Hayden White, and others have argued, our perceptions of the environment are all "distortions" of the phenomenal field because all of us, according to our innate expectations and learned cultural traditions, choose to include or exclude objects in the field of perception, to put certain objects in the foreground or background, to assign some events as causes and others as effects, and to juxtapose or disjoin some events in the field of perception. Whereas one viewer, for instance, posits the Kid's boyhood spent on the lawless frontier as the cause for his violent acts, another might emphasize the Kid's yearning for a father figure like Tunstall as the motivating force behind the Kid's actions. The point is not that one explanation is more true, but that each explanation offers a different truth using the same data, that each, in short, distorts the field to tell a story. Because we all see what we know as individuals in a cultural context, there can be no innocent eye, ear, or language.

The implications of these assumptions for the Kid's interpreters are enormous and serve to remove the notion of the historian's task that pervades the Kid's bibliography. In the first place, if reality can be considered a transaction between mind, environment, and community, then the interpreter of the Kid is not subservient to any data but is rather a participant in the creation of his evidence. Since facts are no longer conceived as pre-existing things that only need to be found, the interpreter cannot be a mere finder, but is rather a maker who endows the perceptual field of potential "facts" with significance. Third, the interpreter's narrative presentation of his facts can no longer be expected to correspond to external reality; rather, the narrative is "the structure of a particular mode of thought and rendered expression," a symbolic structure mediating between events as known by evidence and the possible plot structures a culture employs to make sense of them. [15]

With these different assumptions it becomes meaningless to criticize Burns or any of the old-timers for not making their narratives reflect reality, for that reality, that one Billy the Kid, eludes a final definition; it is now more to the point to discover the kinds of truth offered or concealed within each narrative and to understand how the cultural context and the individual have shaped or been shaped by that vision. Furthermore, we can now realize that the historian's style, regardless of any consciously-stated intentions, is always indissolubly linked to its content, and thus provides an index of both the writer's individual preoccupations and his cultural tradition: what one says is bound up with how one says it. The question becomes not whether Ramon Adams' style is more truthful than Walter Noble Burns's style; rather, the question is why, at that particular time, each author's stylistic techniques gained a following.

Given these conclusions, we can return to the Kid's bibliography and detail emerging possibilities for further study of the Kid. We can conclude, for instance, that an author's sole preoccupation with criticizing previous error-prone interpreters has become as trivialized as any of the stereotypes about the Kid as noble bandit or adenoidal moron. Such criticism has often constituted an end in itself and has yet to offer a means to understanding the Kid in his own historical context or to understanding the images of the Kid in our own historical context. The question to address now, in other words, is not who the Kid was or how a book like Burns's *Saga* distorted the historical record, but why and how it succeeded in establishing itself as the standard biography, and under what conditions its explanation of the Kid would fail to satisfy an audience and thus give way to a different image of the Kid.

We can also conclude that the Kid's interpreters' preoccupations with separating history from legend, a preoccupation which simplifies human cognition and the nature of language, has created a sense of the past reality, but has not yet reconstructed that past reality in its entirety in any published work. As a result, we have seen separate articles informing us of the Kid's real name and the real number of men he killed, but we have had few conceptions of the Kid that understand more than such elementary human motivation as one laughs when one is happy and one scowls when one is angry. For all the accumulated biographical details that have come to light in the past quarter-century, the Kid's interpreters have offered him, particularly since 1973, as an inarticulate Clint Eastwood-type movie character or as a nonentity who can be found in the reproduced facts. It is not that these visions are untruthful, it is rather than these visions are incomplete.

I agree with J. Frank Dobie that the *Trial and Death of Socrates* is a more important document than all the books on Billy the Kid,[16] but I also believe that the elements of the Kid's life, his trial and his death, have their own kind of importance that has eluded his interpreters. And the absence of this perspective should have nothing to do with whether the writer is a professor or a cowboy. For the interpreter of the Kid to become, in Joseph Conrad's words, "the preserver, the keeper, the expounder of human experience,"[15] he or she must refuse to be sidetracked into quarrels over historical errata, and refuse to distrust the imagination's role in creating history. In the final analysis it will take all the resources of the interpreter's imagination to perceive the network of relationships that exists within and among the evidence unearthed by Burns, Rasch, Koop, Keleher, and Mullin, and to see the Kid as something other than a bundle of reflexes or a terrible speller. In short, I am assuming it will take the interpreter who cannot only perceive the Kid as a human consciousness in his own historical context, but who is also, in Américo Castro's words, "willing and able to enter into the living consciousness of others through the door of his own life and consciousness—that is to say, he must dedicate his sense of life (and of being alive) to the lives of others."[18] In this manner, the Kid interpreter can offer a perspective on both the past and the present, for understanding the Kid in a frontier environment of sagebrush and six-shooters is only the first step in discovering the Kid's existence in the century's worth of hearts and minds.[19]

If we are not preoccupied with distinguishing legend from history, and if we realize that the quest for the definitive Billy the Kid is fruitless, then we can examine the ideas and images of the Kid as they are and attempt to understand their significance as indices of the changing preoccupations of the Kid's observers and audience. Whereas before it was important to describe and identify who the Kid was, and to criticize those who did not have a clue to who he was, now it is important to address why we have seen him in a certain way at a certain time, and to account for how the changing perceptions of the Kid relate to a specific cultural context. In essence, this shift from identification questions (who is he?) to epistemological questions (why have we seen him this way?) is possible whenever we consider two points: that legend and myth are forms of reality; that historical interpretation is the provisional agreement of an audience to select one of several possible competing accounts because that particular manner of presentation more completely satisfies an audience's moral and aesthetic desires. Thus, we can examine the predominance of a certain image of the Kid not for what it disguises about the Kid's historical presence, but for what it reveals about the interpreter, his audience, and his cultural context.

At various junctures in the Kid's bibliography observers have realized that legends about the Kid are as central to an understanding of his appeal as any so-called objective history, and that the importance of the Kid is revealed in the "seer" and not just the "seen." Maurice Fulton, for instance, concluded that the Kid's "true significance lies in the legendary figure into which the American people have chosen to make him."[20] In *Pardner of the Wind*, Jack Thorp believed the legend's phenomenal growth was the result of our efforts "to make him fit the role according to the way we'd like to have him be," and that the growth of his legend "might shed light on the deification of certain other 'heroes' in our modern world, such as Adolph [Hitler] of Berchtesgaden and John Dillinger."[21] In his efforts to debunk the image of the violent Wild West, Peter Lyon imagined the Kid as a kind of western Rorschach ink blot: "the face is blank, but it comes complete with a Handy-Do-It-Yourself Kit so that the features may be easily filled in."[22]

Besides seeing the Kid as fulfilling the needs of his viewers, others have accepted myths and legends as inevitable components in the Kid's bibliography and, consequently, have thought them worthy of serious study. Because of the natural confusion of fact and legend, and because of legend's universal appeal to humans, Kent Steckmesser stated that "to ignore legends simply because they are by definition historically unfounded is an error which too many professional historians have made. Legends are of great importance in any interpretation of our national past."[23] In his study of the gunmen's historiography, Gary L. Roberts concluded that "what people believe to be true is often as important as reality. It may, in fact, be part of the truth . . . the myth must be understood and appreciated—not for its gross distortions of history but as a reflection of American aspirations, ideals, and traditions."[24] The point here is that while Roberts and Steckmesser are as interested in discovering the reality of the historical Kid, they are, unlike Ramon Adams,

refreshingly willing to acknowledge and not disparage the inevitable importance of how we have interpreted the Kid in the century since his death.[25]

Although these comments point us in the right direction toward a study of
the images of the Kid as clues to American popular attitudes, they have not
yet resulted in such a study because of certain assumptions implicit in these
comments. It is one thing, for example, to view the Kid's significance as
residing in the popular creation of a legendary figure; it is quite another thing
to see that creation as a dynamic process and not as a static condition. Fulton
takes the initial step in accepting the invented Kid's importance, but then,
having assumed the Kid's legendary figure as a given, devotes his attention
to how Hough's accounts of the Kid have varied from the facts of the Wallace-
Bonney correspondence and thus reveal Garrett's personal influence. In effect,
Fulton's method is similar to those who also wish to distinguish history from
legend, but the difference is that whereas others have traditionally assumed the
historical figure as a given and have thus examined the legendary deviations
from this figure, Fulton reverses this perspective by examining the deviations from the legendary Kid as established by Garrett-Upson. The changes in
the legendary figure as well as the context in which Hough wrote his accounts
are ignored because Fulton assumes that we accept the legend's importance
and the legend itself as outside of time.

It is one thing, furthermore, to say that the images of the Kid fit our needs
and reflect our aspirations; it is quite another thing to specify what those
needs and aspirations were at a given time, and to recognize the interplay of
social and aesthetic concerns in a particular cultural context. Whereas Fulton
was interested in the Kid's legendary figure as a constant, Thorp and Lyon
assume that the aspirations reflected in images of the Kid are both self-evident
and constant. The point is that such aspirations have never been grounded in
a specific context. We can easily say that the Kid's endurance in our imagination is due to a characteristically American preoccupation with the relationship of the individual to society, but this leads us to a minimal distance into
the permutations of the theme in specific accounts of the Kid, into examples
of this theme in a context of the popular Western, and into examples of this
theme's predominance in a larger popular context. Without such an exploration, in other words, our naming a theme is as limited as our labelling the
Kid as a "saint" or "satan" and not asking why each image was popular at a
certain time. This view that images reflect aspirations also posits a simple
determinism—aspirations condition image—and fails to consider the possible impact of image upon aspiration. It is not just, for instance, that the
cultural context shaped the image, but that an image of the Kid, say the Kid
in the 1930 MGM movie, also shaped or changed aspirations of future Kid
interpreters. The further point is that perhaps the Kid himself shaped his

own life so as to conform to the growing legend of his exploits, to a self-concept which turned out to be fatal.

Finally, let me preface my own discussion of these interpreters who have indicated the proper direction for study, but who have not started the journey for various reasons of interest and format, by referring to Steckmesser's study *The Western Hero in History and Legend.* In this study Steckmesser devotes one section to the Kid, and in that section he identifies the contrasting manner in which audiences have shaped the Kid into a saint or satan before he concludes that the Kid is an American Robin Hood. Throughout this section his strategy is to document the growth of legendary accounts of the Kid, accounts which possess an "inherent social truth." All this is well and good, yet it appears that what Steckmesser is doing with the legend is similar to what previous interpreters were doing with the history. That is, whereas earlier interpreters were intent, as we have seen, on examining the bibliography and sorting the material into the categories "fact" and "fiction," Steckmesser divides the legend into the camps of "saint" and "satan."

Although others have been disturbed by the blurring of distinctions between these extremes, we might at this point criticize him for desiring to inform us how people made the Kid, and yet neglecting to place those visions of the Kid into a historical context. That is, Steckmesser's main interest appears rather to be to trace the growth of the legend through two separate traditions. Yet those traditions, although given dates to mark their origins, are not ultimately related to any historical context, and the parallels or relationships between his traditions and the popular Western and the popular culture in general are not studied. Still, this problem is no doubt explained by Steckmesser's larger focus on the Western hero, a focus that also includes a study of Hickock, Custer, and Carson. It is also explained by the fact that Steckmesser, writing in the early 1960s, was himself a part of a cultural context, one which was more receptive to the kind of initial problem he set out to solve in his research.

In the process of discovering the Kid and his legend from their own scholarly perspectives, if interpreters like Steckmesser and others mentioned have indicated the first step in discovering the Kid's significance, then this study inevitably builds on their earlier work. That the present study of the Kid addresses a different problem, or attempts to fulfill others' directions for future study, indicates again that the work springs from a different cultural milieu than its predecessors. Even if the purpose here were to distinguish history from legend in the manner of earlier interpreters, this study would reveal the striations of recent cultural preoccupations. For, as our experiences of the 1960s and the Watergate coverup have taught us, objectivity is a pose—not a reality.

I have sought to complete the step that Steckmesser initiated by recognizing the dynamic changes in the images of the Kid, and by speculating on the functional relationship between a cultural context and a particular image. While this is not any clearly superior ontological stance to assume, it does represent a different position in terms of the Kid's bibliography, one that reveals different truths about the Kid, his interpreters, and his American audiences in the years since his death.

Throughout this study I have assumed that images and ideas of the Kid are not autonomous or exist only in the mind, but that the invented Kids are strategies for coping with certain situations, strategies which reveal—not simply reflect—an encounter between an individual and cultural and historical tradition. I have assumed, in other words, that we must examine our invented Kids not simply to discover what he was but to discover how a particular observer in a particular era using a particular medium explained the Kid. I would maintain that such an examination will offer a sense of the Kid's existence and legend that is far richer than any survey of adjectives that have been applied to the Kid. Thus, the task has been not just to identify, say, Burns's image of the Kid as that of a "saintly" school, but also to understand this image's emergence, its acceptance, its relationship to other events, the eventual strains upon its usefulness as an explanation, and its ultimate failure as a dominant explanation form for events in the historical field. I contend that, just as one observer has said of the larger Western historical experience, in discovering the Kid in this manner we discover ourselves. Perhaps by understanding the Kid and his interpreters in this manner we can also, like Peckinpah's *Pat Garrett and Billy the Kid,* pave the way for visions of the Kid that break out of the constraints of traditional preoccupations.

8 *Vamos a Ver* and the Outlaw Figure

A Conclusion

"Vamos a ver." It was a good old Mexican saying he had made his own. We are going to see. He would have to wait and see. He might have to wait a long time.
—Harvey Fergusson, *The Conquest of Don Pedro*, 1954

" . . . today you are very perspicacious, Santo."
"Maybe. But I feel perfectly all right, Alley."
"It will catch you up later in the day, Santo."
"Vamos a ver."
"What's that?"
"We shall see, Alley, what we shall see."
—William Eastlake, *The Bronc People*, 1958

In the 1930 MGM *Billy the Kid,* Wallace Beery's amiable Pat Garrett figure purposely misses shooting the Kid (Johnny Mack Brown) fleeing on horseback at the film's end and thus allows the Kid to escape into a new life across the border. In the 1941 remake of *Billy the Kid,* however, Brian Donlevy's combination Garrett-McSween figure shoots a more sinister Kid (Robert Taylor) who—after killing the villain who both murdered his parents and defrauded the U.S. Army—draws wrong-handed and meets death with a smile on his face. In the 1958 *The Left-Handed Gun,* John Dehner's Garrett returns home a troubled man after shooting the Kid (Paul Newman), a psychologically-troubled outlaw who had drawn on his empty holster after betraying his own inflexible sense of justice. In Michael Ondaatje's imaginative *The Collected Works of Billy the Kid* (1970), Pat Garrett, crouching near Pete Maxwell's bed and barely suppressing a laugh as he hears the Kid's excited questions, shoots the Kid from such close range that the explosion both leaves "a powder scar on Maxwell's face that stayed with him all his life" and drives the Kid backward into a bedroom wall—where he dies slumped against the wall and with one arm dangling through a broken windowpane.[1] And in Sam Peckinpah's 1973 *Pat Garrett and Billy the Kid,* James Coburn's Garrett, after spending a sleepless night in Maxwell's porch swing as others prepared the Kid for burial, departs from Fort Sumner a victorious, yet spent man, and—in an ironic reversal of such cinematic Westerns as *Shane*—is pelted in the back by a rock thrown by an unadmiring youth.

However one ultimately explains the events of that July 1881 night in Pete Maxwell's place—whether one sees the closing circle of Destiny or the pure caprice of Chance—Garrett in both history and the cinematic and poetic interpretations of history lived to see another day. Yet what he in his own life came to see and what we indeed have seen in our own lives were that, following the Kid's death in 1881, Garrett—like Ondaatje's Maxwell—acquired a scar that stayed with him the rest of his life. For as Garrett lived out his life and watched his dreams fade and his plans go awry, the Kid, of course, became "America's immortal legend" because, as Garrett's most recent biographer states, "more movies, books, and magazine articles have featured him than any other frontier figure."[2] The continuing irony present in the Kid bibliography, of course, is that Garrett himself ensured the Kid's life after death in legend by authorizing Ash Upson to write *The Authentic Life of Billy, the Kid* in 1882. Unlike the Kid, Garrett did not awake the morning after his death by betrayal in 1908 and—to use another Ondaatje image—wash the nicotine out of his mouth and inhale the lingering smell of gunsmoke in his burned shirtfront. Unlike the Kid's, Garrett's death would not occur in circumstances that could lead an old-timer like "Brushy Bill" Roberts to claim to be the real Pat Garrett.

Just as Peckinpah in 1973 realized that Garrett's ironic fate made him the more dramatically interesting figure, so too a few years earlier a poet imaginatively captured an aging Garrett reflecting upon the Kid's resurrection in a legend that has eclipsed any of the brief fame accorded Garrett after his shooting of the Kid. In "Lines To Be Spoken By Pat Garrett, When Older," Ramona Week's Garrett soliloquizes on the outlaw who, as it turns out, "can hold his breath longer than light in summer":

> you ferry back on the wave
> lengths of cowardly rainbows.
> They have chipped your headstone
> to pieces. You rise out of the
> pieces: a hero coming home
> to the land he lost, a winner,

spinning a smoking pistol,
a beautiful, cardboard sinner.

a caricature of a badman:
William Bonney mixed up with
Prince Charlie: and both of you rowing
over the foam of Jordan
and talking about time and places.[3]

As this Pat Garrett realizes in these lines, the Kid defeats death and evades the underworld in a manner analogous to a classical figure who returns from Hades after first ferrying across the river Styx with Charon, the infernal ferryman of dead souls. Unlike Orpheus, however, the Kid does not look back and lose his dream, for the classical river Styx becomes in the next stanza the river of life that supports this "caricature of a badman," who is both combined and confused in the imagination with a bonny Prince Charlie (the dual connotation of the phrase "mixed up with").

Whether we say the Kid still rides or the Kid still rises out of the chips of his tombstone like a Southwestern Lazarus, the question as to *why* the Kid has become "America's immortal legend" has interested numerous observers since 1881. In 1908, for example, William Macleod Raine was "moved to wonder that among so many superlative ruffians one so young could have achieved preeminence." "What was there about this killer of men, this pariah of society, this product of Bowery slum and Western lawlessness," asked J. Frank Dobie in 1929, "that has made him the object of such wide and undimming interest?" In 1952 Marshall Fishwick argued that indictments of the Kid as an adenoidal farm boy don't "explain why Billy remains the most fascinating bad man in American history, and the basis of a whole series of legends and shrines." And from a larger perspective, another observer has wondered in recent years what it is about *all* outlaws, not just the Kid, "that makes everybody say it's wrong, yet . . . eat it up in pulp magazines, comics, movies, television, and radio scripts?"[4]

However the questions are phrased, those doing the asking are essentially interested in understanding reasons for the Kid's popularity, the legend's endurance, and the purposes the legend has served for its creators and consumers. Thus, to simplify the matter, we ask such questions as these: Why was the Kid singled out for notoriety instead of other "superlative ruffians" of his time and place? Why has the Kid's legend endured for at least a century and appealed to international audiences? Exploring such questions should increase our understanding of the phenomenon known as Billy the Kid. Such an exploration, furthermore, will also move us toward a fitting conclusion to this study, because examining such questions inevitably leads us into a summary of the relationships the visions of the Kid have borne to their cultural contexts.

To understand why the Kid and not an outlaw like Jesse Evans became the pre-eminent outlaw of New Mexico and, in the eyes of some observers, of the American West, we need first to examine historical circumstances at the close of the nineteenth century, and then discuss certain personality traits, both real and imagined, which observers discovered in the Kid during the first period of his bibliography.

Both Jesse Evans's and the Kid's activities as outlaws at the close of the nineteenth century lend credence to Eric Hobsbawm's belief, as he states in his *Primitive Rebels,* that episodes of banditry seem most likely to occur when a traditional social equilibrium is upset "during and after periods of abnormal hardship, such as famine or wars, or at the moments when the jaws of the dynamic modern world seize the static communities in order to destroy and transform them."[5] Thus, Hobsbawm further argues, banditry reveals the crisis and tension within a society resistant to the rise of new social and economic structures. The most famous American outlaws—the Kid, Jesse James, and the Daltons—emerged in the disruptive period following the Civil War, in which political and economic dislocations coincided with the emergence of an urban-industrial world, a development which eroded and transformed familiar ways of life in rural America. In New Mexico, where the Kid acted out his life and death as an outlaw, Anglos like John Chisum and J. J. Dolan personified the new economic order that was transforming a familiar Spanish way of life; in New York, where the Kid was apotheosized immediately after his death, the modern financial world in the form of trusts and holding companies was transforming America's market economy.

Both Harvey Fergusson and Walter Noble Burns believed the Kid's importance resided in the fact that he was a symbolic figure of a vanished agrarian era in American history. According to Fergusson, the Kid "was the key figure of an epoch—the primitive pastoral epoch in the history of the West, which began after the Civil War and ended with the completion of the first trans-continental railroads in the early eighties."[6] For Burns, the Kid's life and death symbolized "a transitional period in American history. His life closed the past; his death opened the present."[7] Although these statements written in the mid-1920s accurately reflect a familiar idea about the reason for the legendary Kid's endurance, they are of interest in the first place because the sentiments here recapitulate a theme newspapers elaborated on at the time of the Kid's death. Second, by realizing that Burns's and Fergusson's statements were written after a period of social disruption caused by World War I, we can also understand that just as the Kid rose to prominence during the turbulent period of the Lincoln County War and after the disruptions of the Civil War, so too his revival in the 1920s occurred when a traditional social equilibrium was upset and when doubts were being expressed about the direction of American society in the modern world.

There have been numerous bandits and outlaws in American history, of course, just as there have been frequent periods of social disruption and abnormal hardship. If Hobsbawm's observations help us understand why outlaws like the Kid and Jesse James appeared when they did and proceeded to attract the sympathies of dispossessed social groups, we need to consider further why it happens that the outlaws of this era—rather than, say, the outlaws of an earlier era—dominate the American pantheon of outlaws. Here we can be more specific about the historical circumstances that not only produced outlaws but popular ones like the Kid and Jesse James.

If such outlaws were ultimately considered to be defiant opponents of the dynamic, modern world's destruction of a rural agrarian epoch, the very audience they appealed to was one created out of the social and technological changes occurring after the Civil War. In the first place, following the Civil War great numbers of rural Americans and foreign immigrants entered American cities in search of employment, and in the process created new urban markets for reading entertainment. Between 1865 and 1900, furthermore, with the spread of public primary and then secondary schools, the percentage of people in America who could read was higher than ever before. The industrial revolution, which spawned an urban America at the close of the last century, also transformed the printing and publishing industry. As a result of these changes, more people who could read were living closer to one another, which meant that more reading entertainment was sought by larger audiences. Unlike outlaws who operated before the Civil War, in short, the Kid and his colleagues appeared at the right time in American history: more Americans who could read of an outlaw's exploits did so because their stories filled such widely-circulating and inexpensive publications as the penny newspapers, the dime novels, and *The National Police Gazette.*

Even with greater numbers of available readers and with more efficient methods for meeting the readers' interests, the Kid and other outlaws would still not have made the nearly immediate transition from regional folk figures to national figures had it not been that the outlaws' activities occurred when the nation was intensely interested in Western happenings. The outlaw, in short, rose to prominence as part of the West's rise to prominence.

That the American West held great importance at the close of the nineteenth century was the result of several factors. The very railroads and telegraphs that signalled the end of a primitive agrarian epoch facilitated travel and communications in the West, and travelers' diaries and journals detailing Western adventures among Mormons, Indians, grizzly bears, and desperadoes regularly graced the pages of Eastern newspapers and periodicals. Historical romances and masculine adventure stories set in Western landscapes regularly became popular books. Several commercial magazines—*Outing, Overland Monthly, Cosmopolitan,* and *Harper's*—regularly published Western material by Owen Wister, Frederick Remington, and Emerson Hough. And at the same time the West was a prominent feature of the era's print media, Buffalo Bill Cody's Wild West Show was introducing one version of the Western experience to both national and foreign audiences.

The rise of the West and the Western story to cultural significance can be traced to several psychological and sociological factors. As several scholars have demonstrated, the West—whether in the writings of Mark Twain and Owen Wister or in the paintings of Remington and J. N. Marchand—appealed to great numbers of Americans at the close of the nineteenth century because it offered a spiritual landscape of freedom into which urban man could imagine himself, like Huckleberry Finn, "lighting out" for, when the constraints of civilization became too overwhelming.[8] Along with this psychological appeal of the West as an avenue of vicarious escape, the story of the West emerged as a subject of cultural significance because it was identified as America's unique national epic. At the close of the century, with this epic apparently drawn to a close when the continent was settled, numerous observers speculated about America's future as a modern urban-industrial world power as they simultaneously were attempting to define America in relation to its recent frontier achievements. Just as outlaws flourished during periods of economic and social transition, so too the West and the Western story rose to significance as America was in transition to a new social and economic order. Defining the West became for many an important task for not only educating newly-arrived immigrants, but also for defining the qualities America and Americans would need to confront the challenges of a "new" frontier.

The Kid's popularity at the close of the nineteenth century was inextricably linked with such historical circumstances. In the first place, the West's emergence as a source of entertainment and as subject for cultural commentary meant that Western happenings would be scrutinized; the development of the telegraph and cheap printing techniques, along with an increasing literacy rate, meant that more frequent and cheaper publications reached more readers. The Kid's emergence as a notorious outlaw, then, can be explained partially by the fact that he operated in the right place at the right time and appealed to the right constituency. As Robert N. Mullin and Charles E. Welch have argued recently, "by a twist of fortune Billy's death and some of his exploits, real and imagined, happened to receive almost country-wide publicity, while the deeds and misdeeds of others were . . . reported only regionally."[9] In the second place, if this "twist of fortune" usefully explains why the Kid was, unlike Jesse Evans, an immediate sensation at the time of his death, examining the era's historical context further enables us to understand that after an initial flurry of publicity had passed, the Kid was later revived in this century's first decade as observers like Hough and William

Macleod Raine attempted to explain the significance of the frontier in American history to a country enduring an identity crisis.

Nevertheless, whether we believe "fortune" and the industrial revolution conspired to create notorious outlaws like the Kid and Jesse James, and whether we believe the century-long fascination with romantic heroes made historical outlaws interesting subject matter, we can understand more precisely why "fortune" favored the Kid's cause by turning to discuss the Kid's real and imagined personal characteristics. "Fortune" certainly favored the Kid by publicizing his deadly deeds, to be sure; yet "fortune" at the close of the last century was not just an abstract concept, but was, in the Kid's case, represented by the newspaper writers and editors who realized, perhaps unconsciously, that the Kid's deeds and demeanor made better copy than did the deeds and demeanor of a Jesse Evans or Dave Rudabaugh. In J. Frank Dobie's estimation, for instance, the Kid's legendary growth from folk to popular hero occurred because the Kid was anything but an ordinary killer, thief, or leech on society. Rather, according to Dobie,

> He was an *uncommon* killer, he was an *uncommon* thief. He had something in him that has called to the imagination not only of writers but of the people at large. He was indisputably *brave* and he was, in his own sphere, absolutely supreme. In preserving his own life and in taking the lives of his hunters he was a sheer *genius*. He was as single-minded in this business and as economical as Napoleon; hence his hard way with the dying Charlie Bowdre. He was probably the *quickest and surest man on the trigger* anywhere south or west of Wild Bill Hickock. His *nerve* never broke; his *alertness* never flagged. He had extraordinary *personal magnetism,* for without personal magnetism a mere boy could never have led and held in check a gang of hard, seasoned men. He *controlled himself* as well as he controlled others; never impetuous, he deliberated every act, every robbery, every murder. Although revengeful, he was *generous hearted* . . . and, being generous hearted, he had a certain winsome carefreeness. Above all, he possessed to an unusual degree what Mirabeau finely called *'the art of daring.'*[10] [emphasis added]

I have quoted Dobie at length here because his statement summarizes the personal qualities numerous observers have highlighted to distinguish the Kid from other outlaws of his time and place. Regardless of the observer's overall image and idea of the Kid, ever since the newspaper accounts of the Lincoln County War the Kid has been noted for his charisma, generosity, resourcefulness, bravery, determination, composure, and superior marksmanship and equitation. Through the years since his death, of course, the list has expanded to include the Kid's sense of humor, talents as a dancer and a lover, loyalty to his friends, and his honorable methods in treating enemies. Indeed, both the

Kid's laughter in the face of death and his practical jokes, when combined with the romantic New Mexican setting, have attracted numerous favorable comments since 1881 by those put off by Jesse James's grim pose.

Dobie's statement, however, betrays the fact it was written during the 1920s' transformation of the Kid into a romance hero, for omitted here are the assertions about the Kid that characteristically appeared at the time of his death and served to widen his publicity: that the Kid was the worst outlaw in the history of crime; that the Kid had killed a man for every year of his life. Thus, even though Dobie's statement accurately identifies common notions about the reasons for the Kid's continuing appeal, we need to examine more closely what that "something" was in the Kid's life and deeds which "called to the imagination" of both writers and the general public. As we saw in this study's third chapter, when the Kid died, not everyone was as willing as Dobie to accord him such generous attributes; nevertheless, even the most vehement of the Kid's enemies could not deny the Kid possessed both charisma and the "art of daring." Unlike the Kid, Jesse Evans made no dramatic escape from jail only days before his execution; unlike the Kid, Dave Rudabaugh made no daring escape from a burning house by running a gauntlet of gunfire. Simply stated, the Kid was dramatic in his life and death. Besides his escapes from such precarious circumstances, furthermore, the Kid, unlike outlaws like Clay Allison, did not become respectable, and later die after falling off a wagon loaded with firewood; unlike Dave Rudabaugh, the Kid did not fade into insignificance by leaving the territory or adopting a disguise.

Besides this dramatic quality inherent in the Kid's life and death, his emergence as a notorious national figure was the result of other personal attributes—and his nickname. Unlike Rudabaugh, and to some extent Jesse Evans, the Kid intrigued people because he combined youthful innocence and deadly skills. This most ruthless of desperadoes who supposedly killed a man for every year of his short life, this "outlaw in knickerbockers" who possessed small hands and feet, a high voice, and "the genial apologetic smile of an amiable cherub"—this outlaw learned the art of killing while his contemporaries were still learning the art of reading. We can speculate further that another reason the Kid attracted the attention of the local press, and in turn the national press who reprinted regional events, was the fact that the Kid's most famous names—Billy the Kid; William Bonney—possessed what we can call, for the lack of a better term, a talismanic appeal that was certainly lacking in many other outlaws' names. One wonders, in short, whether the Kid would have been as popular a figure if he had been given or had adopted a more prosaic name. As the Canadian poet bp Nichol wondered in his *The True Eventual Story of Billy the Kid* (1970), would the Kid even have bothered having a fast gun if he had been named "billy the man or bloody bonney?"[11]

In general, the Kid emerged as a notorious figure of national significance at the close of the nineteenth century because his exploits were publicized by both a regional and a national press. Just why this publicity occurred can of course be ascribed to fortune or chance, but we should not underestimate the appeal of the Kid's dramatic escapes, his combination of youthful innocence and deadly experience, and his name. In addition, the Kid's activities between 1876 and his death in 1881 were confined—except for a few side trips to old Tascosa in the Texas panhandle—to a localized area, a factor which no doubt intensified his recognition. Beyond this point, however, we can also understand that the Kid would have remained a regional figure except for the fact that technological advance in communication and publishing during America's industrial revolution meant that his real or imagined exploits could be transmitted quickly and cheaply. Because at this time the West was of considerable cultural significance as both popular historical romance and as subject for cultural commentary, events in the West like the Kid's death served an educational purpose because they seemingly provided reassuring evidence that the past achievements of subjugating a stubborn, recalcitrant wilderness would be duplicated in the future cause of American history.

If this discussion of the Kid's historical context and dramatic personal qualities enables us to understand more clearly why the Kid, unlike Jesse Evans, gained such notoriety at the time of his death, our next task is to understand why the Kid has endured so long after the frontier has closed, so long after his audience had entered the automobile age and the atomic age and had forgotten what the "border shift" was. If the sensationalism inherent in the popular acceptance of the Kid's twenty-one men for twenty-one years formula has reverted to the commonplace as we in this century have whittled away his actual death total and have witnessed a succession of more sensational crimes and criminals, what accounts for his appeal in the popular imagination?

Of course, certain elements present in the Kid's real and imagined deeds and demeanor created his notoriety at the time of his death and also served to sustain it for years after the headlines announcing the news of his death had yellowed with the old newsprint. The "art of daring" which Dobie saw as central to the Kid's appeal prompted him to suggest that "because his daring apotheosized youth—youth in the saddle—youth with a flaming gun—and because his daring kept him running and balancing on the edge of a frightful precipice . . . Billy the Kid will always be interesting, will always appeal to the popular imagination."[12] The Kid as a symbolic figure of an agrarian epoch has continued to appeal to several commentators who through the years have voiced the nostalgia for a pre-industrial America that we also have seen in Burns's and Fergusson's statements. In addition, the Kid's youthfulness and deadliness have persistently attracted the attention of observers who have attempted throughout this century to understand America's youth culture and America's violence. The Western experience has been continually defined and reinterpreted through the years—so that even the words *lawman* and *desperado* occasionally designate designer blue jeans—and the Kid, as part of that Western experience, has also been redefined and reinterpreted.

Practically speaking, the Kid's legend has been sustained because of two other circumstances. In the first place, certain authors and filmmakers have introduced and reintroduced the Kid to national audiences greatly different in both taste and sophistication. No matter what the dramatic quality of his life, and no matter what the historical context, the Kid would not have endured had artists like Burns, Arthur Penn, Sam Peckinpah, and Michael Ondaatje not revitalized the Kid from time to time and saved him from the fate of the Catfish Kid. In the second place, the Kid's popularity is a natural consequence of the controversy surrounding his life and death. If for the moment we refrain from concentrating on the Kid's image as it has developed and changed through the years, we can see that the Kid's early friendship with Pat Garrett, and Garrett's apparent violation of an unwritten Western code that says a man does not shoot another in the dark without warning, have endowed the Kid's bibliography with controversy as numerous contributors through the years have argued over Garrett's actions. These contentions over the manner of the Kid's death, furthermore, extend to several other events in his life, including of course the controversial question asked through the years about whether Garrett actually did kill the Kid in 1881. And, as we saw in the earlier chapters to this study, controversy still surrounds the Kid's date of birth, his father's identity, his actions at several key points in his life, and his exact burial site.

Such obvious responses to the question of the Kid's enduring appeal, however, do not take us very far into an understanding of this problem, for controversy and the extensive reprintings of, say, Charlie Siringo's *A Texas Cowboy* (1885) don't alone explain the Kid's durability in popular culture. Besides the fact that he has attracted the interest of a succession of talented artists, and besides the fact that controversy has sustained his appeal, the Kid has endured because his story has been told in the universal pattern of the quest romance and because his story has appeared in a variety of media from books to ballet. Along with these factors, however, we can understand that the Kid has also endured because visions of the Kid have fulfilled certain strategic purposes for his creators and their audiences. As we have seen throughout this study, such visions cannot be visions of the actual Kid, whoever that was; instead, visions of the actual Kid have been visions filtered through certain sociological and psychological preoccupations.

As we saw in the second chapter, when the Kid's historiographers turned to examine his appeal and his legend's growth, they characteristically explained the Kid's endurance in legend by means of a "need" theory. That is, the Kid as outlaw figure persisted because his life and death were shaped in such a way as to satisfy the need of the moment. Thus, as Jack Thorp stated in 1945, the facts of the Kid's life "have been distorted to make him fit the role according to the way we'd like to have him be." Maurice G. Fulton in 1950 believed the Kid's true significance resided in "the legendary figure into which the American people have chosen to make him." Similarly, another observer believed the Kid's appeal was explained by the fact that he emerges as "a figure freshly refurbished so as to embody the hero who appropriately symbolized the *need* of the hour: brutal killer, avenging angel, mama's boy, slayer of capitalist dragons, bewildered cat's paw, or gay, gallant, carefree cowpoke."[13]

All this is true enough, and the "need" theory enables us to understand how the visions of the Kid appear as strategies for encompassing given cultural situations. We should not be surprised either that the Kid has been susceptible to a variety of interpretations since needs obviously have changed as the Kid's creators have changed. Yet the point is, as C. L. Sonnichsen has stated in regard to the Western's enduring popularity, "everybody is aware that the western is responding to a basic need, but nobody tells us exactly what that need is."[14] In our context, observers have correctly understood that the Kid's image has changed through the years, but they have proceeded to describe that image alone—not the need being satisfied by that image. In addition, it is doubtful if an awareness of an image alone can give us a reliable indicator of a particular need in a particular context, for the Kid's image invariably appears within the context of a larger narrative structure and an implied mode of argument. By solely focusing on the Kid's image in the legend, furthermore, we might be and have been led into making simplistic generalizations about the relationship of image to need, and we might, as is the case with criticism of Garrett's *Authentic Life*, simplify the meaning of the Kid.

By understanding that the Kid's enduring appeal in the popular imagination is linked, along with the other previously-mentioned factors, with the purposes the visions of the Kid have served, we can broaden our inquiry into the problem by examining more specifically what needs or purposes the visions have satisfied. A convenient entry into this problem is provided by Emmett Dalton, the last surviving member of the Dalton gang. Writing in 1931 near the end of his prison term, Dalton was particularly perplexed by the American public's seeming love-hate relationship with its outlaws and criminals. Wondering why the outlaw was both venerated and yet hated, Dalton considered whether the outlaw was famous "because he symbolizes the undying anarchy in the heart of every man."[15] At the same time, Dalton further noted, the outlaw invariably emerges as "the hero of democracy," while men like Pat Garrett are typically distrusted by the public. Like the Kid's observers, Dalton is not entirely specific about how to define the outlaw's appeal or how to understand the public's satisfaction in his failures. Nevertheless, his focus on man's "undying anarchy" and on the outlaw's uncommon defense of the common man points us in the right direction for understanding the Kid's appeal. Dalton's questions and tentative answers, however briefly stated, suggest that the outlaw endures because he satisfies both timeless psychological needs and timely sociological preoccupations. The outlaw, in other words, could be said to endure because his meaning changes to fit the specific needs of the hour, and because his meaning paradoxically does not change but rather satisfies a basic psychological need.

To understand how the visions of the Kid satisfy basic human psychological needs, we must explore what purposes his role as a conventional outlaw figure serves. The Kid's endurance in our own time and in the future, in other words, is and will be due to the thematic elements he shares in common with other notable outlaw figures from other times and other countries. I might have suggested earlier that the Kid's emergence as a national celebrity of dubious morals at the time of his death was because the mystery of his birthplace and his early life invited attention. I think, however, that the very "open" quality of the Kid's birth, life, and death more accurately helps us understand reasons for his endurance, rather than his immediate reception as a notorious desperado. When the Kid was revitalized in the 1920s as old-timers began to talk and as Burns publicized the Kid's oral legend, the mysterious nature of the Kid's existence allowed for several competing visions of the outlaw to coexist without damaging the Kid's basic shape as a noble bandit.

The major motifs or thematic elements of this tradition are familiar to us because they have been associated with outlaws since the time of Robin Hood.[16] In general, this outlaw tradition supports a vision of the person as the people's champion, as their deliverer of justice and righter of wrongs. This outlaw's career in crime typically begins at an early age when the youth is persecuted by society or provoked into violence to avenge an insult or attack on a friend. As a result of this initial crime, the outlaw departs from society and characteristically undergoes a test of survival in the wilderness. During his subsequent career as an outlaw, the outlaw becomes identified as a man of the people and fulfills his sense of justice by robbing from the rich and giving to the dispossessed members of society. Because of such actions—as well as an admiration of the outlaw's skills, gallantry, and audacity—society in turn protects the outlaw from discovery. Due to his own native skills and to such protection, the outlaw avoids capture by conventional means; however, the outlaw eventually (in this tradition) is betrayed by a friend or a lover, is killed, and is mourned by his followers.

Both real and imagined events in the Kid's career approximate these basic motifs, but an elaboration of them is not our purpose here. By understanding the outlines of this tradition, however, we realize that the major reasons offered for the Kid's appeal—his youth, bravery, fight for a just cause, gallantry in defense of the weak, and his final betrayal—all comprise individual elements of this basic outlaw tradition, which transcends national boundaries and temporal restrictions. This fact alone perhaps accounts for the Kid's endurance, since the Kid—like Robin Hood, Jesse James, and Ned Kelly (Australia)—is eventually recognized as, to use Burns's description of this outlaw type, "a heroic outlaw endowed with every noble quality fighting the battle of the common people against the tyranny of wealth and power."[17]

Yet it is important here to recognize that this outlaw tradition apparently requires that the forces of an oppressive society be punished and that the outlaw be betrayed and killed. The outlaw hero who endures in our culture, in other words, endures as both the deliverer and the defeated: what we come to see is that the outlaw only succeeds as he fails. We have with this recognition in a sense returned to Dalton's musings about the public's love-hate relationship with its outlaw heroes—yet until we noted the basic motifs of the heroic outlaw tradition we could not understand the essential correctness of his discussion. Thus, as usual, an opening query leads to further ones: if we can explain the Kid's enduring appeal at least in part to be the result of his legend's similarity to a basic folk outlaw tradition, and if this tradition demands both the outlaw's services and his death, how are we to understand what psychological needs this conventional outlaw figure fulfills?

One way to approach this question is to consider this dialectic of success and failure as related to the apparently basic human need for an intensely exciting, unpredictable world and for an ordered, secure, routine world. These two opposing human needs have been described by Harry Berger in this manner:

> Man has two primal needs. First is a need for order, peace, and security, for protection against the terror or confusion of life, for a familiar and predictable world, and for a life which is happily more of the same. . . . But the second primal impulse is contrary to the first: man positively needs anxiety and uncertainty, thrives on confusion and risk, wants trouble, tension, jeopardy, novelty, mystery, would be lost without enemies, is sometimes happiest when most miserable.[18]

John Cawelti has employed this dynamic tension existing in man's need both for a flight from ennui and for a quest for order to illustrate the appeal of formulaic literature, which offers a high degree of excitement and unpredictability within an ordered world of familiar narrative structures. I would suggest that a conventional outlaw figure like the Kid synthesizes this conflict of primal impulses in the human psyche. That is, in the outlaw's successes as a delivering champion we experience a satisfying escape from the ordered, everyday world; in the outlaw's death by betrayal, however, we find satisfied our desire for an ordered, everyday world in which danger, risk, and threats to stability remain controlled. As a personification of what Dalton called the "undying anarchy in the heart of every man," the outlaw entrances and thrills us with his unrestrained self-assertion; yet what Dalton did not consider was that part of the heart of man requires the outlaw's defeat in fantasy as well as reality to satisfy a human desire for order.

Just why the outlaw figure in his basic conventional tradition must fail can, of course, be explained in Marxist as well as Freudian terms, but I think we can best understand the outlaw figure's psychological appeal as both deliverer and defeated hero by making an analogy to the tragic hero. According to Maud Bodkin in her discussion of classical tragedy in *Archetypal Patterns in Poetry*,

> The experience of tragic drama both gives in the figure of the hero
> an objective form to the self of imaginative aspiration, or to the
> power-craving, and also, through the hero's death, satisfies the
> counter movement of feeling toward the surrender of personal
> claims and the merging of the ego within a greater power—the
> 'community consciousness.'[19]

To make an analogy between the outlaw and the classical tragic hero is not an entirely whimsical act, for like the tragic hero the outlaw is isolated from society and, for better or worse, similarly indulges in unlimited self-expression before ultimately succumbing to defeat. The archetypal pattern of the conventional outlaw hero legend, in short, corresponds to the pattern of tragedy in that both organize the human tendencies of self-assertion and submission. In both dramas the individual's escape into the world of unlimited self-assertion is countered by the self's submission to the community or to destiny, a submission objectified in the hero's defeat or death.

On one level both the outlaw hero and the classical tragic hero must ultimately die in order for the community to exist in the present and to anticipate the future. Nevertheless, perhaps even more significant is the possibility that as audiences of each hero's drama we accept the hero's ultimate downfall because as individuals who realize a prosaic, limited existence we could not live with ourselves if the outlaw or tragic hero succeeded in realizing his dream of making reality match his desires. If the Kid had succeeded in his quest, his very existence would mock those of us who through the years have failed to defy the boundaries imposed on us by time and the environment. The Kid who saves a Mexican woman from the evil designs of Apaches and who yet in story after story falls before Garrett's revolver—this Kid endures in our imaginations as a Southwestern Prometheus whose reward for bringing fire to humankind was suffering. What we come to see in our own experience of *vamos a ver* is that we need the outlaw, yet we are unsure as to whether we can live with him, with any protagonist who confronts us with the reality of total freedom, violence—and death.

When we discover Emmett Dalton's puzzled inquiry into the reasons for the public's love-hate relationship with its outlaws—an inquiry all the more powerful since this aging representative of outlaw freedom contemplates this problem while enduring a life behind bars—we realize that the old childhood dreams of belonging to a band of brothers, to a community of sympathetic spirits, will not fade away or lurch off into the sunset with our advance into maturity. We seemingly desire to know all about the outlaw hero because he is, for a brief moment, imagined to be more alive and more vivid than the common man. Thinking about his escapades, his efficient and meaningless use of violence, and of course his certain death, we experience for a time the unthinkable, perhaps the undoable, and realize in fantasy what it must feel like to range unimpeded throughout the world. By understanding the outlaw's extravagance and wastefulness, by realizing the extremes of pity and fear as we marvel at his disregard for life and as we are yet repelled by his senselessly violent ethic, we discover the outlaw's drama endures because it is in a very important sense our drama of awareness, our drama of discovering also the completed arc of freedom and destiny, of love and death, long before our flesh wears out.

The conventional outlaw hero's fulfillment of such basic psychological needs allows us to understand one reason for the Kid's continuing appeal as a timeless figure of youthful daring. The basic appeal of the outlaw hero as a symbolic figure of escape is of course familiar, but in the above discussion I attempted to suggest that implicit in the outlaw's heroic pattern is a recognition of his ultimate destiny. Thus, I have suggested that this hero, like the classical tragic hero, endures because he objectifies not only the human desire to abolish any obstacles to the free self but also the human acceptance of the limitations imposed on the free self by time and the environment. If the outlaw hero is successful only as a defeated delivering hero in legend, not as a successful hero in history, there is ultimately safety in his defeat, for this subversive figure's challenge to our perhaps too easy acceptance of life as it is becomes removed safely into the legendary past.

If the Kid's perennial appeal can thus be explained in part by the manner in which certain basic psychological needs are fulfilled through his role as a conventional heroic outlaw, it is equally clear that he has endured because he has been a timely *invented* outlaw, because he has been an outlaw whose meaning has changed along with the changing preoccupations of his creators and their cultural context. Certainly the Kid's conflict with and defeat by Garrett can be said to endure because as a human drama it reenacts the perennial conflict between that part of the self that rejects the loss of childhood freedom and self-indulgence and that part of the self which accepts the burdens of maturity and social responsibility. Yet whether this confrontation reminds us of the archetypal conflict between Dionysus and Apollo or the psychological conflict between the superego and the id, this confrontation is and has been grounded in sociological concerns. That is, besides existing as the conflict of father and son or adult and child selves, the Kid-Garrett confrontation is also the continuing conflict between an individual's rejection and yet also grudging acceptance of the dominant middle-class values of his culture.

While the outlaw's appeal is due in part to his being a dramatic figure, he also provides an imaginative escape from the pressures of modern public life in a regimented, bureaucratic society; we should remember that any escape into the outlaw's legendary world is yet vitally connected with the sociological fabric of an audience's everyday world. Critics of the 1950s' so-called Adult Western movie have regularly objected to the filmmakers' imposition of overtly sociological and psychological concerns onto the fabric of the pristine, classical Western of action and adventure. The point is, however, that all Westerns—and by extension all visions of the Kid—possess ideological content. Such dramas ineluctably reveal a particular era's cultural imperatives, and as audiences of such cultural productions we do not simply escape into a completely fantasized world, for we could not relate to such a world unless it was in some manner an extension of our own world's fears and fantasies. While the basic plot of the Kid movies may invariably follow a similar sequence of events, for example, the differences between the 1930 landscape of open range and expansive vistas and the 1950s landscape of darkened interiors and circumscribed horizons, between the earlier portrayal of the Kid's justified and necessary violence and the later portrayals of the Kid's anguished encounter with the consequences of violence, or between the earlier Kid's community of sympathizers and the later Kid's isolation from friends—such differences as these reveal how within an adventure story that has perhaps no bearing on anyone's sense of the Kid there is yet evidence of a particular generation's social conflicts of value and feeling.

What we have come to see in our own discovery of the Kid is that to survey how the Kid has been seen in the years since his death is only the necessary first step to take in discovering the Kid's ultimate significance. By understanding how the Kid's meaning has been contained and released in a formula combining an archetypal story pattern and specific social concerns, we have seen how exploring the Kid has meant exploring a changing modern America's preoccupation with the relationship of the individual to society, the meaning of and often the discrepancy between civil law and moral law, and the uses and consequences of violence.

Between 1881 and 1925, as we have seen, the Kid emerged as a villain in a romance story dramatizing civilization's triumph over a stubborn, resistant, and savage wilderness which protected and contained outlaws and Indians. At a time when American village values were being threatened by America's transition to an urban-industrial society and by America's growing participation in world affairs, the Kid's story essentially reaffirmed a benevolent historical process for audiences searching for a way to understand the forces of change and disorder at home. Garrett emerged as a hero who synthesized the conflicting values of civilization and wilderness, East and West, and the individual and society. Garrett's triumph resolved any doubts about the validity of the democratic social contract, for his actions—however potentially anarchic and violent—established society on a just basis and furthered its existence by eliminating those savages who desired only selfish goals. Whether in the persons of a Roosevelt, who balanced the needs of a strong central government and a strong self-reliant individual, or in a Garrett, who balanced society's needs with his own individual aggression, the heroes of this era demonstrated that continuing American progress was not only possible, but inevitable.

Between 1925 and 1955, however, the Kid's creators revealed a more ambivalent response to the results of manifest destiny, and the invention of the Kid as a romance hero and as a tragic figure responded to this change. Disillusioned by governmental corruption and the gangster's rise to prominence, and yet hopeful that the traditional values of the past would help shape the present society of materialistic Babbitts, the Kid's most influential creators invented the outlaw as a preferable alternative to either criminals like Capone or weak legal and judicial agents of society. That the inventions of the Kid were characteristically offered in the romance story revealed the similar reaffirmation of the continued American dream of a classless, church-centered participatory democracy composed of self-reliant individuals. Yet because society is in these visions of the Kid unable to defend itself or recognize the evil within its own ranks, the outsider like the Kid enters the scene to save the day and restore a society of common people being threatened by evil bankers and their henchmen. Yet no matter how noble his actions, in this era the Kid is not integrated into society at story's end. Thus, the inventions of the Kid become pointed social criticism at the same time they reaffirm the establishment of true justice. Society cannot exist without the Kid's protection, nor can it exist with the Kid in its midst.

Whether invented as a villain, hero, or as a tragic figure, the Kid or Garrett as the protagonist of the story opposed the savage forces threatening the establishment of the good society. Yet because either hero—Garrett in the bibliography's first period, the Kid in its second period—employed violence that was legitimated because it regenerated both society and the heroic individual's self, the story of the Kid's conflict with Western society in a romance story-form dramatized how the hero's personal code of honor and sense of justice were aligned ultimately with the dominant society's best interests. In the years after 1955, however, this finely wrought balance between the self and society, and between civil law and moral justice, was upset. Unlike the romances and tragic romances of the earlier eras, inventions of the Kid after 1955 typically omit the romance framework of civilization's progress or foundation, and instead present a dehumanizing society at odds with an authentic individual's personal code. Although in the previous eras there was hope that a troubled world could be made better by the hero's struggles to transform the world, after 1955 the Kid appears in works that dramatize the individual at odds with society, a civil law unrelated to moral law, and a violence hardly legitimated or regenerative. By the early 1970s, when both the Kid and the frontier society are shown in a virtually meaningless conflict, visions of the Kid approach a fully ironic *mythos* that denies the redemptive nature of tragedy. Such darkly ironic visions of the Kid's insignificance, it should be noted, interestingly appear at a time when Westerns like *Blazing Saddles* were popularizing a benignly ironic vision of the Western movie's conventions, a development which in terms of the Kid's bibliography can be said to have begun with Howard Hughes' *The Outlaw* and to have been continued by the 1960s movie confrontation of the Kid and Dracula. As we move through the years from Pat Garrett's *Authentic Life* to Sam Peckinpah's *Pat Garrett and Billy the Kid,* as we move from romance stories to ironic narratives, we witness how the visions of the Kid reveal the American dream evolving into the American nightmare: a society that could at least in the early visions agree on the definitions of good and evil and of civilization and savagery has become a society that cannot even agree on the definition of the Kid. As we saw earlier, such ironic visions and such a lack of consensus illustrate the splintering of the once-cherished concept of a homogenous American society.

Given the declining number of Kid items appearing in recent years coupled with recent statements as to the Western's demise, the status of the Kid needs clarifying. When we consider the factors creating the decline of the Kid and the Western, we can probably find as many factors as there are observers discussing the situation. Nevertheless, certain factors need to be highlighted, particularly as they bear upon visions of the Kid. In the first place, those who predict the end of the Western basically refer to the Western movie's lack of audience interest and studio production. On a practical level, this development has been accounted for in economic terms: Western movies are more expensive to film, and in times of economic uncertainty they are risky investments. This seems undeniable, but to then relegate the Western to extinction due to this factor alone obscures the fact that recent popular movies involving extensive location shooting and/or technological hardware also have had tremendous budgets and difficult technical problems. It would seem that other factors are at work here, including the lack of a popular star associated with the Western in the manner of John Wayne, or—more importantly—the failure of directors to demonstrate competence in handling the genre even with a large budget.

From this perspective, the decline of the Western and perhaps the Kid in films is both an economic and a creative issue, and in the directors' and actors' seeming self-indulgence and wastefulness we discover another support for Christopher Lasch's concept of the American culture of narcissism. In addition to these failures of economy and creativity, however, we should add a consideration of how changes in the film audience and in the Western's story-form have contributed to the decline in its popularity. It is well-known that contemporary movie audiences are predominantly younger than audiences of the past. For those pioneering in the high-technical world, so the argument goes, the Western's sense of time and place is irrelevant for a generation lacking a sense of history, and particularly a sense of American history as a destined adventure in overcoming a recalcitrant wilderness and native population. By recognizing these changes in the age and experiences of contemporary audiences, we can further suppose that the cultural conflicts and anxieties traditionally displaced and resolved in the Western do not in themselves attract the appeal of recent audiences. Recognizing this thematic change, we can move from a consideration of economic matters, creative failures, and audience demographics into a consideration of the Western story's form. At least on the basis of developments in the Kid's bibliography, the shift from the mode of romance to that of irony, and from the highly formulaic story to the highly mimetic story has meant that resolutions to the Kid's story have become less escapist and more painful because any meaningful action is seemingly impossible. Instead of reaffirmation, visions of the Kid are nonsensical or nihilistic. When we add to this development the parodies of the Western's traditional forms, we can see how visions of the Kid and the West have in the past two decades increasingly undercut their own significance at a time when audiences became younger, budgets tighter, and directors more extravagant.

Given the Kid's century-long endurance in the popular imagination because of his dual appeal as a timeless conventional outlaw and a timely invented outlaw, I do not think it too much to suggest that as an extended metaphor the Kid and Garrett together are America, that their violent skirmish in the last century will always provide, as is the case with the visions of Jesse James and General Custer, an index to the American scene. Even though the Kid and the Western have declined in appearances during the 1970s, it is, as one observer has commented, as foolish to prophesy the death of the Kid and his West as it is to predict the death of the novel. After Lindbergh's flight in the 1920s the Western and the Kid still rode; after the leather holsters worn by the *Star Wars* heroes have disintegrated, the Western will still exist and the Kid will still fall before Garrett's bullet. It may be that the nineteenth-century West of the epic cattle drive will not demand attention, but the contemporary West of desert, mountains, cities, nuclear waste deposits, missile sites, and environmental battles will eventually attract the vision of a spokesman with talent, and fictional outlaws like those created by Edward Abbey will perhaps be seen as the Kid's descendants.

It may also be the case that the Kid has, after Peckinpah's film, received little attention. Yet we can predict that while the ironic vision that permeates his film reveals the bankruptcy of previous visions of the Kid, it has yet in the process opened the way for a revitalized Kid to emerge. Even now, as I write this conclusion in the centennial year of the Kid's death, rumors abound about a new film and a new novel of the Kid. Whatever the validity of these rumors, it seems to me that perhaps future visions of the Kid may reveal three different strands of meaning. We may discover again a young outlaw traipsing across the landscapes of New Mexico or even Jupiter and performing exploits vaguely familiar to us who know the Kid's story, but—given the notoriety of the Kid's name—this outlaw would not be called Billy the Kid or William Bonney. Given the recent fascination with supply-side economics and social conservatism and given the fact that an imaginative consideration of Garrett's role remains to be accomplished, we might discover again a respected Santa Fe Ring and an admirable Pat Garrett crusading to eliminate the disrespectful veterans of the Lincoln County War who refuse to participate in lawful and productive vocations. And given the perhaps predictable future reaction to a bureaucratic society that continues to invoke the spirit of frontier America as it arms itself for Armageddon, we may again discover a Kid as hero who possesses the Garrett-like physical prowess of 1881 and who lacks the debilitating self-awareness of the 1950s Kid.

Yet whether we envision the Kid as a symbol of the vanished worlds of childhood freedom and the pre-industrial society; whether we envision him as a troubled juvenile delinquent or as an avatar of the creative artist; or whether we envision him as an adenoidal farm-boy with a nervous trigger finger—however we see the Kid at whatever date it is pertinent to recall here Michael Ondaatje's Kid. When asked during an imagined jail interview whether he thinks people will remember him, Ondaatje's Kid replies: "I'll be with the world till she dies."[20]

Even as the Kid now graces the labels of children's clothes and chili packets and even as a Roswell, New Mexico, research committee attempts to prove the Kid never died in 1881, what we have seen for such a long time, what we shall see in the future—no matter how long we have to wait—is this: Ondaatje's Kid speaks the truth.

Notes

Chapter 1

1. John L. Sinclair, "Dusting Off Billy's Ghost," *Westways*, 68 (August 1976): 33.

2. In Haniell Long's *Piñon Country* (New York: Duell, Sloan & Pearce, 1941), we learn that two young immigrants—one German, the other French-Irish—plead guilty to a second-degree murder committed during the pair's attempted robbery of a passenger train. Before the robbery the pair lived in El Paso for three weeks, and while there bought cowboy clothes and Western adventure magazines, and frequently visited the local cinema to see Western movies.

3. Lois Telfer of New York City petitioned in 1962 for the removal because, she claimed, the grave was in bad repair and was overcommercialized. Telfer also claimed to be the Kid's only living relative by tracing her kinship to a branch of the Bonney family that migrated to Michigan. On 12 March 1962, Judge E. T. Hensley, Jr., of

the De Baca County district court, denied the petition because "the exact location of Bonney's grave was not known; that in order to disinter Bonney's remains it would inevitably lead to disturbing the remains of those buried in adjoining gravesites." The Lincoln County commissioners supported the petition; the De Baca County commissioners opposed it, no doubt because they did not want to lose any revenue from the tourist trade. See William A. Keleher, *The Fabulous Frontier* (Albuquerque: University of New Mexico Press, 1962), pp. 73–74.

4. James D. Horan, *The Great American West* (New York: Crown, 1978), p. 223; Leon Claire Metz, *Pat Garrett* (Norman: University of Oklahoma Press, 1974), p. 15; Dee Brown and Martin F. Schmitt, *Trail Driving Days* (New York: Scribner's, 1952), p. 162.

5. Arthur Chapman, "Billy the Kid—A Man All 'Bad'," *Outing,* 46 (1905): 501; Marshall Fishwick, "Billy the Kid: Faust in America," *Saturday Review,* 11 October 1952, p. 11.

6. J. C. Dykes, *Billy the Kid: The Bibliography of a Legend* (Albuquerque: University of New Mexico Press, 1952); Introd., *Billy the Kid: The Trail of a Kansas Legend,* by W. E. Koop (n.p.: privately printed, 1965), p. xii.

7. Walter Noble Burns, *The Saga of Billy the Kid* (New York: Ballantine Books, 1973), p. 53.

8. Las Vegas (N.M.) *Gazette,* 28 December 1880.

9. W. R. Burnett, "Nobody's All Bad," *Collier's,* 7 June 1930, pp. 20–21.

10. See Orrin E. Klapp, "The Folk Hero," *Journal of American Folklore,* 62 (1949): 17–25; Alfred Adler, "Billy the Kid: A Case Study in Epic Origins," *Western Folklore.* 10 (1951): 143–52.

11. Joseph G. Rosa, *The Gunfighter* (Norman: University of Oklahoma Press, 1969), p. 47. For interesting treatments of the legend's chronological growth see Kent Steckmesser, *The Western Hero in History and Legend* (Norman: University of Oklahoma Press, 1965), and his "Joaquin Murietta and Billy the Kid," *Western Folklore,* 21 (1962): 77–82; and John Oliver West, "To Die Like a Man: The 'Good' Outlaw Tradition in the American Southwest," (Ph.D. diss., University of Texas, 1964).

12. Amy Hogeboom, *The Boy's Book of the West* (New York: Lothrup, Lee and Shepard, 1946), p. 235.

13. Maurice G. Fulton, "The Apochrypha of Billy the Kid," in *Folk-Say, a Regional Miscellany,* ed. B. A. Botkin (Norman: University of Oklahoma Press, 1930), pp. 88–101. The biography Fulton discovered appeared toward the close of 1882 in the Las Vegas *Optic.*

14. Lloyd Lewis, *It Takes All Kinds* (Freeport, N.Y.: Books for Libraries Press, 1947), p. 101. Lewis reprints the statements Tom Blevins made on 1 November 1930.

15. Kyle S. Crichton, *Law and Order, Ltd.* (1928; rpt. Glorieta, N.M.: The Rio Grande Press, 1970), p. 19.

16. Bertram C. Broome, "'Nuff Said'," *New Mexico Highway Journal,* 9 (1931): 15.

17. Metz, p. 33.

18. See, for example, Erna F. Fergusson, *Murder and Mystery in New Mexico* (Albuquerque: Merle Armitage, 1948), p. 71.

19. G. G. Price, "Billy the Kid," in *Death Comes to Billy the Kid,* ([Greensburg, Kan.: Signal Publishing Co., 1940]), n.pag.

20. Frank G. Applegate, "New Mexican Legends," *Southwest Review,* 17 (1932): 199–208.

21. W. Eugene Hollon, *Frontier Violence* (London: Oxford University Press, 1974), p. 188.

22. Klapp, pp. 24–25.

23. "Walk-along" Smith told J. Frank Dobie that Pat Garrett, the Kid, and Lew Wallace staged the Kid's death and buried two bags of sand in the coffin. See Dobie's *Apache Gold and Yaqui Silver* (1939; rpt. Albuquerque: University of New Mexico Press, 1976), pp. 188–89. "Brushy Bill" Roberts claimed to be the Kid in 1950, and petitioned then New Mexico Governor Mabry for a pardon (it was denied). See C. L. Sonnichsen and William V. Morrison, *Alias Billy the Kid* (Albuquerque: University of New Mexico Press, 1955).

24. F. Stanley, *Desperadoes of New Mexico* (Denver: World Press, 1953), pp. 97–98.

25. Las Vegas (N.M.) *Optic,* 25 July 1881.

26. Phil Lenoir, *Rhymes of the Wild and Wooly* ([Santa Fe, N.M.: privately printed, 1920]), n. p.

27. J. W. Hendron, "The Haunted House of Lincoln Town," *New Mexico,* 25 (1947): 22–23, 41; Edwin Corle, "The Ghost of Billy the Kid," in *Mojave* (New York: Liveright, 1934), pp. 163–69; N. Howard Thorp, *Pardner of the Wind* (Caldwell, Id.: Caxton, 1945), p. 168.

28. Some readers will perhaps recognize echoes here of John G. Cawelti's influential work on formula art, as well as Gene Wise's version of a mode of historical explanation that employs the theories of Kenneth Burke. My own use of their ideas will become more apparent in later chapters. See Cawelti's *Adventure, Mystery, and Romance* (Chicago: University of Chicago Press, 1976); Wise's *American Historical Explanations* (Homewood, Ill.: Dorsey, 1973).

Chapter 2

1. Erna F. Fergusson, *Murder and Mystery in New Mexico* (Albuquerque: Merle Armitage, 1948), p. 53.

2. Arthur Chapman, "A Cowboy War," *Outing,* 58 (1911): 448.

3. Pat Garrett, *The Authentic Life of Billy, the Kid* (1882; rpt. Norman: University of Oklahoma Press, 1954). William A. Keleher's *The Fabulous Frontier* (Albuquerque: University of New Mexico Press, 1962; reprinted 1982) devotes attention to the publishing and biographical facts of the Upson-Garrett work. Upson's "authority" as biographer of the Kid rests solely on his claim to have met the Kid and his mother during his years in New Mexico; as we shall see in the next chapter, this has been enough evidence for many interpreters to accept *The Authentic Life* at face value and to regurgitate the volume's errors of fact.

4. As Jack Potter tells the story on page ten of his *Lead Steer and Other Tales* (Clayton, N.M.: Leader Press, 1939), "the Mexican population were superstitious and claimed their cattle did not drift prior to the death of Billy the Kid and his bunch. They called one of these drifts El Partido de los Animos (The Herd of Spirits) and claimed that the spirits of Billy the Kid and followers O'Folliard and Bowdre were causing the trouble." Sister Blandina Segale tells of her request in *At the End of the Santa Fe Trail* (Milwaukee: Bruce, 1948); William Keleher notes Manuel Moraga's

story about the circus on page 352 of his *Violence in Lincoln County* (Albuquerque: University of New Mexico Press, 1957; reprinted 1982).

5. Philip J. Rasch and R. N. Mullin, "New Light on the Legend of Billy the Kid," *New Mexico Folklore Record*, 7 (1952–53): 1–5. This article presents the documents of Catherine McCarty's marriage to William Henry Antrim in Santa Fe on 1 March 1873.

6. Just to write this first paragraph so effortlessly disguises the labor behind the efforts to establish the Kid's true name and parentage. I am indebted in the following chronicle of the Kid's boyhood to the following articles and books. Besides the previously cited "New Light" article, Rasch and Mullin also published together "Dim Trails: The Pursuit of the McCarty Family," *New Mexico Folklore Record*, 8 (1953–54): 6–11. Relevant articles by Rasch alone include "The Twenty-one Men He Put Bullets Through," *New Mexico Folklore Record*, 9 (1954–55): 8–14; "*Amende Honorable:* The Life and Death of Billy Wilson," *West Texas Historical Association Year Book*, 34 (1958): 97–111; and "The Olingers, Known Yet Forgotten," *Corral Dust*, 8 (1963): 3–6. Relevant publications by Mullin include *The Boyhood of Billy the Kid* (El Paso: Texas Western Press, 1967), and *A Chronology of the Lincoln County War* (Santa Fe, N.M.: Press of the Territorian, 1966). Besides Mullin and Rasch's efforts, also of importance are W. E. Koop, *Billy the Kid: The Trail of a Kansas Legend* ([Kansas City]: privately printed, 1965); Peter Hertzog, *Little Known Facts About Billy, the Kid* (Santa Fe: Press of the Territorian, 1963); and James D. Horan's reproduction of documents in his *The Authentic Wild West: The Gunfighters* (New York: Crown, 1976).

Some observers, most notably Denis McLoughlin in his *Wild and Woolly* encyclopedia of the West, suggest that the Kid was the son of Patrick Henry McCarthy (McCarty) and his wife Catherine, and was born on 17 September 1859. In the light of Catherine McCarty's response to the Indianapolis city directory people, it seems that more concrete evidence, if there is any to be found, is needed before we can accept Patrick McCarthy as the Kid's father. See *Wild and Woolly* (Garden City, N.Y.: Doubleday, 1975), p. 335. Researchers have also discovered one Joseph McCarty of Cass County, Indiana, who fathered two sons around this time.

7. Koop, p. 8.

8. In "Dim Trails" Rasch and Mullin briefly trace Joseph Antrim's later movements. Although Upson believed the Kid's brother died in 1882, Antrim died of apoplexy on 25 November 1930, at 1617 Larimer Street in Denver. He was 76 years old; his assets totaled $1.50. In 1928 Joe Antrim told a Denver reporter that he arrived in Denver in 1871. Also see Koop, p. 13.

9. Koop suggests that the prolonged courtship may have been due to Catherine's observance of the traditional mourning period for her husband, who may have been a Civil War casualty.

10. Mullin, *Boyhood*, pp. 11–12; James D. Horan, *The Great American West* (New York: Crown, 1974), p. 220.

11. "Dim Trails," p. 10; "A Man Named Antrim," p. 51. Ed Moulton soon figured into the Kid's legend as the man who was saved in a saloon fight when the Kid supposedly plunged a knife into Moulton's antagonist. At this point it should be stressed that the research accomplished in the last twenty-five years suggests several revisions of the traditional conception of the Kid's boyhood. In the first place, the notion of the Kid's poverty-stricken boyhood needs to be revised in the light of evi-

dence concerning the McCarty activities in Wichita. Perhaps it was always easier to believe in the poor Irish tenement story because of an Irish ethnic stereotype—not the circumstances of the Kid's life. Second, the view that Antrim abused the Kid and his mother needs revision. George Coe, for example, believed that Billy's first act of violence was his clubbing of his stepfather with a chair because the latter was abusing the Kid's mother; however, Koop and Rasch believe Antrim (1842–1922) to be anything but a cruel stepfather. Rather, they suggest that while Antrim may not have been endeared to his stepchildren, he was a hard-working man who attempted to provide for the family's welfare. One wonders what Antrim thought of the Kid when the youth used the new jacknife Antrim gave him to behead a neighbor's cat.

12. See J. Fred Denton, "Billy the Kid's Friend Tells for First Time of Thrilling Incidents," *Tucson Daily Citizen,* 28 March 1931.

13. As Rasch was so informed by Lloyd F. Rabjohn and Roy L. Wood, nephew and son of Sheriff and Justice of the Peace M. L. Wood, who also convened the coroner's jury, owned the hotel, and arrested the Kid. See "Twenty-one Men," p. 9.

14. Rasch and Mullin, "Dim Trails," p. 9. Although Rasch and Mullin conclude here that the Kid met and probably rode with Jesse Evans during this period, Mullin later suggests in *Boyhood* that perhaps local newspapers were already beginning to attribute area crimes to Kid Antrim. Maurice G. Fulton, with whom I am inclined to agree, believes that the notion of Jesse Evans influencing the Kid at this time is "one of questionable credibility." See his *History of the Lincoln County War,* ed. Robert N. Mullin (Tucson: University of Arizona Press, 1968), p. 67. Denis McLoughlin's *Wild and Woolly* entry on the Kid mentions the Kid's participation with Evans in a stage robbery in October 1877 near Fort Cummings.

15. My account of events in the chronicle of the Kid's days in Lincoln County is indebted to the previously mentioned works by Rasch, Keleher, and Mullin, plus the following publications: Frederick W. Nolan, *The Life and Death of John Henry Tunstall* (Albuquerque: University of New Mexico Press, 1965), and Maurice Garland Fulton's aforementioned *History of the Lincoln County War.*

16. Nolan, p. 213.

17. As another indication of the complexity of motivations surrounding events in territorial New Mexico, we need to remember that Rynerson and Bristol were anti-McSween at this time and anti-Lew Wallace at a later time. Chisum, McSween and Tunstall's silent partner, was placed in jail at this time on account of a suit brought against him by Thomas Catron. Chisum decided not to post bond and thus remained in jail as events were heating up in Lincoln.

18. Warren Beck claims that Brady and his cohorts attached approximately $100,000 worth of McSween property and $50,000 worth of Tunstall property. See his *New Mexico* (Norman: University of Oklahoma Press, 1962), p. 166.

19. Maurice G. Fulton column in the *Roswell* (N.M.) *Daily Record,* 7 October 1937.

20. Nolan, pp. 272ff. Fulton mentions posse member George Kitt's affidavit to Judge Angel, which names Jesse Evans as the one who fired the second shot at Tunstall. See Fulton's *History,* p. 118.

21. This is the date cited in Mullin's *Chronology;* Rasch, in his "Twenty-one Men" article, gives the date as 10 March.

22. One possibility is that after Dr. Ealy fixed the wound Sam Corbet hid Billy,

along with a revolver and blanket, in a hole sawed in the floor underneath a bed; another version has the Kid concealed inside a barrel while a Mexican woman mixes tortillas on top of it as men search her home for the Kid. See Ruth R. Ealy, *Water in a Thirsty Land* (n.p.: privately printed, 1955), p. 66; Paul Trachtman, *The Gunfighters,* Time-Life Series on the Old West (New York: Time-Life, 1974), p. 186. Fulton accepts the initial story as advanced by Ealy and includes it in his *History.*

23. Ealy, p. 78.

24. Rasch, "Olinger," p. 1; "Twenty-one Men," p. 11.

25. Billy the Kid, Letter to Lew Wallace, 13 March 1879, as quoted in Keleher, *Violence in Lincoln County,* p. 211.

26. There is the additional possibility that Chapman caught fire because the powder burns at such close range ignited the lawyer's clothes.

27. Fulton, *Roswell* (N.M.) *Daily Record,* 7 October 1937.

28. Jess G. Hayes, Letter to Rasch and Mullin, 19 June 1952, as quoted in "Dim Trails," p. 9.

29. Hertzog, *Little Known Facts,* p. 6; Homer Croy, *Jesse James Was My Neighbor* (New York: Duell, Sloan and Pearce, 1949), pp. 145–47. According to Croy, who bases his account on Hoyt's story in *A Frontier Doctor,* James went to Las Vegas by train in late-July 1879 to see W. Scott Moore. The Kid took a Sunday dinner at the Old Adobe Hotel in Hot Springs, N. M., and while there met James (who posed as a Mr. Howard from Tennessee). Croy says that the Kid suggested the two join forces, but that James was put off by such a common killer and rustler. Those more partial to the Kid have seen the Kid put off by James's Quantrill-like deeds and serious demeanor.

30. Keleher, *Fabulous Frontier,* pp. 72–73.

31. The chronology of events differs here among several writers, but all place this sequence of events in late November. Although legend has it that the Kid shot Carlyle, we should consider Rudabaugh's statement that all three men—himself, the Kid, and Billy Wilson—shot Carlyle.

32. *Las Vegas* (N.M.) *Gazette,* 27 December 1880.

33. *Las Vegas* (N.M.) *Gazette,* 28 December 1880.

34. Billy the Kid, Letter to Lew Wallace, 4 March 1881, as quoted in Keleher, *Violence,* p. 301.

35. *Las Vegas* (N.M.) *Gazette,* 5 April 1881.

36. Keleher, *Violence,* pp. 318–19.

37. This is Fulton's generally accepted version of the jailbreak. In brief, here are the major alternatives offered for the jailbreak's success: 1) on the way back to the room from the outdoor privy, the Kid managed to outrace Bell and obtain a weapon from the jail's guncloset; 2) while playing cards with Bell the Kid dropped one on the floor—when Bell reached down to pick up the card, the Kid retrieved Bell's revolver; 3) the Kid starved himself so he could slip his small wrists through the cuffs and then clobber Bell over the head with the loose handcuff; 4) the Kid surprised Bell one day by crossing a line drawn down the center of the room, a line the Kid was never to cross; 5) the Kid's girlfriend smuggled in a knife concealed in a tortilla or empenada so the Kid could whittle a key to the cuffs.

38. Besides Garrett's account, see John W. Poe, *The Death of Billy the Kid* (1919; rpt. Boston: Houghton-Mifflin, 1933), and Fulton's *History,* pp. 399ff.

Chapter 3

1. Las Vegas, N.M. *Daily Optic,* 18 July 1881, as quoted in *Billy the Kid: Las Vegas Newspaper Accounts of His Career, 1880–1881* (Waco, Tx.: W. M. Morrison Books, 1958), p. 25.

2. Peter Hertzog, *Little Known Facts About Billy, the Kid* (Santa Fe, N.M.: The Press of the Territorian, 1963), pp. 20–21.

3. Marshall Fishwick, "Billy the Kid: Faust in America," *Saturday Review,* 11 Oct. 1952, pp. 11–12.

4. For the New York City newspaper accounts of the Kid's death I am indebted to Edwin Corle's *Billy the Kid* (1953; rpt. Albuquerque: University of New Mexico Press, 1979), pp. 285–87.

5. *Las Vegas Newspaper Accounts,* p. 27. The *Daily Optic* happily reprinted the *Tribune's* verdict for its own audience.

6. *Las Vegas Newspaper Accounts,* p. 28.

7. *The Times* (of London), 18 Aug. 1881, p. 5.

8. Kent Steckmesser, *The Western Hero in History and Legend* (Norman: University of Oklahoma Press, 1965).

9. My discussion of the romance is indebted to the following sources: Northrop Frye, *Anatomy of Criticism* (Princeton: Princeton University Press, 1957), pp. 186–206, and *Fables of Identity* (Baltimore: Johns Hopkins University Press, 1973), pp. 7–20; Hayden White, *Metahistory* (Baltimore: Johns Hopkins University Press, 1976), pp. 7–11; John Cawelti, *Adventure, Mystery, and Romance* (Chicago: University of Chicago Press, 1976), pp. 37–41. Cawelti uses the term "adventure" to designate what Frye and White mean by "romance," but I have used the latter term since, unlike Cawelti, I am not additionally interested in the evolution of a story-form which centers on developing love relationships called "romances."

10. Frye, *Anatomy,* pp. 187–88.

11. As Cawelti defines the "formula" in popular art, one must not only examine the presence of "a more universal story form or archetype," but also any "number of specific cultural conventions" which are combined or synthesized within the story-form. See his *Adventure,* p. 6. When my study emphasizes the words "vision," "invention," or "explanation," I am basically talking about a formula for interpreting the Kid and his cultural significance. Yet because my study is not confined to printed matter, I do not want to rely solely upon the word "formula." In addition, by occasionally using a word like "invention," I am attempting to stress the act of imagination involved in creating the Kid regardless of time or place. I do not mean to imply by the word that the Kid was "invented" out of thin air, but that the formula for inventing the Kid involves an interpreter's conscious and unconscious manipulation of fact and fiction so as to give the Kid's story a truth which will perhaps be accepted by the interpreter's audience.

12. See Cawelti, *Adventure,* pp. 192–93; Jim Kitses, *Horizons West* (Bloomington: Indiana University Press, 1969), pp. 11–14.

13. My discussion of the dime novel in the next few paragraphs is indebted to the following studies: Daryl Jones, *The Dime Novel Western* (Bowling Green: The Popular Press of Bowling Green State University, 1978); Albert Johannsen, *The House of Beadle and Adams and Its Dime and Nickel Novels* (Norman: University of Oklahoma Press, 1950); Russel Nye, *The Unembarrassed Muse: The Popular Arts in America* (New

York: The Dial Press, 1970); Henry Nash Smith, *Virgin Land* (Cambridge: Harvard University Press, 1971); and Cawelti, *Adventure,* pp. 209–15.

14. J. C. Dykes, *Billy the Kid: The Bibliography of a Legend* (Albuquerque: University of New Mexico Press, 1952), p. 13.

15. John W. Lewis, *The True Life of Billy the Kid,* Wide Awake Library, No. 451 (New York: Frank Tousey, 1881), p. 3.

16. Edmund Fable, *Billy the Kid, the New Mexican Outlaw; or, The Bold Bandit of the West!* (Denver: Denver Publishing Co., 1881), pp. 9, 40.

17. Francis W. Doughty, *Old King Brady and Billy the Kid; or, The Great Detective's Chase,* New York Detective Library, No. 411 (New York: Frank Tousey, 1890), p. 4.

18. Thomas F. Daggett, *Billy LeRoy, the Colorado Bandit, alias The Kid* (New York: Richard K. Fox, 1881), p. 8.

19. Daggett, p. 16.

20. Lewis, pp. 14–15.

21. *The Cowboy's Career; or, The Daredevil Deeds of Billy the Kid* (by "One of the Kids"), as quoted in B. A. Botkin, *Folk-Say, A Regional Miscellany* (Noman: University of Oklahoma Press, 1930), p. 101.

22. Lewis, p. 15.

23. Doughty, p. 29.

24. Nye, for instance, suggests that such was the case when dime novelists created outlaw heroes in order to meet the fantastic demand for the product. See *The Unembarrassed Muse,* p. 203.

25. Lewis, p. 16.

26. See Fable, pp. 20, 55–56.

27. See Jones, pp. 81, 97.

28. Pat Garrett, *The Authentic Life of Billy, the Kid, Noted Desperado of the Southwest* (1882; rpt. Norman: University of Oklahoma Press, 1965), p. 3.

29. Barton W. Currie, "American Bandits: Lone and Otherwise," *Harper's Weekly,* 12 September 1908, p. 15; John Milton Scanland, *Life of Pat F. Garrett and the Taming of the Border Outlaw* (El Paso, Tx.: Carleton F. Hodge, 1908), p. 36.

30. See, for instance, Frank Hall, *History of the State of Colorado,* III (Chicago: Blakely Printing, 1891), p. 259; Arthur Chapman, "Billy the Kid—A Man All 'Bad'," *Outing,* 46 (1905): 73–77; William Macleod Raine, "Billy the Kid," *Pacific Monthly,* 20 (1908):37–45; and J. L. Hill, *The End of the Cattle Trail* (Long Beach, Cal.: George Moyle, 1924), p. 44.

31. J. E. Sligh, "Billy the Kid," *Overland Monthly,* 52 (1908): 47.

32. Emerson Hough, "Billy the Kid, The True Story of a Western 'Bad Man'," *Everybody's Magazine,* 5 (1901): 306; Albert E. Hyde, "The Old Regime in the Southwest," *Century,* 43 (1902): 699; Raine, p. 40; Currie, p. 15; R. B. Townshend, *The Tenderfoot in New Mexico* (London: John Lane, 1923), pp. 234–35.

33. Currie, p. 15.

34. O. S. Clark, *Clay Allison of the Washita* ([Attica, Ind.]: Privately Printed, [1922]), p. 80.

35. Garrett, p. 3.

36. Francis Rolt–Wheeler, *The Book of Cowboys* (Boston: Lothrop, Lee & Shepard, 1921), p. 371; Frederick R. Bechdolt, *Tales of the Old Timers* (New York: Century, 1924), p. 40; Edith M. Bowyer, *Observations of a Ranchwoman in New Mexico* (London: Macmillan, 1898), p. 256; Walter Woods, *Billy the Kid,* in *America's Lost Plays,* ed.

Garrett H. Leverton (1940; rpt. Bloomington: Indiana University Press, 1964), p. 255. This melodrama indicates the beginning of a vision of the Kid as romance hero, but it barely lasted through the war years. I shall discuss this melodrama's importance in the next chapter. The point to make here is that except for this melodrama and the gradual softening of the Kid's image in Siringo's treatments, visions of the Kid at this time stressed his villainous aspects as an opponent of settled society. When the cultural situation was different, as it was after the World War I years and during Prohibition, then the kind of vision of the Kid offered by Woods becomes anything but an isolated example.

37. Forbes Heermans, *Thirteen Stories of the Far West* (Syracuse, N.Y.: C. W. Bardeen, 1887), p. 108.

38. Emerson Hough, *The Story of the Outlaw* (New York: Outing, 1907), p. 14; Scanland, p. 14.

39. Hough, "Billy the Kid," p. 309.

40. Hyde, p. 700.

41. Scanland, p. 36.

42. Hough, "Billy the Kid," p. 310; *Outlaw*, pp. 259–60.

43. Hyde, p. 698.

44. Hough, "Billy the Kid," p. 305; Raine, p. 43; Chapman, p. 73.

45. Hyde, p. 700.

46. Charles A. Siringo, *A Lone Star Cowboy* (Santa Fe, N.M.: Privately Printed, 1919), p. 151; Frederick W. Grey, *Seeking Fortune in America* (London: Smith, Elder & Co., 1912), p. 119.

47. Scanland, p. 37; Raine, p. 579. The Kid was also called "the most desperate and bloody-minded civilized white man that ever cursed the border with his crimes" (Hall, p. 259); "the most daring, reckless and famous outlaw who ever terrorized the Southwest" (Sligh, p. 47); "the most uncompromising and reckless man killer in all the west" (Clark, p. 126); and "the most dreaded kid outlaw that ever terrorized the border lands of the West" (Hill, p. 44).

48. Chapman, p. 77.

49. Arthur Chapman, "A Cowboy War," *Outing*, 58 (1911): 498.

50. Hough, *Outlaw*, p. 273.

51. Scanland, p. 12.

52. See Hyde, p. 691.

53. Hyde, p. 701.

54. P. S. McGeeney, *Down at Stein's Pass* (Boston: Angel Guardian Press, 1909), p. 86.

55. Garrett, p. 156.

56. Frederick R. Bechdolt, *When the West Was Young* (New York: Century, 1922), p. 309.

57. Chapman, "Billy the Kid," p. 77; Hough, "Billy the Kid," p. 310.

58. Scanland, p. 31; Raine, p. 39.

59. Hough, *Outlaw*, p. 2. For more on Hough and *The Story of the Outlaw*, see Carole M. Johnson's interesting "Emerson Hough's *The Story of the Outlaw*," *Arizona and the West*, 17 (1975), 309–26; and Delbert E. Wylder's *Emerson Hough* (Austin, Tx: Steck–Vaughn, 1969).

60. Hyde, p. 698.

61. Hough, "Billy the Kid," pp. 307, 309.

62. Hough, *The Story of the Cowboy* (New York: Appleton, 1897), p. 308.

63. Hough, *Outlaw,* p. vi.

64. I am indebted to the following sources for the themes developed in the next few paragraphs about the era's cultural preoccupations: Robert H. Wiebe, *The Search for Order: 1877–1920* (New York: Hill and Wang, 1967); James D. Hart, *The Popular Book* (Berkeley: University of California Press, 1963); G. Edward White, *The Eastern Establishment and the Western Experience* (New Haven: Yale University Press, 1968); Daniel J. Boorstin, *The Americans: The National Experience,* II (New York: Vintage Books, 1965); Samuel Eliot Morison, *The Oxford History of the American People* (New York: Oxford University Press, 1965); Cawelti, *Adventure,* pp. 209–30; and Richard Etulain, "The Historical Development of the Western," *Journal of Popular Culture,* 7 (1973): 717–26.

65. Hart, p. 201.

66. Forrest G. Robinson, "The Roosevelt-Wister Connection," *Western American Literature,* 14 (1979): 95–114.

67. Theodore Roosevelt, *The Winning of the West,* I (New York: Putnam's, 1889), pp. 274–75. See Robinson, p. 108.

68. Owen Wister, "The Evolution of a Cowpuncher," in his *Red Men and White,* Vol. 1 of *The Writings of Owen Wister* (New York: Macmillan, 1928), p. xxxiv. The essay first appeared in 1895.

69. Robinson, for example, demonstrates how the tumult of the 1890s led Wister to stress the virile qualities of a Specimen Jones, but that the more stable Progressive years of the new century's first decade saw Wister emphasize the Virginian's socially responsible stance. See "The Roosevelt-Wister Connection," p. 114. As I shall suggest in the next few pages, the images of the Kid did not undergo such change for he never had a piece of society in the first place, and, unlike the Virginian or Specimen Jones, was symbolic of the elements that the tough, self-reliant cowboy-heroes were attempting to hold in check.

70. "The Great West," *Century,* 43 (1902): 150.

71. Hough, *Outlaw,* pp. 397–98.

72. Hough, *Outlaw,* p. x.

73. The exception to this general trend is the Woods melodrama which will be discussed next chapter.

74. See John G. Cawelti, "The Gunfighter and Society," *The American West,* 5 (1968): 76; Jones, *The Dime Novel Western,* p. 75.

75. Hough, *Heart's Desire* (New York: Macmillan, 1905), p. 367.

76. Clark, p. 80.

Chapter 4

1. Harvey Fergusson, "Billy the Kid," *American Mercury,* 5 (1925): 224.

2. O. S. Clark, *Clay Allison of the Washita* ([Attica, Ind.]: Privately Printed, [1927]), p. 80.

3. William Macleod Raine, *The Fighting Tenderfoot* (Garden City, N.Y.: Doubleday, Doran & Co., 1929), p. 266.

4. See Gene Wise's discussion in his *American Historical Explanations,* 2nd ed. (Minneapolis: University of Minnesota Press, 1980). I should add here that if the

newer explanation accords with experiences of a larger audience, it will be accepted as a truthful version of reality. When this happens, in short, creator, context, and culture agree, provisionally, on what is truth.

5. Emerson Hough, *The Story of the Outlaw* (New York: Outing, 1907), p. 397.

6. Neill M. Clark, "Close Calls: An Interview with Charles A. Siringo," *American Magazine*, 107 (1929): 129.

7. Walter Woods, *Billy the Kid,* in *The Great Diamond Robbery and Other Recent Melodramas,* America's Lost Plays, Vol. VIII, ed. Garrett H. Leverton (1940; rpt. Bloomington: Indiana University Press, 1964), pp. 199–255. According to Leverton, Woods's melodrama opened its run of twelve seasons at the New Star Theatre in New York City on 13 August 1906. At the opening of the melodrama's seventh season, its managers announced that six million people had seen the melodrama in the past six years. I should mention here that Kent Steckmesser in his *The Western Hero in History and Legend* (Norman: University of Oklahoma Press, 1965) discusses this melodrama as a turning point in the Kid's legendary image. My own assumptions behind my different periodization of the Kid bibliography are stated in this chapter's text.

8. Fergusson, p. 224.

9. Fergusson, p. 228.

10. Fergusson, p. 224.

11. *Dictionary of American Biography,* ed. Allen Johnson (New York: Scribner's, 1929), Vol. II, p. 271.

12. "Billy the Kid: In Two Films About Him Hollywood Fakes History," *Life,* 4 Aug. 1941, p. 65; William A. Keleher, "In 'Re' Billy the Kid," *New Mexico Folklore Record,* 4 (1949–50): 11.

13. Frederick Lewis Allen, *Only Yesterday* (1931; rpt. New York: Harper & Row, 1964). I am also indebted to the following works for the themes developed in the paragraphs on the cultural preoccupations of this era: Allen, *Since Yesterday* (1939; rpt. New York: Harper & Row, 1972); Andrew Bergman, *We're in the Money: Depression America and Its Films* (New York: New York University Press, 1971); John G. Cawelti, *Adventure, Mystery, and Romance* (Chicago: University of Chicago Press, 1976); Richard H. Pells, *Radical Visions and American Dreams* (New York: Harper & Row, 1973); Garth Jowett, "Bullets, Beer, and the Hays Office," in *American History/American Film,* ed. John E. O'Connor and Martin A. Jackson (New York: Frederick Ungar, 1979), pp. 57–75; and John E. O'Connor, "A Reaffirmation of American Ideals: *Drums Along the Mohawk,*" in O'Connor and Jackson, *American History/American Film,* pp. 97–119.

14. William G. Shepherd, "Flat-wheeled Justice," *Collier's,* 14 Nov. 1925, p. 7.

15. See Bergman's chapter, "The Gangsters," in *We're In the Money,* pp. 3–17; Jowett, pp. 65–75.

16. O'Connor, pp. 97–98.

17. Mary Day Winn, *The Macadam Trail* (New York: Knopf, 1931), p. 176.

18. Nelson C. Nye, *Pistols for Hire* (New York: Macmillan, 1941), p. 61; J. Marvin Hunter and Noah H. Rose, *The Album of Gunfighters* (Bandera, Tx.: Rose & Hunter Publications, 1951), p. 2.

19. N. Howard Thorp, *Pardner of the Wind* (Caldwell, Id.: Caxton, 1945), p. 182.

20. Owen White, *Trigger Fingers* (New York: Putnam's, 1926), pp. 26–27.

21. Fred E. Sutton, *Hands Up!* (Indianapolis: Bobbs–Merrill, 1927), p. 187.

22. Eugene Cunningham, *Triggernometry* (New York: The Press of the Pioneers, 1934), p. 132; George D. Hendricks, *The Bad Man of the West* (San Antonio, Tx.: Naylor, 1942), p. 156.

23. Hunter and Rose, p. 2.

24. Frank M. King, *Mavericks* (Pasadena, Cal.: Trail's End, 1947), p. 228; Frederick Watson, *A Century of Gunmen* (London: Ivor Nicholson & Watson, 1931), p. 193.

25. Sutton, p. 187; Watson, p. 193.

26. Cunningham, p. 132.

27. White, p. 18.

28. These contrasts between the old and the modern criminal are voiced between Owen White's 1925 *Trigger Fingers* and F. Stanley's 1953 *Desperadoes of New Mexico* (Denver: World Press, 1953), pp. xii–xiii.

29. Emmett Dalton, *When the Daltons Rode* (Garden City, N.Y.: Doubleday, Doran & Co., 1931), p. 201.

30. Wilbur Smith, "The Amigo of Billy the Kid," *New Mexico Magazine,* 11 (1933): p. 26.

31. Haniell Long, *Piñon Country* (New York: Duell, Sloan & Pearce, 1941), p. 186.

32. Dee Harkey, *Mean as Hell* (Albuquerque: University of New Mexico Press, 1948), p. 218.

33. John Hays Hammond, "Strong Men of the Wild West," *Scribner's,* 77 (1925): 115–25; 246–56.

34. Watson, pp. 193–94.

35. F. Stanley, *Soccorro* (Denver: World Press, 1950), p. 118.

36. George Washington Coe, *Frontier Fighter* (1934; rpt. Albuquerque: University of New Mexico Press, 1951), p. 220; James B. O'Neill, *They Die But Once* (New York: Knight, 1935), p. 134.

37. Fred M. Griffin, "Them Good Old Days," in *New Mexico in Verse,* ed. William Felter and John L. McCarty (Dalhart, Tx.: Dalhart Publishing Co., 1935), p. 50.

38. Dalton, p. 277.

39. See Cawelti's discussion of the West as created by Grey and Hart on pages 230–41 of his *Adventure, Mystery, and Romance;* also helpful is Gary Topping's "Zane Grey: A Literary Reassessment," *Western American Literature,* 13 (1978):51–64.

40. Zane Grey, *Nevada* (New York: Harper, 1928), p. 362. My emphasis.

41. Sam P. Ridings, *The Chisholm Trail* (Guthrie, Ok.: Co–Operative Publishing Co., 1936), p. 54.

42. Harvey Fergusson, *Rio Grande* (1933; rpt. New York: Morrow, 1967), p. 246.

43. Harry C. Gibbs, *Chico,* in *Twenty Short Plays on a Royalty Holiday,* Vol. II, ed. Margaret Mayorga (New York: Samuel French, 1940), p. 475.

44. Miguel Antonio Otero, *The Real Billy the Kid* (New York: Rufus Rockwell Wilson, 1936), p. 215.

45. Frank Collinson, "Tongue River's First Ranch," *Ranch Romances,* 6 (1936): 547.

46. Owen P. White, "Billy the Kid," *Collier's,* 14 Nov. 1925, p. 49.

47. Similarly, in his killings of Deputies Olinger and Bell during his escape from custody only days before his hanging date, the Kid was justified in his violence,

according to many interpreters at this time, because Olinger was viewed as an imitation badman who liked to shoot tobacco juice at people, and because Bell made the mistake of running for help instead of letting the Kid go free when the latter had the drop on him.

48. See "The American Robin Hood" chapter of Steckmesser's *The Western Hero in History and Legend.*

49. G. G. Price, *Death Comes to Billy the Kid* ([Greensburg, Kan.]: Signal Publishing, [1940]), p. 6.

50. Eric Hobsbawm's study of the bandit in an international context *only* mentions the Kid as a type of Robin Hood noble bandit. See his *Bandits* (New York: Delacorte Press, 1969), p. 38.

51. Burnett, p. 30.

52. Forbes Heermans, "The Wedding at Puerto de Luna," in *Thirteen Stories of the Far West* (Syracuse, N.Y.: C. W. Bardeen, 1887); Frank G. Applegate, "New Mexican Legends," *Southwest Review,* 17 (1932): 149.

53. Thomas Marion Hamilton, *The Young Pioneer* (Washington, D.C.: Library Press, 1932), p. 149.

54. Smith, p. 27.

55. See, for instance, Henry F. Hoyt, *A Frontier Doctor* (Boston: Houghton–Mifflin, 1929), p. 90; *Life,* 4 Aug. 1941, p. 66; Eve Ball, "Billy Strikes the Pecos," *New Mexico Folklore Record,* 4 (1949–50): p. 10; John L. McCarty, *Maverick Town* (Norman: University of Oklahoma Press, 1946), p. 78; Erna F. Fergusson, *Murder and Mystery in New Mexico* (Albuquerque: Merle Armitage, 1948), pp. 49–50.

56. Otero, pp. 13–14.

57. Erna F. Fergusson, pp. 49–50; Coe, p. 33.

58. Roscoe Logue, *Under Texas and Border Skies* (Amarillo, Tx.: Russell Stationery Co., 1935), p. 87.

59. Ramon F. Adams, "Billy the Kid's Lost Years," *Texas Monthly,* 4 (1929): 207.

60. Harold Hersey, "Billy Thuh Kid," in *Singing Rawhide* (New York: Doran, 1926), p. 128.

61. Coe, p. vii.

62. Although not all contributors accepted these notions as their stated conclusions about the Kid, many nevertheless advanced stories and images which revealed the Kid as a noble robber or romance hero. Since we have already discussed Fergusson's idea of the Kid, and since in a few paragraphs we shall discuss Burns's popular image of the Kid, I shall for the sake of brevity select a few other examples from the Kid bibliography to illustrate the acceptance of this interpretation of the Kid. See, for instance, Ike Fridge, *History of the Chisum War* (Electra, Tx.: Smith, [1927]), pp. 33–34; Kyle S. Crichton, *Law and Order, Ltd.* (1928; rpt. Glorieta, N.M.: Rio Grande Press, 1970), pp. 16–19; Cunningham, *Triggernometry,* p. 13; Paul I. Wellman, *The Trampling Herd* (New York: Carrick & Evans, 1939), p. 343; E. B. Mann, "Billy the Kid," *American Rifleman,* 95 (1947): 23; Ann Merriman Peck, *Southwest Roundup* (New York: Dodd, Meade & Co., 1950), p. 32; J. Frank Dobie, *A Vaquero of the Brush Country* (Dallas: The Southwest Press, 1929), p. 177.

63. Walter Noble Burns, *The Saga of Billy the Kid* (1926; rpt. New York: Ballantine, 1973).

64. Archie Green, "Commercial Music Graphics: Number Twenty-Eight," *John*

Edwards Memorial Foundation Quarterly, 10 (Spring 1974): 21. This valuable document reproduces three pieces: the letter Polk C. Brockman mailed to the Rev. Andrew Jenkins in which Brockman requested Jenkins write a new song based on the information contained in the Book-of-the-Month Club flyer for the *Saga*; the Club flyer publicizing the *Saga*; and the typescript of the song "Billy the Kid" which Jenkins wrote. Vernon Dalhart, "one of the best-known recording stars of the 1920's," recorded Jenkins's song in 1929 for RCA; in 1973 Ry Cooder re—recorded the song on his album *Into the Purple Valley*. Jenkins (1885–1956) composed over 800 songs in his life, most of them sacred songs; his 1925 song "The Death of Floyd Collins" was a popular hit also recorded by Dalhart. The judgment about Dalhart's popularity is from Bill C. Malone's *Country Music U.S.A.*(Austin: University of Texas Press, 1968), p. 56.

65. Burns, p. 41.

66. Burns, p. 41.

67. Burns, pp. 21, 41.

68. Burns, pp. 219, 223.

69. That is, Fate no more explains the Kid's actions than do the witches of *Macbeth* force Macbeth to perform his crimes.

70. Burns, pp. 42–43.

71. Burns, p. 43.

72. Burns, p. 42.

73. If Western critics and Kid historians have not been able to accomplish this perspective, certainly ballet critics have. Where Peter Lyons in his book about the Wild West thought that the ballet "glorified its [America's] most pathological killer," ballet critic Grace Robert thought rather that the Kid came off in the ballet as a "George Raft type." See Lyons' *The Wild, Wild West* (New York: Funk & Wagnalls, 1969), p. 23; Robert's *The Borzoi Book of Ballets* (New York: Knopf, 1946), p. 55. My own introduction to the ballet occurred in April 1980 when Ballet West (Salt Lake City) revived the dance.

74. See John Tuska, *The Filming of the West* (Garden City, N.Y.: Doubleday, 1976), pp. 193ff.; George N. Fenin and William K. Everson, *The Western: From Silents to the Seventies,* rev. ed. (New York: Penguin Books, 1977), p. 178.

75. Tuska, p. 194.

76. Unless otherwise noted, I shall place the historical name of the movie characters in parentheses after the first mention of the movie character's name.

77. See John H. Lenihan's excellent study *Showdown: Confronting Modern America in the Western Film* (Urbana: University of Illinois Press, 1980), p. 96.

78. For a very helpful discussion of Hughes' film and its notorious production problems and censorship troubles, see Thomas H. Pauly's "Howard Hughes and his Western: The Maverick and *The Outlaw," Journal of Popular Film*, 6 (1978): 35-69. Fenin and Everson suggest that the post-World War II period channeled disillusionment and gloom into Westerns which were more psychologically complex, more erotic, and more interested in the problems of racial conflict. *The Outlaw* is of interest, of course, because it first introduced the sexual emphasis in the Western film instead of the emphasis on action and adventure fare. When viewing this film during the preparation of this book, I found it impossible not to consider this the *Blazing Saddles* of the Kid bibliography, and in this sense the film also anticipates the parody of the

Kid and the Western genre which we see in later years in such productions as *Billy the Kid versus Dracula* (1966). James Robert Parish and Michael R. Pitts, in their *The Great Western Pictures* (Metuchen, N.J.: Scarecrow, 1976), state that *The Outlaw* grossed five million dollars on an investment of 3.4 million dollars (original budget was $440,000). In 1976 *The Outlaw* was rated suitable viewing material for general audiences. See Fenin and Everson, pp. 265–68; Parish and Pitts, pp. 250–51.

Chapter 5

1. N. Howard Thorp, *Pardner of the Wind* (Caldwell, Id.: Caxton, 1945), p., 193.

2. James Farber, *Texans with Guns* (San Antonio, Tx.: Naylor, 1950), pp. viii–ix.

3. See Erna F. Fergusson, *Murder and Mystery in New Mexico* (Albuquerque: Merle Armitage, 1948), pp. 52–53; Maurice G. Fulton, "Billy the Kid in Life and Books," *New Mexico Folklore Record,* 4 (1949–50): 1–6; Dee Brown and Martin F. Schmitt, *Trail Driving Days* (New York: Scribners, 1952), pp. 161–78.

4. Kent Steckmesser, *The Western Hero in History and Legend* (Norman: University of Oklahoma Press, 1965), pp. 95–102; Gary Roberts' entry on the Kid appears in *The Reader's Encyclopedia of the American West,* ed. Howard Lamar (New York: Crowell, 1977), pp. 95–96.

5. Chesmore Eastlake, "Typing the Western Gunman," *1948 Brand Book* (Denver: The Westerners, 1949), p. 210; Orrin E. Klapp, "The Folk Hero," *Journal of American Folklore,* 62 (1949): 20.

6. Besides Steckmesser's two chapters on "The Saintly Billy" and "The Satanic Billy," see W. A. Keleher, "In 'Re' Billy the Kid," *New Mexico Folklore Record,* 4 (1949–50): 11–13.

7. My objective here is not to argue for this as the sole metaphor for describing historical change. However, the active notion of a wave cresting and receding is to my mind a more useful trope than the "current," "stream," or "flow" metaphors which too often connote a placidity of thought and feeling. Similarly, "dialectic" in this context I think suggests a set of rigid oppositions which belies the mixing together (some might say "confusion") of ideas and images in the Kid material. See Hayden White's *Metahistory* (Baltimore: Johns Hopkins University Press, 1973), p. 19, for more on the wavelike motion of history as it is perceived by what White calls the "contextualist" historian.

8. See John G. Cawelti, *Adventure, Mystery, and Romance* (Chicago: University of Chicago Press, 1976), p. 251; John H. Lenihan, *Showdown* (Urbana: University of Illinois Press, 1980), pp. 10–23.

9. See also John G. Cawelti, "The Gunfighter and Society," *American West,* 5 (March 1968): 30–35, 76–78.

10. C. L. Sonnichsen and William V. Morrison, *Alias Billy the Kid* (Albuquerque: University of New Mexico Press, 1955).

11. I am indebted to this contrast of Sophoclean and Aeschylean tragic senses to Hayden White's discussion of Toqueville's work. See *Metahistory,* p. 194.

12. Frazier Hunt, *The Tragic Days of Billy the Kid* (New York: Hastings House, 1956), pp. 2, 186–87, 195, 208.

13. Hunt, p. 303.

14. Hunt, p. 302.

15. Charles Neider, *The Authentic Death of Henry Jones* (New York: Harper's, 1956).

16. See Lewis Nordyke, *New York Times*, 26 Aug. 1956, p. 26; Martin Levin, *Saturday Review*, 29 Sept. 1956, p. 16.

17. Neider, pp. 177–78.

18. White, p. 194.

19. Considerations of space prevent me from discussing the differences of the film and teleplay. In addition, while I shall mainly refer to Penn in the text, the film's Kid is obviously a collaboration of Penn, Newman, and Leslie Stevens.

20. As quoted in *Hollywood Directors, 1941–1976* (New York: Oxford University Press, 1977), p. 361. See also Eric Sherman and Martin Rubin, *The Director's Event* (New York: Signet, 1972), p. 104.

21. Sherman and Rubin, p. 111.

22. Will Wright suggests the opposite view: that Brando's Rio has accepted traditional values and will return in the future. See his *Sixguns and Society* (Berkeley: University of California Press, 1975), p. 68. Both of us can be correct since we are indulging in speculation, perhaps irrelevant, about the lives of fictional characters after the work in question has concluded.

23. My discussion of this era's cultural criticism is indebted to the following studies: William E. Leuchtenburg, *A Troubled Feast: American Society Since 1945* (Boston: Little, Brown & Co., 1973); Alexander Kendrick, *The Wound Within: America in the Vietnam Years, 1945—1974* (Boston: Little, Brown & Co., 1974); Lawrence S. Wittner, *Cold War America: From Hiroshima to Watergate* (New York: Praeger, 1974); William L. O'Neill, ed., *American Society Since 1945* (Chicago: Quadrangle Books, 1969); Morris Dickstein, *Gates of Eden: American Culture in the Sixties* (New York: Basic Books, 1977); Cawelti, *Adventure*, pp. 250–59; Lenihan, *Showdown*, pp. 116ff.

24. Thomas H. Pauly, "The Cold War Western," *Western Humanities Review*, 33 (1973): 258.

25. Lenihan, pp. 116–17.

Chapter 6

1. Gary L. Roberts, "The West's Gunmen," *American West*, 8 (March 1971): 18.

2. Leon Claire Metz, *The Shooters* (El Paso, Tx.: Mangan Books, 1976); James D. Horan, *The Authentic Wild West: The Gunfighters* (New York: Crown, 1976); Harry Sinclair Drago, *The Great Range Wars* (New York: Dodd, Mead & Co., 1970); and Joseph G. Rosa, *The Gunfighter: Man or Myth?* (Norman: University of Oklahoma Press, 1969).

3. Leon Claire Metz, *Pat Garrett* (Norman: University of Oklahoma Press, 1974).

4. Rosa, p. 47; Drago, p. 35.

5. Harry Sinclair Drago, *Road Agents and Train Robbers* (New York: Dodd, Mead & Co., 1973), p. v.

6. Ramon Adams, *A Fitting Death for Billy the Kid* (Norman: University of Oklahoma Press, 1960), p. 3.

7. Charles Olson, "Billy the Kid," in *Human Universe and Other Essays*, ed. Donald Allen (New York: Grove Press, 1967), p. 139.

8. Olson, p. 137.

9. bp Nichol, *The True Eventual Story of Billy the Kid* (Toronto: Weed Flowers Press, 1970), n.p.

10. Michael McClure, *The Blossom,* in his *The Mammals* (San Francisco: Cranium Press, 1972); and *The Beard* (New York: Grove Press, 1965).

11. Jack Spicer, *Billy the Kid* (1958; rpt. San Francisco: Oyster Press, 1975); Michael Ondaatje, *The Collected Works of Billy the Kid* (New York: Berkley, 1975). My reading of Spicer's poem has been aided by Frank Sadler's "The Frontier in Jack Spicer's 'Billy the Kid'," in *The Westering Experience in American Literature,* ed. Merrill Lewis and L. L. Lee (Bellingham, Wash.: Bureau for Faculty Research, 1977), pp. 159–60.

11. See Joseph Frank, "Spatial Form in Modern Literature," in *The Widening Gyre* (Bloomington: Indiana University Press, 1968), pp. 3–62.

12. Besides the facts of his violent career, his publicity, and, presumably, his sex appeal.

13. McClure, *Mammals,* p. 4.

14. Ondaatje, p. 10.

15. For more on Nichol and Ondaatje see Stephen Scobie, "Two Authors in Search of a Character," in *Poets and Critics,* ed. George Woodcock (Toronto: Oxford University Press, 1974), pp. 225–46.

16. Ondaatje, p. 71.

17. Charles Olson, "Projective Verse," in *Selected Writings of Charles Olson,* ed. Robert Creeley (New York: New Directions, 1966), p. 24; McClure, *Mammals,* n.p.

18. Will Henry, "A Bullet for Billy the Kid," in his *Sons of the Western Frontier* (Philadelphia: Chilton, 1966), pp. 165–209.

19. John G. Cawelti, *Adventure, Mystery, and Romance* (Chicago: University of Chicago Press, 1976), p. 256.

20. Nixon saw *Chisum* on 3 August 1970. The next day he told the convention of lawyers and judges that he admired the film because, in a time when respect for law and order was being eroded, it was pleasing to see the "good" guys like Chisum win out in the end and restore justice. By calling Manson one of the "bad guys" Nixon, some thought, endangered the trial's outcome since he publicly declared Manson guilty before the trial had been completed.

21. My understanding of this element of the film is indebted to Paul Seydor's excellent study *Peckinpah: The Western Films* (Urbana: University of Illinois Press, 1980), pp. 202–22.

22. Northrop Frye, *Anatomy of Criticism* (Princeton: Princeton University Press, 1973), p. 192. In his discussion of irony Frye distinguishes two forms. There is a relatively benign form of irony which is intent on unmasking folly and pretense within a framework of a satisfaction with current social institutions. Where this benign form tends in the end towards a comic mode, a second more extreme form of irony tends toward tragic and absurd views of the world. As it should be clear from my text, the ironic visions of the Kid as I see them reveal the presence of the second form of irony. My understanding of irony has also been enhanced by Hayden White's discussion of the historian Burckhardt's ironic vision. See *Metahistory* (Baltimore: Johns Hopkins University Press, 1973), pp. 230–37.

23. Frye, p. 224.

24. Jack Nachbar, "Riding Shotgun: the Scattered Formula in Contemporary Western Movies," in *Focus on the Western,* ed. Jack Nachbar (Englewood Cliffs, N.J.: Prentice-Hall, 1974), pp. 101–12.

Chapter 7

1. Gary L. Roberts, "The West's Gunmen," *American West,* 8 (1971) no. 1: 10; no. 3: 61. For an indication of the "monumental size" of the outlaw's bibliography, see Ramon Adams' *Six-Guns and Saddle Leather* (Norman: University of Oklahoma Press, 1954), *Burs Under the Saddle* (Norman: University of Oklahoma Press, 1964), and *The Adams One-Fifty* (Austin, Tx.: Jenkins, 1976).

2. See also W. Eugene Hollon, *Frontier Violence* (London: Oxford University Press, 1974), and Joseph G. Rosa, *The Gunfighter: Man or Myth?* (Norman: University of Oklahoma Press, 1969).

3. See, for example, Harry S. Drago, *The Legend Makers* (New York: Dodd, Mead & Co., 1975); *The Gunfighters,* Time-Life Series on the Old West (New York: Time-Life Books, 1974), p. 186; Richard Elman, *Bad Men of the West* (New York: Ridge Press, 1974), pp. 122–31; and James D. Horan, *The Authentic Wild West: The Outlaws* (New York: Crown, 1977).

4. This is my paraphrase and slight modification of a sentence G. K. Chesterton wrote to describe the mind of Macaulay in his *The Victorian Age in Literature* (1913; rpt. London: Oxford University Press, 1966), p. 10.

5. William Brent, *The Complete and Factual Life of Billy the Kid* (New York: Frederick Fell, 1964), n.p.

6. Edmund Fable, *Billy the Kid, the New Mexican Outlaw* (Denver: Denver Publishing Co., 1881), n.p.; Charlie Siringo, *History of "Billy the Kid,"* (Santa Fe, N.M.: privately published, 1920), p. 3; N. Howard Thorp, *Pardner of the Wind* (Caldwell, Id.: Caxton, 1945), pp. 168–69; Ramon Adams, *A Fitting Death for Billy the Kid* (Norman: University of Oklahoma Press, 1960), pp. 17–18, 30; Rosa, *The Gunfighter,* p. 47; Peter Lyon, *The Wild, Wild West* (New York: Funk and Wagnalls, 1969), p. 24.

7. Pat Garrett, *The Authentic Life of Billy, the Kid* (1882; rpt. Norman: University of Oklahoma Press, 1954), p. 4.

8. Annie D. Tallent, *The Black Hills* (St. Louis: Nixon-Jones, 1899), p. vii.

9. Nat Love, *The Life and Adventures of Nat Love, Better Known in the Cattle Country as "Deadwood Dick"* (Los Angeles: Wayside Press, 1907), n.p.

10. This account is a shorthand version of Gene Wise's introduction of Thomas Kuhn's view of the scientific (and historical) enterprise. See Books I and II of Wise's *American Historical Explanations* (Homewood, Ill.: Dorsey, 1973). Bruce Kuklick describes this model of approaching the historian's task as the "ideal observer" model. See his "The Mind of the Historian," *History and Theory,* 8 (1969): 315. My discussion here is also indebted to Carolyn R. Miller, "A Humanistic Rationale for Technical Writing," *College English,* 40 (1979): 610–17. Whether or not this model serves as the goal for most professional historians writing in America now, this model, whether called "positivist" or "ideal observer," certainly describes the assumptions of the contributors to the Kid's bibliography.

11. Wise, p. 75: "Documents—however many, however reliable—won't give us history *in fact;* they'll give us a few random facts *about* history."

12. See Don D. Walker's elaboration of this problem with the word "reality" in his "Riders and Reality: A Philosophical Problem in the Historiography of the Cattle Trade," *Western Historical Quarterly,* 9 (1978): 163–79.

13. Even if we had a video recorder at the hotel in Hot Springs, N.M., when the

Kid and Jesse James supposedly had their meeting, a video recorder that would not be tainted by language's figurative nature, we—fallible human beings—would have to decide on a camera angle to record the event, and thus would supplement the recorder with our own version of the objects in space.

14. Besides Hayden White's books and essays, I should mention here such primary contributors to this epistemology as E. H. Gombrich (*Art and Illusion*), Peter Berger and Thomas Luckmann (*The Social Construction of Reality*), Kenneth Burke (*The Philosophy of Literary Form*), Ernst Cassirer (*An Essay on Man*), and Thomas Kuhn (*The Structure of Scientific Revolutions*).

15. Harold Toliver, *Animate Illusion* (Lincoln: University of Nebraska Press, 1974), p. 52.

16. J. Frank Dobie, *Guide to the Life and Literature of the Southwest* (Dallas: Southern Methodist University Press, 1942), pp. 1–2.

17. Joseph Conrad, *Notes on Life and Letters* (London: J. M. Dent, 1905), p. 20.

18. Américo Castro, *An Idea of History*, trans. Stephen Gilman and Edmund L. King (Columbus: Ohio State University Press, 1977), p. 305. Believing that no social study has completed its "intellectual journey" until it returns to "the problems of biography, of history and of their intersections within a society," C. Wright Mills in his *The Sociological Imagination* argues that "we cannot adequately understand 'man' as an isolated biological creature, as a bundle of reflexes or a set of instincts, as an 'intelligible field' or a system in and of itself. Whatever else he may be, man is a social and an historical actor who must be understood, if at all, in close and intricate interplay with social and historical structures." One understands this interplay, Mills suggests, by going much deeper than an initial recognition of man as a role-playing social creature. We must also strive "to understand the most internal and 'psychological' features of man: in particular, his self-image and his conscience and indeed the very growth of his mind." See Mills, *The Sociological Imagination* (New York: Oxford University Press, 1959), pp. 6, 157, 161. Given these demands on the historian's talents as stated by Castro, Conrad, and Mills, we see that regardless of their factual errors, Burns, Hunt, and Harvey Fergusson were coming close to understanding the Kid when their works discussed how the Kid may have shaped his life according to the growing legend about his exploits.

19. Where Castro believes only selected subjects are worthy of "history," while other less worthy subjects are fit material for the lesser realms of "description" or "narration," my own view is that "history" depends more on the historian's ability to explore the subject rather than on any *a priori* qualities of a subject that make it fit for "history."

20. Maurice G. Fulton, "Billy the Kid in Life and Books," *New Mexico Folklore Record*, 4 (1949–50): p. 1.

21. Thorp, pp. 169–70, 189.

22. Lyon, p. 123.

23. Kent Steckmesser, *The Western Hero in History and Legend* (Norman: University of Oklahoma Press, 1965), p. vii.

24. Roberts, no. 2, p. 61.

25. Compare and contrast the tone of Steckmesser's and Roberts's comments with this typical one by Adams: "No doubt I will be criticized for taking the glamour from a folk-hero, for denying the people the right to satisfy appetites greedy for thrills and blood." See Adams's *A Fitting Death*, p. 17.

Chapter 8

1. Michael Ondaatje, *The Collected Works of Billy the Kid* (New York: Berkley, 1975), p. 93.

2. Leon Claire Metz, *The Shooters* (El Paso, Tx.: Mangan Books, 1976), p. 15. A comparison of the Kid's bibliography with the bibliographies of Custer and Jesse James will reveal, I believe, that the Kid is an enduring figure—but not that he has been featured in more places than any other frontier figure.

3. Ramona Maher Weeks, "Lines to be Spoken by Pat Garrett, When Older," in *A Part of Space: Ten Texas Writers*, ed. Betsy Feagan Colquiett (Fort Worth: Texas Christian University Press, 1969), p. 86.

4. William Macleod Raine, "Billy the Kid," *Pacific Monthly*, 20 (1908): 37; J. Frank Dobie, *A Vaquero of the Brush Country* (Dallas: Southwest Press, 1929), p. 121; Marshall Fishwick, "Billy the Kid: Faust in America," *Saturday Review*, 11 Oct. 1952, pp. 11–12; F. Stanley, *Desperadoes of New Mexico* (Denver: World Press, 1953), p. xi.

5. Eric Hobsbawm, *Primitive Rebels* (New York: Norton, 1959), p. 20.

6. Harvey Fergusson, "Billy the Kid," *American Mercury*, 5 (1925): 224.

7. Walter Noble Burns, *Saga of Billy the Kid* (1926; rpt. New York: Ballantine, 1973), p. 42.

8. See Eric Hobsbawm, *Bandits* (New York: Delacorte Press, 1969), p. 112.

9. Robert N. Mullin and Charles E. Welch, "Billy the Kid: The Making of a Hero," *Western Folklore*, 32 (1973): 105. Also useful in this regard are Michael Owen Jones, "(PC + CB) X SD (R + I + E) = HERO," *New York Folklore Quarterly*, 27 (1971): 243–60; Roger D. Abrahams, "Some Varieties of Heroes in America," *Journal of American Folklore*, 3 (1966): 341–62; and Mody Boatwright, "The Western Badman as Hero," *Publications of the Texas Folklore Society*, 27 (1957): 96–104.

10. Dobie, pp. 176–77. My emphasis.

11. bp Nichol, *The True Eventual Story of Billy the Kid* (Toronto: Weed Flowers Press, 1970), n.p.

12. Dobie, p. 177.

13. N. Howard Thorp, *Pardner of the Wind* (Caldwell, Id.: Caxton, 1945), p. 189; Maurice G. Fulton, "Billy the Kid in Life and Books," *New Mexico Folklore Record*, 4 (1949–50): 1; Peter Lyon, *The Wild, Wild West* (New York: Funk and Wagnalls, 1969), p. 123. My emphasis.

14. C. L. Sonnichsen, *Fron Hopalong to Hud: Thoughts on Western Fiction* (College Station: Texas A & M Press, 1978), p. 16.

15. Emmett Dalton, *When the Daltons Rode* (Garden City, N.Y.: Doubleday, Doran & Co., 1931), p. 277.

16. My understanding of this folk outlaw tradition has been enhanced by the following publications: Richard E. Meyer, "The Outlaw: A Distinctive American Folk Type," *Journal of the Folklore Institute*, 17 (1980): 93–124; Hobsbawm, *Bandits;* Alfred Adler, "Billy the Kid: A Case Study in Epic Origins," *Western Folklore*, 10 (1951): 143–52; Orrin E. Klapp, "The Folk Hero," *Journal of American Folklore*, 62 (1949): 17–25; and Kent Steckmesser, "Joaquin Murietta and Billy the Kid," *Western Folklore*, 21 (1962): 77–82.

17. Burns, p. 53.

18. Harry Berger, Jr., "Naive Consciousness and Culture Change: An Essay in Historical Structuralism," *Bulletin of the Midwest Modern Language Association,* 6 (1973): 35. John Cawelti's *Adventure, Mystery, and Romance* (Chicago: University of Chicago Press, 1976) introduced me to this essay during his discussion of the appeal of formulaic art.

19. Maud Bodkin, *Archetypal Patterns in Poetry* (London: Oxford University Press, 1968), p. 23.

20. Ondaatje, p. 84.

Bibliography

Adams, Ramon. *The Adams One-Fifty: A Check-list of the 150 Most Important Books on Western Outlaws and Lawmen.* Austin, Tx.: Jenkins Pub. Co., 1976.
———. "Billy the Kid's Lost Years." *Texas Monthly,* 4 (1929): 205–11.
———. *Burs Under the Saddle: A Second Look at Books and Histories of the West.* Norman: University of Oklahoma Press, 1964.
———. *A Fitting Death for Billy the Kid.* Norman: University of Oklahoma Press, 1960.
———. *Six-Guns and Saddle Leather: A Bibliography of Books and Pamphlets on Western Outlaws and Gunmen.* Norman: University of Oklahoma Press, 1954.
Adler, Alfred. "Billy the Kid: A Case Study in Epic Origins." *Western Folklore,* 10 (1951): 143–52.
Allen, Frederick Lewis. *Only Yesterday.* 1931; rpt. New York: Harper Brothers, 1964.
———. *Since Yesterday.* 1939; rpt. New York: Harper Brothers, 1972.
Applegate, Frank G. "New Mexico Legends." *Southwest Review,* 17 (1932): 199–208.
Ball, Eve. "Billy Strikes the Pecos." *New Mexico Folklore Record,* 4 (1949–50): 7–10.
Bechdolt, Frederick R. *Tales of the Old Timers.* New York: Century, 1924.
———. *When the West Was Young.* New York: Century, 1922.
Beck, Warren A. *New Mexico: A History of Four Centuries.* Norman: University of Oklahoma Press, 1962.
Benedict, Ruth. *Patterns of Culture.* 1934; rpt. Boston: Houghton-Mifflin, 1959.
Berger, Peter L., and Thomas Luckmann. *The Social Construction of Reality.* Garden City, N.Y.: Doubleday, 1966.

Bergman, Andrew. *We're In the Money: Depression America and Its Films.* New York: New York University Press, 1971.

"Billy the Kid: In Two Films About Him Hollywood Fakes History." *Life,* 4 August 1941, pp. 65–69.

Billy the Kid: Las Vegas Newspaper Accounts of His Career, 1880-1881. Waco, Tx.: W. M. Morrison Books, 1958.

Boorstin, Daniel. *The Americans: The National Experience.* New York: Vintage, 1965.

Bowyer, Edith M. *Observations of a Ranchwoman in New Mexico.* London: Macmillan, 1898.

Brauer, Ralph, with Donna Brauer. *The Horse, the Gun and the Piece of Property: Changing Images of the TV Western.* Bowling Green, Ohio: Bowling Green University Popular Press, 1975.

Breihan, Carl W. *Badmen of the Frontier Days.* New York: Robert M. McBride, 1957.

Brent, William. *The Complete and Factual Life of Billy the Kid.* New York: Frederick Fell, 1964.

Brininstool, E. A. *The True Story of the Killing of 'Billy the Kid' (Notorious New Mexican Outlaw).* 1919; rpt. Los Angeles: n.p., 1923.

Broome, Bertram C. "'Nuff Said'." *New Mexico Highway Journal,* 9 (1931): 15–17.

Brown, Dee, and Martin F. Schmitt. *Trail Driving Days.* New York: Scribner's, 1952.

Burnett, W. R. "Nobody's All Bad." *Collier's,* 7 June 1930: 20–21, 30.

Burns, Walter Noble. *The Saga of Billy the Kid.* 1926; rpt. New York: Ballantine, 1973.

Castro, Américo. *An Idea of History.* Trans. Stephen Gilman and Edmund L. King. Columbus: Ohio State University Press, 1977.

Cawelti, John G. *Adventure, Mystery, and Romance: Formula Stories as Art and Popular Culture.* Chicago: University of Chicago Press, 1976.

———. "The Gunfighter and Society." *American West,* 5 (1968): 30–35, 76–78.

———. *The Six-Gun Mystique.* Bowling Green, Ohio: Bowling Green University Popular Press, 1971.

Chapman, Arthur. "Billy the Kid—A Man All 'Bad'." *Outing,* 46 (1905): 73–77.

———. "A Cowboy War." *Outing,* 58 (1911): 498–506.

Chesterton, G. K. *The Victorian Age in Literature.* 1913; rpt. London: Oxford University Press, 1966.

Clark, Neill M. "Close Calls: An Interview with Charles A. Siringo." *American Magazine,* 107, no. 1 (1929): 38–39, 129–31.

Clark, O. S. *Clay Allison of the Washita: First a Cow Man and then an Extinguisher of Bad Men.* [Attica, Ind.]: n.p., [1922].

Coe, George Washington. *Frontier Fighter.* 1934; rpt. Albuquerque: University of New Mexico Press, 1951.

Collinson, Frank. "Tongue River's First Ranch." *Ranch Romances,* 6 (1936): 542–48.

Conrad, Joseph. *Notes on Life and Letters.* London: J. M. Dent, 1905.

Cook, Jim (Lane). *Lane of the Llano.* Boston: Little, Brown, 1936.

Copland, Aaron. "Billy the Kid" Piano Solo. London: Boosey & Hawkes, 1944.

Corle, Edwin. *Billy the Kid.* 1953; rpt. Albuquerque: University of New Mexico Press, 1979.

———. *Mojave.* New York: Livewright, 1934.

The Cowboy's Career, or the Dare Devil Deeds of 'Billy, the Kid,' The Noted New Mexican Desperado. Chicago and St. Louis: Belford, Clarke & Co., 1881.

Crichton, Kyle S. *Law and Order, Ltd., The Rousing Life of Elfego Baca of New Mexico.* 1928; rpt. Glorieta, N.M.: Rio Grande Press, 1970.

Croy, Homer, *Jesse James Was My Neighbor.* New York: Duell, Sloan and Pearce, 1949.

Cunningham, Eugene. "The Kid Still Rides." *New Mexico,* 13 (1935): 13–15.

———. *Triggernometry: A Gallery of Gunfighters.* New York: The Press of the Pioneers, 1934.

Currie, Barton, W. "American Bandits: Lone and Otherwise." *Harper's Weekly,* 12 September 1908, p. 15, 35.

Daggett, Thomas F. *Billy Le Roy, The Colorado Bandit; or, The King of American Highwaymen.* New York: R. K. Fox, 1881.

Dalton, Emmett. *When the Daltons Rode.* Garden City, N.Y.: Doubleday, Doran & Co., 1931.

Dickstein, Morris. *Gates of Eden: American Culture in the Sixties.* New York: Basic Books, 1977.

Dobie, J. Frank. *Apache Gold and Yaqui Silver.* 1939; rpt. Albuquerque: University of New Mexico Press, 1967.

———. *Guide to the Life and Literature of the Southwest.* Dallas: Southern Methodist University Press, 1942.

———. *A Vaquero of the Brush Country.* Dallas: The Southwest Press, 1929.

Doughty, Francis W. *Old King Brady and Billy the Kid.* New York Detective Library, No. 411. New York: Frank Tousey, 1890.

Drago, Harry Sinclair. *The Great Range Wars: Violence on the Grasslands.* New York: Dodd, Mead, 1970.

———. *The Legend Makers: Tales of the Old-Time Peace Officers and Desperadoes of the Frontier.* New York: Dodd, Mead, 1975.

———. *Road Agents and Train Robbers.* New York: Dodd, Mead, 1973.

Dykes, J. C. *Billy the Kid: The Bibliography of a Legend.* Albuquerque: University of New Mexico Press, 1952.

Ealy, Ruth R. *Water in a Thirsty Land.* [U.S.A.]: n.p., 1955.

Eastlake, Chesmore. "Typing the Western Gunman." In *1948 Brand Book.* Ed. Dabney Otis Collins. Denver: Westerners, 1949.

Elman, Robert. *Bad Men of the West.* New York: Ridge Press/Pound, 1974.

Etulain, Richard W. "The Historical Development of the Western." *Journal of Popular Culture,* 7 (1973): 717–26.

Etulain, Richard W., and Michael T. Marsden. *The Popular Western: Essays Toward A Definition.* Bowling Green, Ohio: Bowling Green University Popular Press, 1974.

Fable, Edmund. *Billy the Kid, the New Mexican Outlaw; or, the Bold Bandit of the West.* Denver: Denver Pub. Co., 1881.

Farber, James. *Texans with Guns.* San Antonio, Tx.: Naylor, 1950.

Felter, William, and John L. McCarty. *New Mexico in Verse.* Dalhart, Tx.: Dalhart Pub. Co., 1935.

Fenin, George N., and William K. Everson. *The Western: From Silents to the Seventies.* New York: Penguin, 1977.

Fergusson, Erna. *Murder and Mystery in New Mexico.* Albuquerque: Merle Armitage, 1948.

Fergusson, Harvey. "Billy the Kid." *American Mercury,* 5 (1925): 224–31.

———. *Rio Grande.* 1933; rpt. New York: William Morrow, 1967.

Fishwick, Marshall W. *American Heroes: Myths and Reality.* Washington, D.C.: Public Affairs Press, 1954.

———. "Billy the Kid: Faust in America." *Saturday Review,* 11 October 1952: 11–12, 34–36.

Frank, Joseph. *The Widening Gyre: Crisis and Mastery in Modern Literature.* Bloomington: Indiana University Press, 1963.

French, Philip. *Westerns: Aspects of a Movie Genre.* New York: Viking, 1973.

Fridge, Ike, as told to Jodie D. Smith. *History of the Chisum War, or Life of Ike Fridge.* Electra, Tx.: Smith, [1927].

Frye, Northrop. *Anatomy of Criticism: Four Essays.* 1957; rpt. Princeton: Princeton University Press, 1973.

———. *Fables of Identity: Studies in Poetic Mythology.* New York: Harcourt, 1963.

Fulton, Maurice Garland. "The Apochrypha of Billy the Kid." In *Folk-Say, A Regional Miscellany.* Ed. B. A. Botkin. Norman: University of Oklahoma Press, 1930, pp. 88–101.

———. "Billy the Kid in Life and Books." *New Mexico Folklore Record,* 4 (1949–50): 1–6.

Fulton, Maurice Garland. *History of the Lincoln County War.* Ed. Robert N. Mullin. Tucson: University of Arizona Press, 1968.

Garrett, Pat. *The Authentic Life of Billy, the Kid, Noted Desperado of the Southwest.* 1882; rpt. Norman: University of Oklahoma Press, 1965.

Ghent, W. J. "Bonney, William." *DAB* (1929).

Gibbs, Harry C. *Chico.* Rpt. in *Twenty Short Plays on a Royalty Holiday.* Ed. Margaret Mayorga. Vol. II. New York: Samuel French, 1940.

Gombrich, E. H. *Art and Illusion: A Study in the Psychology of Pictorial Representation.* New York: Pantheon, 1960.

Green, Archie. "Commercial Music Graphics: Number Twenty-Eight." *John Edwards Memorial Foundation Quarterly,* 10 (1974): 19–22.

Grey, Frederick William. *Seeking Fortune in America.* London: Smith, Elder, & Co., 1912.

Grey, Zane. *Nevada: A Romance of the West.* New York: Harper and Brothers, 1928.

The Gunfighters. New York: Time-Life Books, 1974.

Hall, Frank. *History of the State of Colorado.* Vol. III. Chicago: Blakely Printing, 1891.

Hamilton, Thomas Marion. *The Young Pioneer: When Captain Tom Was a Boy.* Washington, D.C.: Library Press, 1932.

Hamlin, William Lee. *The True Story of Billy the Kid.* Caldwell, Id.: Caxton, 1959.

Hammond, John Hays. "Strong Men of the Wild West." *Scribner's,* 77 (1925): 115–25, 246–56.

Harkey, Dee. *Mean as Hell.* Albuquerque: University of New Mexico Press, 1948.

Hart, James D. *The Popular Book: A History of America's Literary Taste.* 1950; rpt. Berkeley: University of California Press, 1963.

Heermans, Forbes. *Thirteen Stories of the Far West.* Syracuse, N.Y.: C. W. Bardeen, 1887.

Hendricks, George D. *The Bad-Man of the West.* San Antonio, Tx.: Naylor, 1942.

Hendron, J. W. "The Haunted House of Lincoln Town." *New Mexico,* 25 (1947): 22–31, 41.

———. *The Story of Billy the Kid: New Mexico's Number One Desperado.* Santa Fe, N.M.: Rydal, 1948.

Henry, Will. "A Bullet for Billy the Kid." In his *Sons of the Western Frontier.* Philadelphia: Chilton, 1966, pp. 165–209.

Hersey, Harold. *Singing Rawhide: A Book of Western Ballads.* New York: George Doran, 1926.

Hertzog, Peter. *Little Known Facts About Billy, the Kid.* Santa Fe, N.M.: Press of the Territorian, 1963.

Hill, J. L. *The End of the Cattle Trail.* Long Beach, Cal.: George W. Moyle, 1924.

Hobsbawm, Eric. *Bandits.* New York: Delacorte, 1969.

———. *Primitive Rebels: Studies in Archaic Forms of Social Movement in the 19th and 20th Centuries.* New York: Norton, 1959.

Hogeboom, Amy. *The Boy's Book of the West.* New York: Lothrop, Lee and Shepard, 1946.

Hollon, W. Eugene. *Frontier Violence: Another Look.* New York: Oxford University Press, 1974.

Horan, James D. *The Authentic Wild West: The Gunfighters.* New York: Crown, 1976.

———. *The Authentic Wild West: The Outlaws.* New York: Crown, 1977.

———. *The Great American West.* New York: Crown, 1978.

Hough, Emerson. "Billy the Kid, the True Story of a Western 'Bad Man.' " *Everybody's Magazine,* 5 (1901): 302–10.

———. *Heart's Desire.* New York: Macmillan, 1905.

———. *The Story of the Cowboy.* New York: D. Appleton, 1897.

———. *The Story of the Outlaw: A Study of the Western Desperado.* New York: Outing, 1907.

Hoyt, Henry F. *A Frontier Doctor.* Boston: Houghton-Mifflin, 1929.

Hunt, Frazier. *The Tragic Days of Billy the Kid.* New York: Hastings House, 1956.

Hunter, J. Marvin, and Noah H. Rose. *The Album of Gunfighters.* Bandera, Tx.: Rose & Hunter, 1951.

Hyde, Albert E. "The Old Régime in the Southwest: The Reign of the Revolver in New Mexico." *Century,* 43 (1902): 690–701.

Johannsen, Albert. *The House of Beadle & Adams and Its Dime and Nickel Novels.* 2 vols. Norman: University of Oklahoma Press, 1950.

Johnson, Carole M. "Emerson Hough's *The Story of the Outlaw.*" *Arizona and the West,* 17 (1975): 309–26.

Jones, Daryl. *The Dime Novel Western.* Bowling Green, Ohio: Bowling Green University Popular Press, 1978.

Jowett, Garth. "Bullets, Beer, and the Hays Office." In *American History/American Film.* Ed. John E. O'Connor and Martin A. Jackson. New York: Ungar, 1979, pp. 57–75.

Keleher, William A. *The Fabulous Frontier.* Albuquerque: University of New Mexico Press, 1962.

———. "In 'Re' Billy the Kid." *New Mexico Folklore Record,* 4 (1949–50): 11–13.

———. *Violence in Lincoln County, 1869–1881.* Albuquerque: University of New Mexico Press, 1957.

Kendrick, Alexander. *The Wound Within: America in the Vietnam Years, 1945–1974.* Boston: Little, Brown, 1974.

King, Frank M. *Mavericks: The Salty Comments of an Old-Time Cowpuncher.* Pasadena, Cal.: Trail's End, 1947.

Kitses, Jim. *Horizons West.* Bloomington: Indiana University Press, 1969.

Klapp, Orrin E. "The Folk Hero." *Journal of American Folklore,* 62 (1949): 17–25.

Koop, W. E. *Billy the Kid: The Trail of a Kansas Legend.* [Kansas City]: n.p., 1965.

Koszarski, Richard. *Hollywood Directors, 1941–1976.* New York: Oxford University Press, 1977.

"Last Days of a Gunman: True Story of Billy the Kid; Accounts from Contemporary Newspapers." *Life,* 4 May 1959: 86–88.

Lenihan, John H. *Showdown: Confronting Modern America in the Western Film.* Urbana: University of Illinois Press, 1980.

Lenoir, Phil. *Rhymes of the Wild & Wooly.* [Santa Fe, N.M.: n.p., 1920].

Leuchtenburg, William E. *A Troubled Feast: American Society Since 1945.* Boston: Little, Brown, 1973.

Levin, Martin. Rev. of *The Authentic Death of Hendry Jones,* by Charles Neider. *Saturday Review,* 29 September 1956: 16.

Lewis, John Woodruff. *The True Life of Billy the Kid.* Wide Awake Library, No. 451. New York: Frank Tousey, 1881.

Lewis, Lloyd. *It Takes All Kinds.* Freeport: N.Y.: Books for Libraries Press, 1947.

Logue, Roscoe. *Under Texas and Border Skies.* Amarillo, Tx.: Russell Stationery Co., 1935.

Lomax, John. *Cowboy Songs and Other Frontier Ballads.* New York: Macmillan, 1922.

Long, Haniell. *Piñon Country.* New York: Duell, Sloan & Pearce, 1941.

Loring, Eugene, chor. *Billy the Kid.* Ballet West. Capitol Theater, Salt Lake City, Ut.; 12 April 1980.

Love, Nat. *The Life and Adventures of Nat Love, Better Known in the Cattle Country as "Deadwood Dick."* Los Angeles: [Wayside Press], 1907.

Lyon, Peter. *The Wild, Wild West.* New York: Funk & Wagnalls, 1969.

McCarty, John L. *Maverick Town: The Story of Old Tascosa.* Norman: University of Oklahoma Press, 1946.

McClure, Michael. *The Beard.* New York: Grove Press, 1965.

———. *The Blossom.* Rpt. in his *The Mammals.* San Francisco: Cranium Press, 1972.

McGeeney, P. S. *Down at Stein's Pass: A Romance of New Mexico.* Boston: Angel Guardian Press, 1909.

McLoughlin, Denis. *Wild and Woolly: An Encyclopedia of the Old West.* Garden City, N.Y.: Doubleday, 1975.

Malone, Bill C. *Country Music U.S.A.* Austin: University of Texas Press, 1968.

Mann, E. B., "Billy the Kid." *American Rifleman,* 95 (1947): 21–23, 38.

———. *Gamblin' Man.* New York: William Morrow, 1934.

Metz, Leon C. *Pat Garrett: The Story of a Western Lawman.* Norman: University of Oklahoma Press, 1974.

———. *The Shooters.* El Paso, Tx: Mangan Books, 1976.

Meyer, Richard E. "The Outlaw: A Distinctive American Folk Type." *Journal of the Folklore Institute,* 17 (1980): 93–124.

Miller, Carolyn R. "A Humanistic Rationale for Technical Writing." *College English,* 40 (1979): 610–17.

Morison, Samuel Eliot. *The Oxford History of the American People.* New York: Oxford University Press, 1965.

Mullin, Robert N., and Charles E. Welch, Jr. "Billy the Kid: The Making of a Hero." *Western Folklore,* 32 (1973): 104–12.

Mullin, Robert N. *The Boyhood of Billy the Kid.* El Paso, Tx.: Texas Western Press, 1967.

————. *A Chronology of the Lincoln County War.* Santa Fe, N.M.: Press of the Territorian, 1966.

Nachbar, Jack. "Riding Shotgun: The Scattered Formula in Contemporary Western Movies." In *Focus on the Western.* Ed. Jack Nachbar, Englewood Cliffs, N.J.: Prentice-Hall, 1974, pp. 101–12.

Nash, Roderick. *Wilderness and the American Mind.* New Haven: Yale University Press, 1973.

Neider, Charles. *The Authentic Death of Hendry Jones.* New York: Harper's, 1956.

————. *The Great West.* New York: Coward-McCann, 1958.

Nichol, bp. *The True Eventual Story of Billy the Kid.* Toronto: Weed Flowers Press, 1970.

Nolan, Frederick W. *The Life and Death of John Henry Tunstall.* Albuquerque: University of New Mexico Press, 1965.

Nordyke, Lewis. Rev. of *The Authentic Death of Hendry Jones,* by Charles Neider. *New York Times,* 26 August 1956: 26.

Nye, Nelson C. *Pistols for Hire: A Tale of the Lincoln County War and the West's Most Desperate Outlaw William (Billy the Kid) Bonney.* New York: Macmillan, 1941.

Nye, Russel. *The Unembarrassed Muse: The Popular Arts in America.* New York: Dial Press, 1970.

O'Connor, John. "A Reaffirmation of American Ideals: *Drums Along the Mohawk.*" In *American History/American Film.* Ed. John E. O'Connor and Martin A. Jackson. New York: Ungar, 1979, pp. 97–119.

————, and Martin A. Jackson, eds. *American History/American Film: Interpreting the Hollywood Image.* New York: Ungar, 1979.

Olson, Charles. *Human Universe and Other Essays.* Ed. Donald Allen. New York: Grove Press, 1967.

Ondaatje, Michael. *The Collected Works of Billy the Kid.* New York: Berkley, 1975.

O'Neill, James B. *They Die But Once.* New York: Knight, 1935.

O'Neill, William L., ed. *American Society Since 1945.* Chicago: Quadrangle Books, 1969.

————. *Coming Apart: An Informal History of America in the 1960's.* Chicago: Quadrangle, 1971.

Otero, Miguel Antonio. *The Real Billy the Kid: With New Light on the Lincoln County War.* New York: Rufus Rockwell Wilson, 1936.

Pauly, Thomas H. "The Cold War Western." *Western Humanities Review,* 33 (1979): 257–73.

————. "Howard Hughes and his Western: The Maverick and *The Outlaw.*" *Journal of Popular Film,* 6 (1978): 350–69.

Peck, Anne Merriman. *Southwest Roundup.* New York: Dodd, Mead, 1950.

Pells, Richard H. *Radical Visions and American Dreams: Culture and Social Thought in the Depression Years.* New York: Harper & Row, 1973.

Poe, John W. *The Death of Billy the Kid.* 1919; rpt. Boston: Houghton Mifflin, 1933.

Pomeroy, Earl. "Rediscovering the West." *American Quarterly,* 12 (1960): 20–30.

Potter, Jack. *Lead Steer and Other Tales.* Clayton, N.M.: Leader Press, 1939.

Price, G. G. *Death Comes to Billy the Kid.* [Greensburg, Kan.: Signal Publishing Co., 1940].

Raine, William Macleod. "Billy the Kid." *Pacific Monthly,* 20 (1908): 37–45.

————. *Famous Sheriffs and Western Outlaws.* 1929; rpt. New York: New Home Library, 1944.

————. *The Fighting Tenderfoot.* Garden City, N.Y.: Doubleday, Doran, 1929.

————. "Taming the Frontier: The Apache Kid." *Outing,* 46 (1905): 579–83.

Rasch, Philip J. *"Amende Honorable:* The Life and Death of Billy Wilson." *West Texas Historical Association Year Book,* 34 (1958): 97–111.

————. "A Man Named Antrim." In *1956 Brand Book.* Los Angeles: Westerners, 1957, pp. 48–54.

————. "The Olingers, Known Yet Forgotten." *Corral Dust,* 8 (1963): 3–6.

————. "The Twenty-One Men He Put Bullets Through." *New Mexico Folklore Record,* 9 (1954–55): 8–14.

————, and R. N. Mullin. "Dim Trails: The Pursuit of the McCarty Family." *New Mexico Folklore Record,* 8 (1953–54): 6–11.

————. "New Light on the Legend of Billy the Kid." *New Mexico Folklore Record,* 7 (1952–53): 1–5.

Rascoe, Burton. *Belle Starr: The Bandit Queen.* New York: Random House, (1941).

Rhodes, Eugene Manlove; "In Defense of Pat Garrett." *Sunset,* 59 (1927): 26–27, 85–91.

Ridings, Sam P. *The Chisholm Trail.* Guthrie, Okla.: Co-Operative Publishing, 1936.

Rolt-Wheeler, Francis. *The Book of Cowboys.* Boston: Lothrop, Lee & Shepard, 1921.

Robert, Grace. *The Borzoi Book of Ballets.* New York: Knopf, 1946.

Roberts, Gary L. "McCarty, Henry." In *The Reader's Encyclopedia of the American West.* Ed. Howard R. Lamar. New York: Crowell, 1977.

————. "The West's Gunmen." *American West,* 8, nos. 1 and 3 (1971): 10–15, 64; 18–23, 61–62.

Robinson, Forrest G. "The Roosevelt-Wister Connection." *Western American Literature,* 14 (1979): 95–114.

Roosevelt, Theodore. *The Winning of the West.* New York and London: G. P. Putnam's Sons, 1889. Vol. I.

Rosa, Joseph G. *The Gunfighter: Man or Myth?* Norman: University of Oklahoma Press, 1969.

————, and Robin May. *Gun Law: A Study of Violence in the Wild West.* Chicago: Contemporary Books, 1977.

Rosenberg, Bruce A. *Custer and the Epic of Defeat.* University Park: Pennsylvania State University Press, 1974.

Russell, Charles M. *Pen and Ink Drawings.* Pasadena, Ca.: Trail's End, 1946. Vol. I.

Sadler, Frank. "The Frontier in Jack Spicer's 'Billy the Kid'." Rpt. in *The Westering Experience in American Literature.* Eds. Merrill Lewis and L. L. Lee. Bellingham, Wash.: Bureau for Faculty Research, 1977.

Santee, Ross. *Lost Pony Tracks.* New York: Scribner's, 1953.

Scanland, John Milton. *Life of Pat Garrett and the Taming of the Border Outlaw.* El Paso, Tx.: Carleton F. Hodge, 1908.

Scobie, Stephen. "Two Authors in Search of a Character: bp Nichol and Michael Ondaatje." Rpt. in *Poets and Critics.* Ed. George Woodcock. Toronto: Oxford University Press, 1974, pp. 225–245.

Segale, Sister Blandina. *At the End of the Santa Fe Trail.* 1932; rpt. Milwaukee, Wis.: Bruce Publishing, 1948.

Seydor, Paul. *Peckinpah: The Western Films.* Urbana: University of Illinois Press, 1979.

Shepard, William G. "Flat-wheeled Justice." *Collier's,* 15 November 1925: 7–8, 23.

Sherman, Eric, and Martin Rubin. *The Director's Event: Interviews with Five American Film-makers*. New York: Atheneum, 1970.

Sinclair, John L. "Dusting off Billy's Ghost." *Westways*, 8 (1976): 32 35, 78.

Siringo, Charles A. *A Cowboy Detective*. Chicago: W. B. Conkey, 1912.

———. *History of "Billy the Kid."* Santa Fe, N.M.: n.p., 1920.

———. *A Lone Star Cowboy*. Santa Fe, N.M.: n.p., 1919.

———. *A Texas Cowboy*. 1885; rpt. New York: New American Library, 1955.

Sligh, J. E. "Billy-the-Kid." *Overland Monthly*, 52 (1908): 47–51.

Smith, Henry Nash. *Virgin Land: The American West as Symbol and Myth*. 1950; rpt. Cambridge: Harvard University Press, 1971.

Smith, Wilbur. "The Amigo of Billy the Kid." *New Mexico*, 11, (1933): 26–27; 47–48.

Sonnichsen, C. L. *From Hopalong to Hud: Thoughts on Western Fiction*. College Station: Texas A & M University Press, 1978.

———, and William V. Morrison. *Alias Billy the Kid*. Albuquerque: University of New Mexico Press, 1955.

Stanley, F. *Desperadoes of New Mexico*. Denver: World Press, 1953.

———. *Socorro: The Oasis*. Denver: World Press, 1950.

Steckmesser, Kent. "Joaquin Murietta and Billy the Kid." *Western Folklore*, 21 (1962): 77–82.

———. *The Western Hero in History and Legend*. Norman: University of Oklahoma Press, 1965.

Story of the Great American West. Pleasantville, N.Y.: Reader's Digest, 1977.

Sutton, Fred E., as told to A. B. MacDonald. *Hands Up!* Indianapolis: Bobbs-Merrill, [1927].

Tallent, Annie D. *The Black Hills; or, the Last Hunting Grounds of the Dakota*. St. Louis: Nixon-Jones Printing, 1899.

Thorp, N. Howard. *Pardner of the Wind*. Caldwell, Id.: Caxton, 1945.

Toliver, Harold. *Animate Illusion*. Lincoln: University of Nebraska Press, 1974.

Topping, Gary, "Zane Grey: A Literary Reassessment." *Western American Literature*, 13 (1978): 51–64.

Townshend, R. B. *The Tenderfoot in New Mexico*. London: John Lane, 1923.

Tuska, John. *The Filming of the West*. Garden City, N.Y.: Doubleday, 1976.

Vidal, Gore. *The Death of Billy the Kid*. In *Nine Modern Short Plays*. Eds. David A Sohn and Richard H. Tyre. New York: Bantam Books, 1977, pp. 1–32.

Walker, Don D. "Riders and Reality: A Philosophical Problem in the Historiography of the Cattle Trade." *Western Historical Quarterly*, 9 (1978): 163–79.

Watson, Frederick. *A Century of Gunmen: A Study in Lawlessness*. London: Ivor Nicholson & Watson, 1931.

Wecter, Dixon. *The Hero in America: A Chronicle of Hero-Worship*. New York: Scribner's, 1941.

Weeks, Ramona Maher. "Lines to Be Spoken by Pat Garrett, When Older." In *A Part of Space: Ten Texas Writers*. Ed. Betsy Feagan Colquiett. Fort Worth: Texas Christian University Press, 1969.

Wellman, Paul I. *The Trampling Herd*. New York: Carrick & Evans, 1939.

West, John Oliver. "To Die Like a Man: The 'Good' Outlaw Tradition in the American Southwest." Diss. University of Texas 1964.

White, G. Edward. *The Eastern Establishment and the Western Experience: The West of*

Frederick Remington, Theodore Roosevelt, and Owen Wister. New Haven: Yale University Press, 1968.

White, Hayden. *Metahistory: The Historical Imagination in 19th Century Europe.* Baltimore: Johns Hopkins University Press, 1973.

———. *Tropics of Discourse.* Baltimore: Johns Hopkins University Press, 1979.

White, Owen P. "Billy the Kid." *Collier's,* 14 November 1925: 17, 48–49; 21 November 1925: 11, 44–45.

———. *Them Was the Days: From El Paso to Prohibition.* New York: Minton, Balch & Co., 1925.

———. *Trigger Fingers.* New York: Putnam's, 1926.

Wiebe, Robert H. *The Search for Order: 1877–1920.* New York: Hill and Wang, 1967.

Winn, Mary Day. *The Macadam Trail.* New York: Knopf, 1931.

Wise, Gene. *American Historical Explanations: A Strategy for Grounded Inquiry.* Homewood, Ill.: Dorsey, 1973.

Wister, Owen. *Red Men and White.* Vol. I of *The Writings of Owen Wister.* New York: Macmillan, 1928.

Wittner, Lawrence S. *Cold War America: From Hiroshima To Watergate.* New York: Praeger, 1974.

Woods, Walter. *Billy the Kid.* Rpt. in *America's Lost Plays.* Ed. Garrett H. Leverton. Vol. VIII. Bloomington: Indiana University Press, 1964, pp. 199–255.

Wright, Will. *Sixguns & Society: A Structural Study of the Western.* Berkeley: University of California Press, 1975.

Index

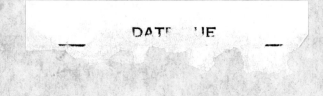

DATE DUE